MW00994289

WAR STORIES OF THE BATTLE OF THE BULGE

WAR STORIES OF THE BATTLE OF THE BULGE

Michael Green and James D. Brown

ZENITH PRESS

First published in 2010 by Zenith Press, an imprint of MBI
Publishing Company, 400 1st Avenue North, Suite 300,
Minneapolis, MN 55401 USA.

Zenith Press titles are also available at discounts in bulk quantity
for industrial or sales-promotional use. For details write to Special
Sales Manager at MBI Publishing Company, 400 First Avenue
North, Suite 300, Minneapolis, MN 55401 USA.

To find out more about our books, join us online at
www.zenithpress.com.

Designer: Helena Shimizu

Editor's note: Contributed passages, including those from the
Bulge Bugle, have been lightly edited for readability.

Front cover image: Courtesy U.S. Army
Back cover image: National Archives

Maps: Patti Isaacs/Parrot Graphics, recreated from U.S. Army
source maps

Library of Congress Cataloging-in-Publication Data

Green, Michael, 1952-
War stories of the Battle of the Bulge / [compiled by] Michael
Green & James D. Brown.
    p. cm.
ISBN 978-0-7603-3667-0 (hbk. w/jkt)
1. Ardennes, Battle of the, 1944-1945--Personal narratives,
American. 2. Soldiers--United States--Biography. 3. United States.
Army--Biography. I. Brown, James D. II. Title.

D756.5.A7G716 2010
940.54'219348--dc22
                2009029284

Printed in the United States of America

CONTENTS

ACKNOWLEDGMENTS

Special thanks are due to the Veterans of the Battle of the Bulge Association and its president, board of directors, and trustees for allowing the editors to use various first-person stories published in their quarterly association newsletter, the *Bulge Bugle*. More information on the Battle of the Bulge Association can be found at their website, battleofthebulge.org. Mention must also be made of the many Battle of the Bulge veterans who were kind enough to send in their first-person war stories to the editors in response to a notice placed in the *Bulge Bugle* requesting such stories. Due to space and format restrictions, not all of them could be used.

Thanks for help in completing this book are also due to Martin W. Andresen and Thomas Sweeney, both U.S. Army retired. Ken Berg was also more than kind in offering his research work on the Battle of the Bulge. Professional research work was done at the U.S. Army Military History Institute, located at Carlisle Barracks, Pennsylvania, by Tim Frank, who is available for hire and can be reached at historian1975@gmail.com.

INTRODUCTION

THE INTRODUCTORY PARAGRAPHS THAT FOLLOW SERVE ONLY TO help the reader gauge the monumental scale and complexity of the fighting that took place during the Battle of the Bulge. Our primary purpose is to share with the reader first-person stories of American soldiers that will provide a feeling for this important time and place. Some of the stories contained within this book are horrifying, which is the nature of combat, while others are sad, and a few humorous. Many detail the utter confusion of war and those who try to make some sense of it. All serve to commemorate the sacrifice and the suffering of those who served their country at one of its most trying hours.

Home by Christmas! In classical warfare, the duration of campaigns and wars could be measured in decades or even centuries. Armies moved as fast as they could walk, and their pace was further slowed by the passage of seasons and the ripening of crops along their route of advance. The Crusades, the Thirty Years' War, and the Hundred Years' War saw legions of soldiers march off to return both literally and figuratively older.

More modern wars, fueled by the efficiency of industrial logistics systems, became so costly in terms of blood and treasure that no nation could afford to stay at war for very long. It was necessary to decide conflicts in, at most, a few years, or they could not be won at all.

And thus it was in the winter of 1944–45 that it became increasingly believable to both the Allies and the Germans that they would be home by Christmas. This held a dark double entendre for the Germans because their lines were contracting so rapidly, it was clear that even if fighting continued into the New Year, most of it would be on German soil. For the Allies, particularly the British and Americans, it seemed certain that even the delusional Hitler would see that all was lost and sue for peace before the German homeland was utterly destroyed.

Hitler proved to be a cynic to the last and decided to gamble on the Western Allies' increasing restlessness to see a quick end to the war. He was sure that one last powerful offensive in the West would accomplish a sorely needed political goal, even if he could not hope for an outright military turnabout. He hoped that an offensive against the British and Americans would give the Allies an excuse to accept an armistice, such as the one that had concluded World War I. Such a political solution would allow the Nazis to redeploy forces to the Eastern Front and stem the Red tide that was rushing ever closer to Berlin.

It may be observed that such a turn of events would not have been completely unwelcome by many leaders in both Washington and London, where concerns over Stalinist expansionism in the postwar era were already being raised. In later months, Gen. George Patton was famously censured for publicly stating the opinion that German forces should be rearmed and made part of a new alliance of British, American, and German forces to stamp out Bolshevism while Soviet forces were nearing exhaustion. In what would be the last winter of the war, however, Hitler was hoping that the Americans and British, even if they would not actively participate in a renewed offensive against the Russians, would at least withdraw their support for their ally.

In the pre-dawn darkness of December 16, 1944, Hitler launched the first wave of his massive surprise offensive, code-named *Wacht am Rhein* (Watch on the Rhine), against the weakly defended eighty-five-mile-long American-held Ardennes sector, which encompassed territory in Belgium, Germany, and Luxembourg. The German forces included 250,000 men, 1,900 artillery pieces, and almost 1,000 tanks and armored assault guns. Although the Allies held almost complete air superiority, Hitler's plan counted on the nullifying factor of poor flying weather to compensate for the Luftwaffe's weakness.

The fierce fighting in the Ardennes Forest, which took place from mid-December 1944 through almost the end of January 1945, is more properly classified as a campaign than a single battle: It consisted of numerous battles spread over a fairly wide area at different times and involved nearly one million soldiers on both sides.

The 250,000 German soldiers that hurled themselves into the Ardennes were divided among three field armies; the Sixth Panzer Army, which was intended to deliver the main blow against the Americans, the Fifth Panzer Army on its northern flank, and the Seventh Army defending the southern flank of both their advances. Among these three field armies were seven corps, which oversaw twenty divisions, including several panzer divisions, plus another five divisions held in reserve.

The Germans' immediate military goal was to reach the Allied-controlled port of Antwerp, Belgium, within a week, but the more realistic political goal was to inflict enough losses to the Western Allies to set the stage for an armistice. This would allow the *Wehrmacht* to concentrate its remaining resources on the Red Army.

On the morning of December 16, 1944, there were ninety-six Allied divisions along the Western Front border of Nazi Germany, which ran 450 miles from the northern tip of neutral Switzerland to the North Sea. It is axiomatic that an offensive operation such as *Wacht am Rhein* should have a force ratio of at least three-to-one in its favor to ensure success. Although Hitler did not have an exact count of the Allied forces arrayed against him, it is a reflection of the true intention of the German offensive that it was mounted with a nearly four-to-one unfavorable-force ratio. The German generals knew that the military objective of retaking Antwerp was not realistic, and Hitler's plan for a political victory was the best that could be hoped for.

The bulk of the Allied divisions were American, divided between the 6th and 12th Army Groups. The American 12th Army Group, commanded by Lt. Gen. Omar N. Bradley, oversaw three field armies on December 16, 1944, these being Lt. Gen. Courtney Hodges' First Army, Lt. Gen. William H. Simpson's Ninth Army, and Lt. Gen. George S. Patton's Third Army.

Each of Bradley's three field armies oversaw three corps. A corps was a relatively small controlling headquarters in World War II, consisting of fewer than 200 men, whose job it was to control the divisions assigned to it. The three American field armies together had a combined total of 815,087 men.

There was also an important British and Canadian contingent, the 21st Army Group, under the command of Field Marshal Bernard Montgomery. Included in the group were the First Canadian Army and the Second British Army.

General Dwight D. Eisenhower, the Western Allied Supreme Commander, long favored a broad front policy along the entire 450-mile front with Nazi Germany, which was a matter of strategic policy arrived at before the German offensive. But there were areas of the front that were perceived to offer little in the way of strategic value to either the Germans or the Allies. One of those was the rural and heavily wooded area, bisected by numerous rivers and streams, known as the Ardennes, which fell within the control of Bradley's 12th Army Group.

It was in the Ardennes front that Bradley, with Eisenhower's approval, took a calculated risk by deciding to use it as an area where his battle-bloodied divisions could recover and refit, and newly arrived and untested divisions could acquire a little combat experience before being shipped off to the more active areas of the front. Because the Allies had no anticipation of German offensive operations in the Ardennes in late 1944, an intelligence failure of some magnitude on the part of the Allies, the infantry and armored divisions assigned to that area were allotted areas of the front that far exceeded their ability to defend.

Not counting assigned nondivisional units, U.S. Army infantry divisions in World War II had an authorized strength of 14,253 men. Each division was divided into three regiments, each containing three battalions. Each battalion was further subdivided into three rifle companies. U.S. Army armored divisions came in two different versions, being classified as either tank divisions (heavy) or tank divisions (light). The tank division (heavy) had an authorized strength of 14,620 men and fielded 158 light tanks and 232 medium tanks, while the tank division (light) had 10,616 men and deployed 77 light tanks and 168 medium tanks. Attached nondivisional units would augment divisional size.

The defense of the Ardennes was assigned to two corps, these being the V Corps under the command of Maj. Gen. Leonard T. Gerow and VIII Corps under the leadership of Maj. Gen. Troy H. Middleton. The V and VIII Corps, as well as the VII Corps, under the leadership of Maj. Gen. Lawton Collins, fell under the control of Hodges' First Army, with a total of 341,659 men.

Gerow's V Corps oversaw part of the northern sector of the Ardennes front with the 2nd and 99th Infantry Divisions. The 8th and 78th Infantry Divisions as well as elements of the 9th Armored Division also formed part of Gerow's V Corps but were not located on the Ardennes front on December 16, 1944. The 99th Infantry Division served as the southernmost shoulder of Gerow's V Corps. Intermixed with that division were elements of the 2nd Infantry Division that were moving westward in preparation for an attack on the Roer River dams.

Middleton's VIII Corps, located to the south of Gerow's V Corps, defended the bulk of the Ardennes front and consisted of three infantry divisions, the 4th, 28th, and the 106th. There were also elements of the 9th Armored Division in the line located between the 28th Infantry Division on its north and the 4th Infantry Division on its south. The 106th Infantry Division was assigned the northernmost shoulder of Middleton's VIII Corps.

Patrolling the boundary between Gerow's V Corps and Middleton's VIII Corps, in an area known as the Losheim Gap, was the 14th Cavalry Group, which was assigned to the 106th Infantry Division. The Losheim Gap was seven miles wide and was the classic invasion route for German armies into France going back to 1870, during the Franco-Prussian War. It was also used as an invasion route by the Germans in 1914, during World War I, and in the summer of 1940, during the early part of World War II. Hindsight is blessed with 20/20 vision, but ignoring the use of this route three times in previous campaigns must be judged as a serious failure on the part of the Allies.

The German Sixth Panzer Army was to punch through the northernmost portion of the Ardennes with its armored and infantry divisions. The shortest path to Antwerp for the Germans was over the Elsenborn Ridge, defended by the 99th Infantry Division, with elements of the 2nd Infantry Division intermixed.

Despite the forces arrayed against them, the American units held on to Elsenborn Ridge and could not be pushed off. The veteran 1st Infantry Division of Collins' VII Corps joined the green 99th Infantry Division and the veteran 2nd Infantry

Division in defense of the Elsenborn Ridge on December 19. A key factor in helping to throw back the German attacks was the large number of divisional and nondivisional artillery units present.

On the southernmost area of the German advance into the Ardennes was the veteran 4th Infantry Division, belonging to Middleton's VIII Corps. It was attacked by a German infantry division from the Seventh Army but successfully repelled all the enemy attacks with the help of a tank battalion from the green 9th Armored Division and an assortment of divisional and nondivisional artillery units.

Defending the area between the 99th Infantry Division on the northern shoulder and the 4th Infantry Division on the southern shoulder were the veteran 28th Infantry Division and the green 106th Infantry Division of Middleton's VIII Corps. These units took the brunt of the German offensive operation and ceased to be effective fighting units after a few days. The badly outnumbered and outgunned 14th Cavalry Group, defending the Losheim Gap, was knocked out of action by December 17.

Acutely aware of the serious threat posed by the German offensive operation, Middleton had sent Combat Command Reserve (CCR) of the 9th Armored Division to the Belgian road junction town of Bastogne on December 16. (It arrived by midnight of December 17.) Middleton also sent the majority of his combat engineer battalions to act as infantry in the defense of the town. In addition, he dispatched Combat Command B (CCB)* of the 9th Armored Division to support the infantry regiment belonging to the 106th Infantry Division.

It became apparent early on the first day of the German offensive that additional forces would be required to stiffen

---

*World War II U.S. divisions were organized into three combat commands, each comprising about one third of the division's fighting strength. They were designated CCA, CCB, and CCR (R for "reserve").

the 28th and 106th Infantry Divisions as well as the 104th Cavalry Group. Eisenhower therefore ordered Patton's Third Army, located south of the Ardennes front, to send the 10th Armored Division to Bastogne. (It arrived on December 18.) Eisenhower further ordered Simpson's Ninth Army, north of the Ardennes front, to send the 7th Armored Division to the Belgian road and rail center of Saint-Vith, located twenty-five miles northeast of Bastogne.

The 7th Armored Division would arrive in the Saint-Vith area on December 19. Both Bastogne and Saint-Vith were major choke points for any offensive operation through the Ardennes, and the Americans had to hold it to prevail. Bastogne did not play an important part in the original German offensive operation plan. It only became important as the German Sixth Panzer Army was blocked at the northern shoulder of the Ardennes front, the shortest route to Antwerp, and the German Fifth Panzer Army became the primary force to head for Antwerp. The Fifth Panzer Army needed Bastogne, because it offered the second best path to Antwerp and resided in their sector of operations.

The German divisions of the Fifth Panzer Army initially took Saint-Vith on the night of December 21. However, the 7th Armored Division and other units defending the city merely pulled back to the surrounding area and kept delaying the German advance until December 23, when they were ordered to withdraw to a more easily defended location. By this time, the Americans had stymied the Germans' plan to reach Antwerp within a week, and their entire offensive operation was permanently thrown off schedule. The delay the vigorous Saint-Vith defense forced on the Germans also allowed the Americans to rush in reinforcements to the Ardennes. The 7th Armored Division would retake Saint-Vith on January 23, 1945.

In response to the growing crisis with Middleton's VIII Corps, Eisenhower sent in his last uncommitted reserves, the 82nd and 101st Airborne Divisions belonging to the XVIII Airborne Corps under the command of Maj. Gen. Matthew B. Ridgway. These divisions moved into the Ardennes front on December 19. The 82nd went to the Belgian town of Werbomont to help seal off the Losheim Gap.

The 101st Airborne Division arrived in Bastogne on December 19 to become part of Middleton's VIII Corps. Other units that would participate in the defense of Bastogne included the 705th Tank Destroyer Battalion and a number of divisional and nondivisional artillery units, as well as elements from a number of units and individual stragglers that drifted into the town and were put into the line.

Despite being surrounded by German forces and suffering countless attacks, Bastogne never fell into German hands. On December 26 the 4th Armored Division, which formed part of Patton's Third Army, would break the German blockade of Bastogne. Patton had launched his rescue of Bastogne from the town of Arlon, Belgium, on December 21 with his III Corps, which, besides the 4th Armored Division intended for Bastogne, included the 26th and 80th Infantry Divisions to its right.

Three days after sending his III Corps toward Bastogne, Patton launched his XII Corps, containing the 4th, 5th, and 35th Infantry Divisions along the right flank of the III Corps into the southern flank of the German bulge. Patton also brought other divisions into the fight, including the 90th and 95th Infantry Divisions along with the 6th Armored Division, to the right of the XII Corps. Eventually, Patton's Third Army would also be assigned the 87th Infantry Division, the 11th Armored Division, and the 17th Airborne Division.

On December 20, Eisenhower reassigned Hodges' First Army and Simpson's Ninth Army (a total of six corps, the V,

VII, XVIII, XII, XVI, and XIX, containing nineteen divisions) to Montgomery's 21st Army Group to enable Monty to commit his strengthened forces to counterattacking the northern flank of the sixty-mile-deep, eighty-mile-wide bulge that the Germans had punched into the American lines beginning on December 16. Bradley's 12th Army Group retained only Patton's Third Army, which consisted of four corps, the III, VIII, XII, and XX, giving Patton's Third Army a total of sixteen divisions.

The 82nd Airborne Division was eventually joined by the 7th Armored Division and 30th Infantry Division, from Simpson's Ninth Army, and formed the XVIII Airborne Corps, which would take responsibility for the Ardennes front sector located between Gerow's V Corps on its north and Collins' VII Corps to its south. As the fight developed, Gerow's V Corps, finally consisting of the 1st, 2nd, 9th, and the 99th Infantry Divisions as well as the 5th Armored Division, took responsibility for the northernmost sector of the Ardennes.

Simpson's Ninth Army sent the 2nd Armored Division into the fray, where it became part of Collins' VII Corps, which would eventually include the 3rd Armored Division; also sent in were the 75th and 84th Infantry Divisions. They would be responsible for the Ardennes sector located between the XVIII Airborne Corps on its north and the British XXX Corps to its south.

On January 3, 1945, Montgomery's 21st Army Group launched Hodges' First Army in a counteroffensive against the northern flank of the Bulge. Its goal was to link up with Patton's Third Army coming up from the south at the Belgium town of Houffalize, located nine miles northeast of Bastogne. Houffalize had fallen to the Germans on December 22, and the American forces recaptured it on January 16, 1945, effectively pinching off the Bulge. It took the Americans another twelve days pushing westward to restore the front lines to those held on December 16. The price the Western Allied armies paid was terribly high. They lost nearly 80,000 men to all causes; of these all but 1,400 were Americans. Estimates on German casualties range from 90,000 to 120,000 people. British Prime Minister Winston Churchill would state in the House of Commons on January 18, 1945, that the Battle of the Bulge was "undoubtedly the greatest American battle of the war, and will, I believe, be regarded as an ever-famous American victory."

1 | THE GERMANS ATTACK

Edward A. Connors
B Battery, 108th Field Artillery Battalion, 28th Infantry Division

The 28th Infantry Division had noticed increased enemy vehicle activity on the nights before the German attack in the Ardennes, but had discounted it as normal frontline relief activity. American soldier Edward Connors almost had a chance to see the German attack preparations.

IN DECEMBER 1944, THE 28TH INFANTRY DIVISION was in a rest area stretching from Wiltz, Luxembourg, to Eupen, Belgium, a distance of twenty-five miles. We had suffered heavy losses in the Hürtgen Forest on October 26 and 27 after having relieved the 9th and 47th Infantry Divisions, and we were in this rest area awaiting the replacements that would bring us up to battle strength.

I was a machine gunner positioned in front of the 155mm howitzers. The weather was bitterly cold, and we were constantly looking through binoculars for any type of movement. The first sergeant sent for me one day and said, "I'm sending you to guard the airstrip at Wiltz. There will be other gunners there, too." He told me that I would stand guard duty only at night and that during the day I would be on my own. This assignment was to be for just one week. One gunner from each of the other batteries was to go with me. I told the sergeant that I didn't like leaving the battery, but he said it was only for a week, it would be a nice break, and besides, he said, it was an order.

The next morning I was on my way to Wiltz with four other GIs. The airstrip was on a plateau halfway up a large hill. Wiltz was down in the valley below, and over the hill was a no man's land, thick with trees. The machine guns were set up on raised tripods so that you had to stand up in order to fire them. This, I thought, is not a good situation, no gunners during the day, only at night, and no protection, not even a foxhole. When I questioned this, I was told, "This is a rest area, no action here."

The fog was too thick for any of the planes to use the strip, but one of the pilots offered to give anyone a plane ride if the fog lifted before we moved out. The fog cleared in the afternoon of December 15, our last day there, so one other guy and I got our airplane ride. The other fellow went first and came back in a short time because he got airsick. The pilot wanted to know if I'd get sick too, and I told him, "No I wouldn't." I didn't know for sure, but I really wanted that plane ride.

The pilot showed me where to place my feet so that they wouldn't interfere with the control cables and told me I could remove my helmet and set it on my knees just in case I got sick. Well, we taxied down to the end of the uneven field, turned around, gunned the engine, and took off down the airstrip— and quickly we were in the air. What a thrill. We turned to the right and flew over the town of Wiltz. I could see the GIs below me grow smaller—what a different world it was from up in the sky. I was doing okay, so the pilot asked if I'd like to fly over the so-called front lines. At the moment, my mother's image flashed before me, and as much as I wanted to fly over the lines, I said "No thanks, my mother would kill me if I got shot down." He laughed, and we circled around Wiltz a few more times. I really enjoyed that plane ride.

Well, the next morning, December 16, we left to return to our outfits. Halfway back to the outfit we ran into heavy shell fire, but what happened on our way back is another story. We later learned that a half-hour after leaving the air strip at Wiltz, the Germans came over the hill area where we had been; it was the beginning of the Battle of the Bulge. We also found out that three of the four aircraft made it out safely. Sadly, though, the 28th Infantry Division Headquarters personnel stationed in Wiltz suffered heavy losses.

To this day I regret the decision I made not to fly over the front lines that day, for surely we would have seen the Germans preparing to attack the next day and maybe, just maybe, we could have made a difference.

—*The* Bulge Bugle, *February 2001*

Harry F. Martin Jr.
L Company, 424th Infantry Regiment, 106th Infantry Division

The 106th Infantry Division had noticed a great deal of movement opposite its frontline positions in the days before the German Ardennes Offensive but was so green to combat it didn't know what threat it might indicate. Soldiers like Henry "Harry" F. Martin Jr. would pay the price for that inexperience.

THE MORNING OF DECEMBER 16, ONE OF OUR LEADERS came charging into our cabin just before dawn, screaming, "The Germans are coming! The Germans are coming! We'll all be killed!" Those exact words are etched in my brain for the rest of my life. Thoughts raced through my head: This had been a quiet sector for almost three months. We had only been here for five days, so why are the Germans attacking us? We grabbed our rifles and steel helmets without wasting a second and got out of the cabin as fast as we could. Bill and I were assigned to the open foxhole on the extreme left flank. The rest of the platoon went to the log bunkers directly in front of them.

As soon as we got into our foxhole, Bill announced that he was going to use a rifle grenade. He sat down in the foxhole and affixed the grenade to his rifle. Seconds later I could see hundreds of shadowy heads bobbing up and down, coming over the crest of the hill just before dawn. They acted like they were drunk or on drugs. They came over the hill screaming and shrieking. Their shrill screams went right through my head. I was absolutely terrified. They had already outflanked our company, and now they were coming to finish us off.

Being on the extreme left flank with nothing on our left and out of sight of our platoon on the right, it felt almost like we were against the entire German army. I was horror-stricken. There was no thought of running away or surrendering; the thought never entered my mind. I had an absolute conviction to fight to the death while being certain that we would be killed. Just about this time, Bill tugged on my leg. I was vaguely aware that Bill had asked me to let him know when the Germans were close enough. Neither one of us had ever fired a rifle grenade before. We did not have the slightest idea of the effective range. There were so many of them storming down the hill coming right for us. There was no way of stopping all of them. I had a feeling of utter hopelessness of surviving the attack. I was panic-stricken. I felt that my entire life force had left my body.

I was already dead and I was fighting like a zombie. Sheer panic set in, causing me to fire my rifle without thinking or aiming. I was unaware of my body, just terror, firing my rifle as fast as my finger could pull the trigger. But they still kept coming as though they were immune to death. Apparently I was not hitting a thing. I was so transfixed with fear and terror, my eyes did not focus on the individual enemy attacking. I was firing blindly as fast as I could without thinking or looking through the sights of my rifle. All hope of living was gone. Bill tugged on my leg again and yelled, "Are they close enough?" I can remember telling him no, but my brain did not register distance or range. I could not even think about what Bill was saying. He tugged on my leg a half dozen times during the battle, and I kept telling him no. In my terror-stricken seizure I continued to fire my rifle frantically in the general direction of the swarming sea of terror. I could only see the huge mass of bodies charging toward me. It appeared as though the entire hillside was alive and moving in with its huge tentacles reaching out to devour me.

Some of the Germans went to their right and stormed the company command posts. I was vaguely aware of hearing hand grenades exploding inside the CP (command post). They killed our company commander. But with the Germans charging closer and closer, still screaming, and bullets zipping by my head, any thoughts of regret for Captain Bartel did not register, and we all would soon be dead anyway.

In the middle of this terrifying battle I heard a very confident calm voice inside my head say, "squeeze the trigger." I instantly calmed down, took careful aim at one of the charging Germans through my gun sight, and squeezed the trigger. He flung his arms up over his head and fell down dead, shot through the head. I felt a sensation surge through my whole body. I was no longer a zombie. My life force had come surging back. I was alive, and for the first time I felt that I had a chance to come out of this battle.

At this very moment I was a veteran combat soldier. I continued to shoot the attacking Germans until they finally stopped coming. The battle was over. After such intense fighting it was very strange how suddenly the battle ended, how quiet everything had become. I had a feeling of disbelief that it was over, but at the same time it seemed like it would never end.

Later I thought about the voice that I heard in my head and told me to squeeze the trigger. I had failed to qualify with the rifle in basic training. I had to go back and do everything by the numbers without live ammunition again. For the next five weeks after supper and on Sundays the practice continued. Over and over they drummed the procedure by the numbers into my head, always ending with, "Squeeze the trigger, do not jerk the trigger, slowly squeeze the trigger, sque-e-e-ze the trigger." After a while at night I dreamt about squeezing the trigger. We made fun of doing things by the numbers, but it saved my life.

The battle was over. I had conquered my worst fears and I had stood to fight the enemy. The battle had started just before dawn. I have no idea what time it was over. It had seemed like an eternity, but now it was over. What a great feeling it was to have survived our first battle. I had just started to relax a little when suddenly I came to the full realization of what had happened when the Germans threw the grenades into our company command post. Captain Bartel was dead and I was responsible. At the beginning of the battle when I was in my terror-stricken stage firing my rifle without thinking or aiming, some of the Germans dispersed to their right and surrounded the CP. If I had not been so terrified, I could have stopped them before they reached the CP. Because of my inability to function in the beginning, Captain Bartel was dead. I let my company commander down, and I felt tremendous remorse.

About thirty minutes later, still feeling remorseful, I looked up as some of the men from the other platoons walked by on their way to our field kitchen. I could not believe my eyes. There, among the men, stood Captain Bartel. He was alive!

Oh, thank God! Captain Bartel was alive! I was very surprised and at the same time very happy to see him. He had not been in the company command post when the Germans threw the grenades in. He had left that post before our 3rd Platoon was alerted. He was already up with the main body of our company. We had slept through the heavy artillery barrage that struck our forward platoons.

—*The* Bulge Bugle, *August 1991*

Leon J. Setter
Headquarters Company, 2nd Battalion, 42nd Infantry Regiment, 106th Infantry Division

Most of the inexperienced 106th Infantry Division was quickly overwhelmed by the German Ardennes Offensive in the first few days. Leon Setter describes the confusion and his frustration during that time and his capture.

I WAS AN AMMO BEARER ON DECEMBER 16, 1944. I was quartered in a wood shack atop the Schnee-Eifel in the first belt of pillboxes of the Siegfried Line, which had been taken the previous fall. The 106th Infantry Division line extended north to include the 1st Battalion and the 14th Cavalry, attached to the 106th, and to the south by the 3rd Battalion and the 423rd Regiment, with the 2nd Battalion in reserve. Continuing to the south was the 424th Infantry Regiment. Initial attacks by the enemy against our division occurred in the 14th Cavalry area and against the 423rd and 424th Infantry Regiments.

My shack was among several built around pillboxes. It was close to a pillbox that served as 2nd Battalion headquarters. In turn, this pillbox was located about two miles east of the town of Schlausenbach, which was headquarters for the 422nd Infantry Regiment. The shacks had been vacated on December 12 by men of the 2nd Infantry Division as they were being relieved by the 106th Infantry Division. Their new assignment was to move north and prepare for an attack by filtering through the 99th Infantry Division. This attack was in progress when the Bulge began.

The shack was big enough to house two people: me and a truck driver. We were awakened early by the artillery fire on the morning of December 16. We had just finished preparing to go outside our hut when our platoon sergeant knocked on the door to inform us that the division had been placed on a class-one alert because of enemy activity in the area.

After chow, the truck driver and I were given orders to go to an ammo dump somewhere in the Schönberg–Saint-Vith area to pick up a truck load of ammo. At the ammo dump we loaded the truck and were resting when a truck from the 423rd Regiment pulled up. The driver explained that his truck guard had just been killed when they came into contact with the enemy near a road junction between Schönberg and Bleialf. He then told us where the incident took place and suggested we be careful on the way back. This was the first time we had heard of an actual attempt to penetrate our lines, even though we had picked up several rumors that an attack would occur soon.

We took off immediately with our loaded truck. We decided that it would be best for us to go back the same way we had come into the dump, rather than trying to determine a different way back. I was in the back of the truck while he was driving. After driving for about an hour we arrived at 2nd Battalion headquarters. During the trip back the driver kept a close lookout to the front as best he could while I kept scanning the area to the rear as we drove. The return trip was successful without coming in contact with the enemy, even though we had to pass near the location where the initial incident occurred.

As we pulled up in front of 2nd Battalion headquarters we learned that all available men from Headquarters Company had been sent to assist with responding to the activity at Auw. By this time, the flank of the 422nd Regiment was exposed and the enemy was beginning to penetrate us to the rear. I spent the afternoon as a guard just outside the 2nd Battalion headquarters pillbox. My orders were to keep scanning the area for the enemy and not to allow anyone outside to enter the pillbox without first getting the permission of one of the officers inside the pillbox. Late in the afternoon when I was on relief from guard duty, General Alan Jones and some of his staff pulled up in a Jeep. After talking to some officers in the headquarters pillbox, he and his staff members proceeded on foot, presumably to visit one of the rifle company areas. Soon thereafter, General Jones, who was the 106th Infantry Division commander, returned and continued his tour.

During the evening of the 16th, our platoon sergeant told us that the company had been ordered to be ready to pull out just after midnight. We were not to take our duffle bags because we would return in a few days. Shortly after midnight, we assembled on the logging road in front of the CP in columns of four. It was pitch dark and difficult to determine how many men in addition to my company were in front of us or behind us. After about twenty minutes, the column began walking down the road we had used to enter the area four days earlier. We walked for what seemed like one or two hours, stopping from time to time to rest and to allow the column to remain together or allow other companies to join us.

Suddenly I realized that I had lost contact with my squad. I noticed that a soldier just in front of me had a Browning automatic rifle (BAR). Also, I knew he was not in my company because no one in my company carried such a rifle. Evidently he was a member of the 2nd Battalion, which was in the process of moving into a wooded area. This soldier shot some rounds into a clump of trees to our front, which reduced the small-arms fire in my immediate area. One soldier got up and ran about a hundred yards into the cover area without getting hit despite the tracer bullets flying in all directions. The second soldier ran the hundred yards into the trees. Next, it was my turn. The fourth man to run the hundred yards I recognized as a member of my squad. Afterwards he showed me his mess kit on the back of his pack. There was a bullet hole through it. He had felt something hit as he was running and considered himself lucky because he was running with his head and shoulders down in a squatted position.

After walking into the woods about fifty yards, I saw Colonel Deschenaux, the 422nd Regiment's commander. Then I went into a shack used by the field artillery. This must have been the 589th Field Artillery Battalion, as they were the support artillery unit for the 422nd Regiment. There, I saw a member of my platoon who had just had a bullet hit him in the front which had just penetrated his overcoat as he was standing parallel with the bullet as it traveled across his chest.

Next, I saw my squad leader. He called my squad together and told us our situation looked bad. He reminded us that we were completely surrounded. He concluded by telling us to dig foxholes to protect ourselves from the shelling and that we would assemble after dark in an attempt to find our way to make contact with American lines again. I spent the next hour digging a foxhole and dodging the shelling. A small fragment hit me in the hand. It was about the size of a toothpick and about a half-inch long. It stuck in my hand, so I pulled it out.

As I finished digging my foxhole, my squad leader came to me and told me that Colonel Deschenaux had ordered the entire 422nd Regiment to surrender to the enemy and that we were ordered to destroy our weapons. Also, we were to form in a group within thirty minutes to walk down the hill in accordance with instructions given by the enemy. Needless to say, I was confused. This had been my first day in actual combat. At first I felt relieved because of the combat pressure. Soon it began to sink in, and another kind of fear set in: that of the unknown. What was going to happen next?

I proceeded to dismantle my carbine after about ten minutes had passed, throwing the parts in all directions. As I walked toward the assembly area, I saw an American soldier that had been wounded and apparently was in shock. A few of the men were trying to make him as comfortable as possible.

By this time I saw a couple of the enemy soldiers who were lining us up in a column of fours to march us down the hill. It took about thirty to forty minutes for the column to get into Schönberg, where we were placed inside a Catholic church. As soon as the church was filled, the rest of the prisoners had to sleep outside on the ground.

On the morning of December 20, we were lined up in a column of four and walked into Germany. I was a prisoner of war until liberation on April 14, 1945. My weight when captured was 160 pounds, which fell to 100 pounds by the time I was liberated 119 days later.

This is my story. When I left the Bulge area, it was growing by the hour. Its containment and eventual elimination is the story of other men. God bless them.

—*The* Bulge Bugle, *November 1991*

Jesse L. Morrison
B Battery, 482nd Antiaircraft Automatic Artillery Weapons Battalion, 9th Armored Division

Combat Command R of the 9th Armored Division had been stationed in Trois-Vierges, Luxembourg, to reinforce the 106th Infantry Division if needed. Jesse Morrison describes how his unit escaped capture during the German Ardennes Offensive.

MANY THINGS HAVE BEEN WRITTEN ABOUT THE BATTLE OF THE BULGE. Some are true, some not. One thing that is not true is that there was a breakthrough and that we had been surprised by the Germans.

My involvement in the campaign began a few days before December 16, 1944. We were dug in on a hill outside Trois-Vierges, Luxembourg. A lieutenant from my Battery B, 482nd AAA SP (self-propelled) 9th Armored, First Army, came to our half-track and told us our planes had spotted a large amount of German equipment assembled just across the border from us. He said our commanders had decided to move us out and open the line for five miles to allow them to come through. Then we would cut them off and starve them. This decision, instead of meeting them head on, was in my opinion the biggest blunder of the campaign. This has been covered up.

We moved to a small town in Belgium and sat waiting for the Germans to move. One morning before dawn, someone knocked on our front door and said, "Get out of town fast, as the Germans are coming in." We got on our vehicles and rode out of town and kept driving until sometime before noon. We received orders by radio to proceed to Saint-Vith, Belgium, and join the 7th Armored Division already there. They had succeeded in having most of the German tanks retreat and were engaged in combat with the ones still there.

In a few hours the town was cleared, but they dug in outside of town and continued to shell us the rest of the day. Our tanks finally succeeded in destroying them all.

We had an order to hold Saint-Vith for twenty-four hours and then move out, and our planes would bomb it. The weather did not permit this. We held it for forty-eight hours. When we decided to withdraw, we found we were surrounded. Both our flanks had withdrawn earlier without our knowledge. We kept moving around to avoid capture. During this time we came upon a half-dozen of our own tanks, crew intact, parked on a paved road. They planned to rescue some of our officers and men that had been captured the day before. Our lieutenant at that time was Howard Jackson from Louisiana. He was ordering us to pass the tanks, and we were reluctant to do this. He walked in the road and was wounded. Then one of the tanks took a direct hit and started burning—then another and another. It was time for us to leave, which we did.

We came upon some units of the 106th Infantry Division. They were tired, cold, and hungry. I remember giving one of them a can of string beans. He cut the can with his bayonet and ate those cold beans with his fingers. These boys were starving.

They received orders to withdraw. We stayed there so they wouldn't get overrun before they got dug in. We learned the Germans were in a town not far from us. The lieutenant we had left was Frank W. Winchester, of Memphis, Tennessee. He decided we would go just outside of this town and wait for the Germans to come our way. We proceeded down a farm road for about two miles, came to the outskirts of town, and positioned our three half-tracks off the side in a field. Our plan was to slaughter them in retribution for their having captured some of our officers and men.

We hadn't slept in days, so, while waiting, the guard went to sleep. You don't have to guess who that was. The Germans woke me going up the road, laughing and talking, their guns being pulled by vehicles and horses. I stayed quiet and watched them until it was time to wake my relief, who was Sergeant Mabry, from West Virginia. The Germans were too close for me to use our radio, so Sergeant Mabry crawled to one of the other vehicles to contact Lieutenant Winchester to inform him of our predicament. He told us to come to the paved road the same way we had gone down. This meant we would have to get in line with the Germans and try to pass them by. They had captured and were using some of our equipment, so we were able to do this. They would move aside and let us pass. We were successful.

Upon reaching the paved road, just at the break of day, we were astonished to see nothing but smoke. We were told later that our planes had spotted us in that pocket. Someone had ordered some part of the 75th Infantry Division to open up that road and smoke it to let us out. We drove fifty miles that day and spent that evening and night in the field. I think that was Christmas Eve. I'm not sure.

Having no maps of the area, Lieutenant Winchester decided we should move farther. About 2 a.m. we proceeded to move. There was a town about a mile away that we would have to pass through. There were Germans in that town, and we had to fight our way through.

The successful holding of the German armored division at Saint-Vith kept them from proceeding to Bastogne. Saint-Vith was the turning point of the Battle of the Bulge.

—*The* Bulge Bugle, *August 1992*

Joseph Jan Kiss Jr.
C Company, 38th Infantry Regiment, 2nd Infantry Division

When the German Ardennes Offensive began, the 2nd Infantry Division was attacking eastward toward the Roer River dams. Realizing that a major attack was taking place, the divisional commander redirected his forces southward to stem the German attack. Joseph Kiss Jr. describes the fighting for the twin Belgian towns of Krinkelt and Rocherath and his division's withdrawal to the Elsenborn Ridge.

ON THE NIGHT OF DECEMBER 15, OUR SQUAD STOPPED and dug in by a firebreak as sort of an outpost. I dug in with Pvt. Bill Horn.

At dawn I saw a small pillbox a hundred feet to the right, and I went to check it out. Going down the stairs, I heard a noise and I peeked around a wall with a grenade in hand, and saw Sergeant Vaughn peeking at me—he was checking also! I talked to Vaughn and returned to the foxhole. Private Stanley Gawronski yelled to me, "Sergeant, I just saw some Germans run across the firebreak about forty yards ahead." I said, "Why didn't you shoot?" He said, "Well, really I couldn't see too good, and besides, I didn't want them to know we were here." I said, "That sounds okay."

By now it was daylight. Next to me in the hole, Bill Horn—a good-looking young man with a thin moustache—had a K-ration open. He said, "Want a cracker, Joe?" I said, "Yeah, I'll pay you back." I took it and heard a bullet hit Bill in the head. His head fell on my shoulder, and blood ran onto my shoulder. He was staring at me, and his mouth was opening and closing fast, like a fish out of water, with a slight gurgle. I felt his pulse: it was quivering and then stopped. I yelled to the other guys, "Bill just got shot. He's dead. Keep your heads down!" (The sniper shot Bill instead of me because he was a little taller and the sniper saw him better, I believe.) Then someone yelled, "Pull back. We're pulling out."

We pulled back in broad daylight, about seven or eight miles from near Wahlerscheid to the twin towns of Krinkelt and Rocherath in Belgium, under artillery fire. I hit the ground near a German foxhole, afraid to get in it, as it may have been booby trapped. A machine gun burst over me, tearing black bark off trees and exposing the white wood underneath, causing me to dive in the foxhole anyway.

We walked into Krinkelt at dark with German tanks on the horizon firing point-blank at us. We could see them on account of light from the burning buildings. We were walking along the road in a ditch two feet deep filled with water. The wounded were falling on the road and into the ditch.

We had orders to help no one. Leave them for the medics. Keep moving. The dead or wounded that fell on the road were mashed by trucks, tanks, and Jeeps, bumper-to-bumper, trying to escape.

I saw men smashed flat as a pancake. You could see the outlines of helmets through bodies twice a normal size, smashed flat. I had to stare at some for a while to figure out that it was once a human being.

Some animals were in a burning barn across the road, and it sounded like the crying of human babies.

At a crossroad someone tapped me on the shoulder and said, "What outfit, son?" I said, "Charlie Company, 38th Regiment, 2nd Division." I saw two stars on his helmet, but I knew from pictures that he was Gen. Walter Robertson, our division commander. He said, "Down this road to the left, about two blocks to a brown brick house on the end." I said, "Yes, sir," called to my squad, and took off. I heard later that he was all over the area trying to build up a good, strong line and gather up stragglers.

I got into the brick house just as a German tank shot an 88 shell above the door, killing one GI, shredding money from his wallet in the process. The Germans were calling, "Hey, Charlie Company," but we had orders long ago never to answer, as they only wanted to locate you. Although 99th Infantry Division and 106th Infantry Division GIs who were shot up badly kept coming through our lines for days and yelling to us, especially the wounded, we wouldn't answer till we positively identified them.

I turned in one tank destroyer crew for not obeying my order to come over and knock out a German tank a block from us. We called them yellow and other things. They said, "Couldn't move till Lt. So-and-So came back." I said, "But we need you right now."

At daylight I was sitting in the barn, back against the straw, with a guard at the door. A sniper in the church across the street shot at the guard. The bullet chipped the barn door and hit the straw next to my left ear. We fought all day and all night. The sniper in the church finally took a shot at Colonel Mildren, our battalion commanding officer. We heard that he had a tank blow off the steeple.

Three German tanks knocked out three of our tanks by the church, which looked like a tank graveyard. German artillery and Nebelwerfer (six-barrel) rockets poured it on. The night of the 17th, Captain Rollings had another guy and me hook anti-tank mines to telephone wires across the road in a ditch. We hid in the cellar across the street. If enemy tanks came down the road, we were to pull the wire and drag the mines onto the road in front of them. None came.

We heard about a massacre at Malmédy (really Baugnez by a tavern); eighty-six were killed and forty-three got away. I walked within arm's reach of that Malmédy sign shown on pictures. Lots of guys said, "No more prisoners," but I never could shoot one in cold blood. In fact, I was awfully happy when they quit shooting and surrendered. I noticed a lot of them had wedding rings on. Some kneeled down and prayed.

One GI shot a German dragging a machine gun out of a clump of trees eight times in the back with his M1; funny how he didn't ask him to surrender. This German seemed to be praying in French as he died.

One prisoner, a wiry guy, stood ramrod straight and wouldn't talk. This kind of gave me a slow burn, so I went to punch him; he ducked his head, and I hit his steel helmet. That taught me something, but I got his brand new Schmeisser machine pistol.

The Germans had a gun with a cardboard barrel. Laugh, but it's true! It was used to propel propaganda leaflets into our lines about one and a half miles.

Their MG42 machine guns could fire 1,500 rounds per minute. It scared the holy hell out of us. It was a vicious, wicked gun. Just went *BBRRRRUUPPPP.* We called it "Hitler's saw." Our air-cooled machine gun only fired six hundred rounds per minute.

Every fourth or fifth German carried a hose about five feet long and a half-inch wide. We wondered why. Then it dawned on me—it was to siphon gas from disabled vehicles; they were short of gas.

German artillery and machine gun fire was awful. German tracers were yellow, ours a reddish pink; they looked like pretty—but deadly—fireflies at night.

This was the coldest winter ever. It hit twenty-seven below one night, and we woke up one morning around December 20 with one foot of snow on us. Son of a bitch, it was cold! We found small Christmas trees in houses. The Germans had tinfoil from cigarette packs and bits of torn colored paper on them. It made us sad.

The Germans yelled at us all the time to surrender, but we fought on. I saw grown men cry, but no one laughed. We all felt bad. I cursed Hitler for the thousandth time.

About 3 a.m. December 18, our 155s (artillery pieces) knocked out a tank 150 yards from us. German tankers in short black jackets, four of them, ran just below us to a drop off, about a foot. But we could see them well from above. We called to them to give up. They said, "Do you surrender, Yanks?" A BAR man next to me shot them. The German soldier is a son of a bitch to fight. You hardly ever get a good shot at one, and he really perseveres. But he seems to have an uncanny ability to know or estimate correctly when the jig is up and it's no use continuing to fight any longer (and judge it better or wiser to surrender). I saw one German with his upper half completely shot off! I also saw a German lieutenant lying 150 feet from me for about four hours not moving. I was sure he was dead. I looked real hard, but I couldn't see any signs of breathing. All of a sudden he jumped up with hands high shouting, *"Kamerad, kamerad, nicht schiessen!"* (Friend, friend, don't shoot!) and surrendered to us.

I saw Captain Rollings, a mean, tough Texan, get shot in the legs, around December 18. He always had a small cigar in his mouth. Whenever he thought the prisoners were too cocky or laughed at him, he put his gun down, donned leather gloves, and beat them badly. He sent me on a suicide mission once to blow a hole in a wall with twenty pounds of dynamite. He covered me with a machine gun from a shell hole in the ground. (Remember, captain?)

Germans were yelling, *"Marschiert schnell! Schnell!"* (Move quickly! Quickly!) But we held. We were dirty, muddy, unshaven, wet, tired, and frozen beyond belief. I wish everyone could see us now!

When bullets came close to your head, they split the air so fast that air coming back together pops like a hard clap of hands. It really pops; only ricochets will buzz or whine or whir—so much for movie phoniness.

On December 17, rumor had it that we (the 2nd Infantry Division) were to hold Krinkelt and Rocherath, while the 99th Infantry Division remnants and some from the 2nd Infantry Division were to go back west to Elsenborn Ridge one and three-quarters of a mile away, to start preparing us a new line. First Infantry Division was on the way to tie in on our right at Elsenborn Ridge. Good news.

At 7 a.m. on December 18, many tanks attacked us. Infantry had crept up at night to the very edge of both towns. We backed up a hundred yards, and our artillery smashed the tanks, and our infantry drove back the German troops.

On the 19th, after wrecking all the usable guns and vehicles we could not take out, we retired to Elsenborn, being shelled all the way in the rain. (After the war, I read that a German spotter with a motorcycle and radio in the woods directed that damn, accurate shell fire. We lost more than one thousand men at the Battle of the Bulge.)

I had a good hole on top of a ridge, with a good, long field of fire. Our 38th Infantry Regiment was on the front line, another regiment behind us manned a second line of defense, and there was another regiment behind them for reserve. Talk about power! Most times there is only one regiment behind you. With 1st Infantry Division on our right and 9th Infantry Division on the left, all of us veterans, we felt pretty good. We had artillery almost hub-to-hub behind us for support: sixteen batteries of division artillery (four were 155s) and seven batteries of corps artillery (155s, 4.5-inch, 105s, and 8-inch). We also had twelve regiments of 105mm howitzers, 348 guns, tank and tank destroyer guns (75mm and 90mm), and also one battery of 4.2-inch chemical mortars. One helluva concentration when they fired all at once, as they did at Krinkelt and Rocherath. It was awesome. Both towns seemed to explode. We really felt sorry for those Germans. We called it a division serenade, as all those different sizes of shells made a different sound going through the air.

Behind my dugout on Elsenborn Ridge was a fence row with trees about ten feet high along it, about two hundred yards from me. Our antitank guns were hidden there. On Christmas, I was talking to a gun crew as we watched buzz bombs going toward Liège, Antwerp, Belgium, and maybe to England. They made a loud, brackish noise. Four German planes started to bomb and strafe back by our artillery. All of a sudden from the southwest, a P-51 Mustang dove onto them and shot all four down in about three or four minutes. We were amazed, of course. They flew over us once, shooting. We dove under an ammo Jeep. I heard a tinkling sound, looked up into the trees, and saw .50-caliber shell casings from the P-51's guns trickling down through the tree branches. I reached and grabbed one for a souvenir, and it burned my hand. It was still hot! I brought it home, but somehow it got lost, like my Iron Cross and other souvenirs.

I decided to build a larger dugout under the trees at the fence row, as an artillery shell caved in the right front of my old dugout. The same barrage had one shell hit dead center on Barnett's hole fifteen seconds after he ran to a buddy's hole on his left, "real luck!"

I had the new hole pretty deep when the new CO, Lieutenant Mode, walked up. He laughingly said, "If you go any deeper, I'll court martial you for desertion!" A half-hour later I leaned back to rest and was looking out and up through the trees over my hole. I heard artillery coming in and heard a tick and a branch wiggled in front of me as a shell whizzed over me and hit about fifty feet back. Evidently the side of the shell scraped the branch. If the nose would have hit it, it would have exploded right above me. I stared at the branch for five minutes and couldn't move. Whew!

We later heard that this was called the "Battle of the Bulge."
—*The* Bulge Bugle, *February 1993*

John B. Savard
G Company, 38th Infantry Regiment, 2nd Infantry Division

The heroic delaying action of the 2nd Infantry Division at the twin Belgian villages of Krinkelt and Rocherath threw off the German Sixth Army's northward advance. John Savard describes the fighting in and around Rocherath.

EACH YEAR OUR MINNESOTA WINTERS TURNED MY THOUGHTS back to 1944 and the Ardennes. As a nineteen-year-old rifleman in G

Company, 38th Infantry, 2nd Infantry Division, I will never forget the cold and snow of that terrible battle. I had been wounded in the arm and chest on June 21, 1944, in Normandy, and after two months in a hospital in England, I rejoined my company near the end of August 1944. The war news was very good, and most of us believed the war in Europe was nearly over. After we helped liberate the French port of Brest, my division was transported across France to the Belgium-Germany border and took over positions in Schnee-Eifel. While in these positions, we were able to replace our Normandy and Brittany losses with new men and returning wounded. On December 11, all our units were relieved by elements of the newly arrived 106th Infantry Division. Our new mission was to move further north, where we were to attack through the 99th Infantry Division lines. Our objective was the Roer River dams.

The division jumped off on December 13 with our 9th Infantry Regiment in the lead. Because of the nature of the terrain, with the lack of roads, the advance began on a regimental front. By December 16, the 9th Regiment had forged a break in the German fortifications at the border town of Wahlerscheid, and my regiment pushed through the gap to continue the attack. As we moved through the Monschau forest, we began to hear the ominous sounds of battle to our rear. Actually, our 23rd Infantry Regiment was already involved in support of the 99th Division and also to cover our only road to safety.

Late on December 16, my company was ordered to hold what we had, but be prepared to continue the attack on December 17. As more information was received, it became apparent that the fighting we could hear was not just a local counterattack. We were told to be ready to withdraw all our men and equipment back down the single road toward the Belgian towns of Rocherath and Krinkelt, for we faced the danger of being cut off.

When the withdrawal orders were given, the 38th Infantry Regiment was leading the advance, and my battalion was assigned the mission of protecting the regiment's withdrawal. The night of the 17th was the beginning of a nightmare. I can vividly recall our withdrawal and our attempts to block the enemy advance. At one point, in pitch darkness, we set up a defense along a firebreak, protecting our line of withdrawal. The ground was frozen, and only shallow holes could be dug. The forest around us was filled with artillery bursts and tracer fire. Luckily, the enemy forces facing us were not able to get much armor forward, and the pair of Sherman tanks that were supporting our position kept the enemy from over-running our line. After things settled down a little, the tanks withdrew down the road to Rocherath and we were ordered to follow.

As G Company fought its way into Rocherath, it seemed like the whole town was on fire. The town was being defended by service troops of the 38th Infantry Regiment, and it seemed that enemy forces occupied half the houses. Regimental headquarters was under attack, and our first mission was to secure the area around this headquarters. When we finally forced the enemy out of the buildings around regiment, I found myself as a temporary guard in a barn-like building attached to regimental headquarters. The road equipment was in operation, and I could hear operators sending and receiving messages. Few people seemed to know what was going on. When the situation in our part of town had stabilized, G Company was given a new mission. We were to fight our way back to the outskirts of town and defend a road junction which friendly troops might use to get into town.

We had had little food and no sleep for about thirty-six hours, and when we finally reached our objective, it was completely dark. We spent the evening of December 18 preparing our defensive position, which was a junction where two roads met on their way into Rocherath. After the position around some farm buildings was secured, a patrol was sent out to attempt contact with any friendly troops still heading for Rocherath. None of the patrol returned, and all were listed as killed in action. As the night passed, metallic sounds were heard in front of my platoon and reported to the captain. We were told there was at least one knocked-out German tank at the edge of a farm field and perhaps the enemy was trying to relieve it. We called for artillery fire, and the noise stopped. Soon after, under cover of darkness, a group of men approached our position walking down one of the roads. Our outposts believed it was our returning patrol, and before they could react, an enemy force of about a dozen men were inside our perimeter, spraying the area with automatic fire. First Sergeant Embody gathered some company headquarters men and began to clean out the enemy. We had already heard that the SS troops we were facing were killing American prisoners and therefore none of the attackers were taken prisoners. The burp gun fire by the original enemy force must have been a sign, for the whole line erupted in battle.

My foxhole buddy Norman Martz was hit in the head. Others along the line suffered similar fates, but with mortar and machine gun fire, we held our position. As the Germans pressed forward, Captain Skagg called for artillery fire on our position, which probably turned the tide of battle. When the Germans withdrew, my squad was down to five men. The rest of the company was about the same. As daylight came, a relief column reached us and we withdrew into town, where we formed teams to hunt down the German tanks which had forced their way into town under cover of darkness.

While hunting down German tanks on December 19, on one occasion I stepped out the door of one house and found myself looking almost down the gun barrel of a Mark IV tank. I dove back inside and down the cellar as part of the building exploded. A bazooka team knocked out the tank and killed the crew as they emerged. During the night of December 19, the remaining defenders of the two towns were ordered to with-draw to new positions prepared by our engineers on Elsenborn Ridge. From these positions we fought off all enemy attacks. The remains of the German panzers slipped off to the west, where they were stopped by other American units.

—*The* Bulge Bugle, *February 1992*

Rollo J. Moretto
C Company, 26th Infantry Regiment, 1st Infantry Division

Once the German Ardennes Offensive struck the V Corps front lines, the command post of its northern neighbor, the VII Corps, sent the 26th Infantry Regiment of the uncommitted 1st Infantry Division as reinforcements. Rollo Moretto relates how American artillery saved his unit from being overrun by the enemy.

ON APPROXIMATELY DECEMBER 9, 1944, WE WERE RELIEVED, and it was rumored that the 1st Division would be returning to England for a much needed rest. By then, we had been in com-bat for six months, starting with the Normandy Invasion on June 6, 1944. Our ranks depleted and badly in need of all sorts of equipment, the rumor sounded good. We were pulled back to the Liège-Verviers area.

After less than a week, the Germans had broken through the U.S. defenses, and my unit was immediately alerted and rushed to the breakthrough area. C Company was attached to the 2nd Battalion of the 26th Infantry Regiment for the move. We traveled both on foot and by truck in a shuttle-type move, and our target was Bütgenbach. On our way we encountered many American troops who had been overrun and were disorganized and in full retreat.

Some of the troops were on foot and some were in vehicles, including some tanks. Some of the men related some weird accounts of what was going on. The one account that has always stuck in my mind was that Tiger tanks were being dropped by parachute in the breakthrough area. On the way we had also been advised by S2 (military intelligence) that the Germans had dropped paratroopers dressed in American uniforms who spoke perfect English. This and other stories we heard made us wonder what we were headed for.

We arrived in Bütgenbach late at night on December 16 and immediately started to set up a defense. Outposts were set up along C Company's front, with the main line of resistance approximately seventy-five yards behind the outposts.

At the break of dawn the following morning all hell broke loose. As far as your eye could see, German tanks were coming over the rise, firing their machine guns as they came. German infantry followed the tanks on foot. After a short time the tanks overran our outposts. They ran right over the foxholes in some cases, and in other instances the enemy tank personnel motioned for the men to surrender.

Everyone as far as I could judge began to withdraw piecemeal. I and some of the others finally sought refuge in the cellar of an extremely large building.

Lieutenant Colonel Derrill M. Daniel, commander of the 2nd Battalion, and his headquarters personnel were the occupants of this building. Two tanks soon penetrated to about twenty yards of the building, and by this time there appeared to be over a hundred soldiers in that cellar. At one point a rifle went off, and someone yelled out, "They're throwing hand grenades down the cellar," and boy did that start a scramble.

Colonel Daniel was personally directing artillery fire over the radio. He was in communication with all sorts of artillery units, including our own 33rd Field Artillery Battalion and division's 5th Field Artillery Battalion with their 155s. He even was asking for corps artillery, and at one point he yelled over the radio, "Get me all the dammed artillery you can get." There is no doubt in my mind that Colonel Daniel almost single-handedly slowed the German advance until reinforcements arrived and began to build on our positions. Thanks to Colonel Daniel and fortunately for us, the German infantry had taken all sorts of casualties from the artillery fire and were unable to penetrate our defenses in any number.

When Colonel Daniel was advised about the two tanks that had penetrated to within twenty yards of the building, he asked to be kept advised of their movements. I would inch up the cellar stairs, and when the tank crews would spot me, they would turn the 88s and fire a round. But before they did, I would come flying down those cellar steps. The situation remained that way, it seemed, for an eternity.

Colonel Daniel called for volunteers to knock out the tanks with a bazooka. One young soldier somehow with help managed to get on the roof of the building and miraculously disable one tank. It seemed like an impossible task but somehow that kid got the job done. The remaining tank stayed for a while and then turned tail, probably realizing he was sticking out like a sore thumb without support.

It was fortunate for us that our artillery inflicted so much damage to the German infantry. Otherwise, we surely would have been outflanked.

During the Bulge, I understand that forty-three enemy tanks were knocked out in the 26th Infantry Regiment's area. In succeeding days the Germans attacked our positions numerous times, with artillery supporting their infantry, but by then we were solidly in place and never budged an inch. Toward the end of December the action slowed somewhat, and patrols from both sides operated in the area.

—*The* Bulge Bugle, *February 1991*

Charles Haug
B Company, 112th Infantry Regiment, 28th Infantry Division

Prior to deployment to the Ardennes front, the 28th Infantry Division had distinguished itself in the bloody battles of the Hürtgen Forest, which had begun in September 1944. The Ardennes was intended to be a rest area for the division. Charles Haug got very little rest in the Ardennes.

IT WAS A COLD, CLEAR NIGHT, AND THE ONLY NOISES I heard during the couple hours of guard duty were a few coughs from our own men, who were in holes farther down the line. Warren Quimby came to relieve me at midnight just like always, and I remember I told him there was one thing I didn't see during my two hours guard that I had always seen before: there hadn't been a single German flare shot up over our lines. We didn't think any more of it, and I went back to the dugout and crawled in beside Frankie.

At 2:00 a.m. Frankie Jordano went out to relieve Quimby, who told him there hadn't been a single flare shot up while he was on guard also. It didn't take long and it was 4:00 a.m.— my turn to relieve Frankie again. He said too that no flares had been shot up during his two hours. This meant a whole night without a single flare. I was pretty sleepy, and I was wishing it would soon be 6:00 a.m. so I could go back and sleep a little bit again. Little did I know then I had had my last real sleep I was to get for the next ten days.

Ten minutes past 5:00 a.m., December 16, 1944—what the hell happened? Who turned on the light switch? What am I seeing? At first I thought I had fallen asleep, but no! The whole sky had just become light, just like the dawn was breaking, and it was two hours early. This was no German flare, because you could always see them come sailing over you, hanging from their white parachutes. This was something much bigger than a flare. Something we had never seen before. The end of the world, maybe! It took about a minute before we finally got our mouths closed again. By now everyone had seen it, and there was a big commotion in our little town. Believe it or not— it was like bright moonlight over our positions. However, when we looked directly in front of us into the German lines, all we could see was the cold black night. We couldn't hear a sound anywhere, and it made chills run up and down our spine. Our watches ticked on. Soon it was 5:30 a.m. and no change. We were in bright moonlight, and five hundred yards in front of us it was completely dark. But, by now we had partly solved the big mystery. We realized the Germans had set up about ten or twelve gigantic searchlights on the hills about two or three miles in front of our positions. They aimed the beams of the lights up into the fog and clouds. This caused the lights to reflect down from the fog onto our positions and made it seem almost like moonlight. We immediately called back to our artillery and asked them to fire their long-range shells into the hills and try to knock out the lights. Our artillery let loose with everything they had, and I mean everything. In fact, they shot every shell they had. Next they shot up all their reserve shells, and then there was silence. They called and told us they were completely out of ammunition and they wouldn't be getting any more for a day or so, so it would be no use for us to call on them for the next forty-eight hours. That was just dandy. One of the search lights went out (perhaps from the artillery), so now there were only about ten or eleven of them still shooting their Hollywood premier beams up into the heavens.

By now it was 6:15 a.m., and everything was quiet. Suddenly, in the distance we could hear artillery shells being fired. We assumed it was the Germans who were firing this time. None of the shells landed in our immediate area. We could hear the shelling in the distance for about a half hour. Everything was still quiet in front of us. Our eyes were as big as saucers as we stared into the still darkness ahead of us.

About this time the phone in the command post rang. It was from the three fellows in our outpost we called "88." They talked fast and were scared. They could see Germans approaching their position in the early dawn. About this time we could hear German "burp guns" (submachine guns) firing and hand grenades exploding. The phone went dead. Five minutes later the fellows in our second outpost called and reported Germans throwing hand grenades at their position. More shots were fired, and we were minus another three men. This was our initiation to the famous Battle of The Bulge. We didn't realize yet, but we had been caught directly in the middle of the German attack.

Now we were next in line. There were about 190 of us in our positions around Lützkampen. We had no idea of what was coming, but by now we knew they weren't coming over to sing Christmas carols to us.

Frank Jordano, Warren Quimby, and I each had a foxhole just to the east of the company CP where Captain Deck, Lt. Mayer Goldstein, and 1st Sgt. Ralph McGeoch were located. George Knaphus and Ken Janne also had positions near us. Frank, Warren, and I were all messengers for our platoons, and we were put on the alert to contact our commanding officers in anticipation of messages.

From 7:00 to 7:30 a.m. there was complete silence in front of us. We later realized that it was during this time the Germans were moving their men up to begin their surprise attack on our positions around Lützkampen. It was still semi-dark, except for the light beams which were aimed into the sky. A few minutes past 7:30, we experienced what was perhaps the biggest hair-raising scare of our entire army career. Out of the darkness came the awfullest screaming and yelling you would ever want to hear. The Germans were coming! They were screaming like a bunch of wild Indians. They were less than a hundred yards in front of us. How they ever got so close without us hearing them, we'll never know. But there they were. They were coming, running as fast as they could, directly toward our positions. There was a steady stream of lead pouring from their guns. It seemed that about half of their bullets were tracer bullets, and the red streaks snapped in all directions. We immediately opened up on them, and the battle was on.

The first sergeant called Frankie and me to his dugout immediately. He wanted us to be ready to leave with the first message he could think of. As soon as our men started firing at the Germans, they took cover in the ditch of the road they were advancing on. At some points, they were as close as fifty feet to some of our men. All shooting was close-range stuff, and it was just a matter of who could shoot first.

By now, the dawn was just starting to break, and we could make out pretty well just where the Germans were. We estimated that there must have been about two hundred krauts attacking our positions, so we figured we could give them a pretty even match. However, we had one distinct advantage. We were in holes and dugouts. They were in the open field and in the ditch. During the first half hour of the battle, our men had pretty easy picking, and many Germans were killed.

Captain Deck was getting pretty nervous in his dugout, as we all were. For some reason, he suddenly decided that he had to be up closer to the other men in order to direct their fire. He was the first one of our men to leave his hole, and he ran fast in a low crouch toward the 1st Platoon men. He had run about fifty yards when the Germans spotted him. Just two shots and our company commander, Captain Deck, fell to the ground in front of us. We had only two medics in the company, and they rushed out to the captain as soon as they saw him fall, but they never made it. Both of them were shot down and killed before they had gone twenty yards. Our captain was also dead when we finally reached him.

The shooting back and forth kept up continuously for over an hour. The Germans would attack in groups of about six or seven men each. But we were usually able to knock them off before they could get very far. They did make some progress though. We saw a group of Germans attack one of our machine gun positions. They killed our guys, and that left us with only one machine gun in the company.

About this time the first sergeant sent both Frankie Jordano and me with messages to our platoons. My platoon was scattered along a hedgerow on the edge of town, and it seemed to be the longest run I have ever made. I had to run right past the place where Capt. Deck had been killed, and I figured sure I would be spotted. But by now, there were so many of our men running around that the krauts didn't know which one of us to shoot at. When I reached the 2nd Platoon and found Lt. John Peetz, he was busy directing the fire of his men. He told me to tell 1st Sgt. Ralph McGeoch they would soon have the krauts under control. So I carried the message back to McGeoch and waited for him to think of some other question for me to run and ask. Right then I wasn't too excited about being a platoon runner.

About ten o'clock the small-arms fire in our area finally stopped. In the ditch where the Germans had been attacking from, we could see a bunch of white handkerchiefs waving. By this time we had killed about 135 of the Germans, and one of our men had just picked off their captain, who had been ordering his men to attack. The remaining thirty or forty Germans decided to call it quits. As they came out of the ditch with their hands up, we were surprised to see that most of them were a bunch of young boys. The oldest was perhaps about eighteen, and they went down to about fourteen years old. This was part of what we had been fighting all morning. They must have been good shots, though, because our losses were by no means light. Out of our original two hundred men, we now had fewer than ninety men left. As soon as we had finished searching the krauts, they started to ask us questions. The main one seemed to be, "Will we be sent to New York?" Two of our men took the prisoners and headed for the battalion CP in the rear.

While one group of our men was busy with the German prisoners, another group was busy carrying our wounded into a building near the CP. There must have been about forty of them, and we could give them very little help. Both of our medics were dead, and we had no vehicles in which to transport the wounded to the rear. I will always remember their moans of pain and their pleas to help them to an aid station. But we could do nothing for them. Germans had pushed through the outfits on both the right and the left of us, and by now they were moving rapidly to the rear. Nearly all of our rear reserves had been captured by noon of this day, and that left us sitting in a little piece of land about a mile wide and a couple miles deep. We had licked the first wave of the enemy that hit us, but we knew by now that the Germans had made up their minds that they were going to win the war, and that there would soon be more Germans moving in en masse. We could hear frantic fighting going on all around us all morning, and as the day grew on, the shots came from farther and farther behind us. Our lines had crumbled.

We still had some faith left in the American army, though, and we prayed that other outfits in the rear would be able to stop the Germans and push back up to us. Early in the afternoon of this day we began to hear many vehicles and tanks approaching on the roads in front of us. As we watched through our field glasses, we could see hundreds of German tanks, trucks, and half-tracks coming down the winding roads. We knew that we didn't have a chance, but we had lost all contact with the rest of our division, and we had not had any orders to withdraw, so we had to sit tight. We did, however, move out of Lützkampen and into our old positions in the hills just behind Lützkampen. Our wounded were all left in Lützkampen, and we never heard from them again.

About 3:00 in the afternoon, the second wave of Germans reached Lützkampen. They stopped their trucks and tanks in town, and hundreds of Germans unloaded from the vehicles and began searching the houses. We heard many shots, and I suppose they killed all of our wounded that we had just left. About 5 p.m. their work was done, and we knew that they would soon be coming from the town toward us. We had nothing to defend ourselves with except our rifles. Our artillery was completely out of ammunition, and our machine gunners had all been killed. About 5:15, the dreaded moment came. Six small German tanks headed out of Lützkampen in our direction. Behind the tanks came hundreds of Germans on foot. The tanks seemed to crawl along about two or three miles an hour. We bit our lips and prayed. There were still about ninety of us on the hillside. As the first tank reached our first two guys in a hole, we witnessed the most horrible thing that any GI dreams of. The tank was equipped with a flamethrower.

It stopped about fifty feet from the hole, and as the two kids sat there helplessly, a gigantic stream of roaring fire shot in on them. Their worries were over. They had been burned to a crisp.

All of us on the hillside saw this, and we knew we were next. It terrified our guys, and many of them jumped up from their holes and ran back over the hill and into the thick woods in back of us. As the seconds ticked on, more and more of our men kept running to the rear. It was a sight that would hang heavy on any American's heart. It was a sight of defeat—our own men running to the rear in no organized manner. I guess the only reason Frankie, Quimby, and I didn't get up and run was that we were too scared to get out of our holes. Also, the first sergeant was nearby, and we were supposed to carry messages for him. Remember?

It wasn't long before the tanks once more started moving slowly in our direction. By now they were less than two hundred yards from us. We were scared and shaking. But just at this instant a miracle happened. From a hillside about a quarter of a mile to our left, we heard a series of sharp cracks from an antitank gun, it was shooting tracer shells, and we could see the streaks of fire coming from the hillside toward the tanks. The first few shells missed, but the third shell made a direct hit on the first tank, and it burst into flames. The streaks of fire kept coming from the hillside, and soon the second and third tanks were also in flames. About this time the German ammunition in the burning tanks started exploding. Did we ever have fireworks, shells exploding in every direction, and it was only a matter of seconds and the fourth and fifth tanks were also hit. Their tracks were knocked off, and they weren't able to move. The sixth tank must have got scared out. We saw it turn around and head back into Lützkampen. The Germans coming on foot also turned around and ran back to Lützkampen. They made no further attempt to attack that night. I'll always remember Lieutenant Peetz, my platoon officer, jumping from his hole and yelling, "We licked 'em! We licked 'em!"

Up until the time we heard the first shots from the hillside, we had no idea there were any of our antitank guns up there. We later found out they were with the 106th Infantry Division, and we were mighty glad to have them on our side.

Darkness soon came upon us, and the tanks were still burning. About 9 p.m. our first sergeant, Ralph McGeoch, decided that he wanted to know just how many of our men were still on the hillside with us. He sent Frankie and me out into the darkness to bring back all of our men that we could find. He wanted to organize all of his men so we would be ready for the attack we knew was coming the next morning. Frankie and I checked every hole where we knew our men were dug in. Most of them were empty. When we finally got through about midnight, we reported back to the first sergeant. Counting ourselves, we now had only eighteen men left on the hillside.

Many of the rest had gone deep into the woods behind us, where we could not find them. Yes, we now had one lieutenant and seventeen enlisted men left in our company. We hadn't had any contact with the rest of our division since early in the morning. Our company commander was dead, and Lt. M. Goldstein took over his command. He said that since we had no orders to withdraw, we would have to stay on the hillside and fight to the last man.

All of us paired off in twos and crawled into holes to take up our positions. I was in a hole with Frankie. Throughout the night, we could smell the awful smell of burned flesh. It was that of the Germans who had been caught inside of the first three tanks. They never had a chance to get out. About 3:00 in the morning, Frankie and I noticed a black object moving back and forth in the snow about a hundred yards is front of our hole. It looked to us like the body of a man crawling up the hill on his stomach. As we strained our eyes and listened, we could imagine that he was moaning and calling to us. Both Frankie and I kept our rifles on fire and were ready to shoot. It was a long night. As the dawn started to break, we could see that our black object was only a clump of weeds that had been blowing back and forth in the wind.

Soon it was daylight, and much to our surprise the Jerries stayed in Lützkampen and were making no effort to attack. Lieutenant Peetz kept repeating that he wished we could get our artillery outfit to shell the town; he figured with all those krauts in Lützkampen, we had a wonderful target in front of us. All of our communication wires back to the artillery units had been cut, so we had not had any contact with them since they called and said they were out of ammunition. Suddenly our first sergeant, Ralph McGeoch, got a wild idea. He figured that maybe by now, they had been able to get some sure ammunition, and if we could get word to them to shell Lützkampen, we could knock out a lot of Germans. He asked for a couple of volunteers to act as a patrol to contact the artillery. None of us responded to his call. We figured things were bad enough without having to chase around by ourselves in the daylight. But, his finger pointed—and Ken Janne and I had been ordered to contact the artillery. Ken was from Wichita, Kansas, and he came over on the boat with Frankie and me. This meant that there would now be only sixteen men left to defend our positions around Lützkampen. Ken and I said good-bye to Frankie, and we wished each other luck.

We knew that the artillery was supposed to have a forward observer on a hill about a quarter of a mile to our right. We crawled from our holes and ran as fast as we could for the hill. We hadn't gone over two hundred yards when we were spotted from the town. They started firing mortar shells on the hillside we were climbing. About fifteen of the shells landed around us, but we were not hit by any of the shrapnel. It seemed like a long climb, but we finally got to the clump of trees on the hill, where we were supposed to find the forward observer. But we didn't find our artillerymen. What we found were two GI helmets, two army rifles, and two cartridge belts lying in a pile on the ground. This meant only one thing: our two artillerymen had been captured during the night. It also meant that the Germans had taken this ground, and they probably had men around very close. Ken and I decided we'd get the hell out of there. We knew that the artillery had been dug in about a mile or so behind our lines, so we decided we'd try to get back to them with the message from the first sergeant. We made our way to the edge of the clump of trees, and we came upon a big field. We had to get across this field in order to get to the wooded area behind our lines that led to our artillery positions. Just as we started across the field, we heard a roaring sound to our left. We took one look, and our hearts jumped to our throats. What we saw was a huge, black German tank. Its men must have seen us coming from the woods, and it was moving itself into a better firing position. We made a mad dash for the opposite side of the field, but as we ran we heard a machine gun open up from the tank. As the bullets hit the ground, we could see the snow jumping about thirty feet from us. They had missed, and we were soon deep in the woods headed for the rear. We didn't stop running until we were so tired that we could hardly breathe. Then we slowed down to a walk, and our only thoughts were that we wished we would soon bump into some GIs.

We must have wandered around in the woods until about 2:00 in the afternoon without seeing a soul. We came across many fresh tracks of GI boots in the snow, though, so we knew that we were headed in the right direction. About 2:30, we suddenly saw two GIs standing on a hill in front of us. We rushed up to them, and they said they were with the artillery outfit. We had reached our goal. With the artillery outfit, we also found the rest of the guys in our company who had jumped up and ran as the tanks were coming the night before. We got in with them and started to dig ourselves a hole so we could have some protection in case the Germans should start shelling our area. The artillerymen told us that they were still all out of ammunition and had no hopes of getting any more. Most of them left their big guns and grabbed their rifles. They were now to be riflemen with the infantry. All together we now had nearly one hundred men again, and we each wondered what would happen next. Ken and I knew that we should by right try to get back to our first sergeant, but we decided that we would stick with these men. We figured it would be stupid to run up to our old positions.

All was quiet on the hill where we were dug in until about 4:00 in the afternoon. We must have been spotted by some German artillery observer, because all of a sudden, a terrific artillery barrage started coming in on us. It lasted about twenty minutes, and we stayed deep in our holes. As soon as it was over, we were ordered to retreat into a valley behind the hill. About this time, it started to get dark, and we were told to head west. We knew that if we went west far enough we would eventually hit the English Channel. Our big joke at the time was that if we ever got there, we were going to swim right over to England.

We hadn't walked far when we came to a small road running east and west. We didn't know if the Germans had gone up this road yet or not, but it was easier walking, so we headed west on the road. By now, it was about 8 p.m. There was no moon, and the night seemed cold and black. We must have followed the road through the hills for about a mile, when we came to a small bridge over a river about fifty feet wide. Just as we got to the bridge, we heard someone yell, "Halt!" in front of us. The first few guys in our line saw that it was two German guards standing by the bridge. Our guys fired three shots, and the two krauts dropped to the ground without firing a shot. The rest of us ran across the bridge as fast as possible and into the hills on the other side. We knew now that the Germans had taken this road and that we would probably be meeting more of them soon.

We cut across country for about a mile, and by now we were all getting mighty tired. We finally stopped, and we each started to dig ourselves a hole so that we could have some protection in case we were attacked again. By this time, about two-thirds of our guys had lost their shovels from their belts, so we had to take turns digging. We stayed in these holes until about 4:00 in the morning. We had no blankets, and by this time we were all so cold that we felt numb all over. There was about six inches of snow. It was now the morning of December 18. Most of us had lost overcoats on the first day of the attack, and the light jackets we were wearing had no lining. The Germans were now beginning the third day of their attack.

As we sat in our holes, we watched a patrol of about twelve Germans pass through the woods a short distance from us. We were told to hold our fire, and the Jerries didn't spot us. As soon as they were gone, one of our officers told us to crawl out of our holes and head west once more. It would soon be light, and we had to go someplace where we would have more cover. We started walking. About 6:00 a.m. we came to a small town, and three of our men went into the town to see who was in it. After about twenty minutes, they came back all excited. They said that there were about a hundred men from our division in the town, and our morale was lifted 100 percent. Once we were in there, we found that our battalion commander, Col. Gustin M. Nelson, was in charge of these men. They had been driven from another town the day before, and they were happy to have us join them. We now had a few men from almost every company in our 112th Infantry Regiment. Everyone told the same story. They had all been attacked on the first morning, December 16, and most of their men had been either killed or captured.

It didn't take long and it was daylight again. Colonel Nelson and his men had managed to save two of their machine guns, and they set one up at each side of the town. He ordered nearly all of the men to dig in around the town, and the rest of us were to stay in town and help him. Twelve of us were ordered to take care of the ammunition he had saved for the machine guns. He told us that in case we were attacked, it was our job to see to it that we carried plenty of ammunition out to the machine guns. By 8:00 everything was still quiet, and we thought our job was going to be easy. The twelve of us started to hunt around in the house where the ammunition was stored. We found a trap door that led to a basement. In the basement we found a wine cellar. Everybody had a drink.

While we were in the cellar, we heard our machine gun on the far side of the town start firing. This meant that the Jerries must be coming again. Wouldn't they give us any peace? Must they attack all the time?

It wasn't long until we heard big shells coming into the town, and our riflemen opened up near the machine gun that was firing. We knew now that the German were close. We soon found ourselves running and crawling toward the machine gun with extra belts of ammunition.

We got to the machine gun all right, but what we saw coming was not a very pleasant sight: German tanks coming up a road directly in front of us and German infantry headed for our town on foot to our left.

Our riflemen and machine guns were firing everything they had at the infantrymen coming across the field, but they kept advancing steadily. By the time the twelve of us were back in town to get our next load of ammunition, the krauts had knocked out our machine guns. Our colonel could tell that we were outnumbered about ten to one, and it wasn't long until our whole outfit was once more on the retreat. The tanks rolled into town from one side, and we withdrew into the woods on the other. We lost many men.

We made our way into the woods behind the town, and the Germans lost contact with us. Our colonel led us through the woods for about five miles before we lay down to rest. It was now about 3:00 in the afternoon. We all threw ourselves on the ground, and no words were spoken. As we lay there, we realized for the first time that we were mighty hungry. Some of our guys had not had a bite to eat for three days now. Many of the rest of us had found food in the basements of the houses in the town we had just been in. Some of us still had hunks of bologna stuffed in our pockets, and we had been eating on it as we had been walking. Our colonel decided that each of us should share alike. He made everyone empty all the food we were carrying in our pockets into one pile. He then split it up, and each of us got a little something to chew on.

It was now drawing near to the third evening of the German breakthrough. Our colonel told us that we would have to spend the night in the woods. Each of us started to dig a shallow hole. We were in a small wooded area which was surrounded by fields on three sides. In the field were standing many grain shocks which had never been taken in from the last harvest season. Each of us got one of these grain shocks and dragged it into the woods. We lined the bottom of our holes with the straw, and as we crawled into the hole, we pulled the remainder of the straw over us to serve as a blanket. We knew that we were going to have another cold night ahead of us.

Just as we were settled for the night, we saw about five GIs coming on foot across the open field. As they got nearer, I suddenly recognized Frankie as one of them, and I ran out to meet them. Besides Frankie, there was Quimby, our first sergeant, and a couple others. We were all together once again. They told Ken and me that the Germans had attacked them just a short time after Ken and I had left on the patrol to the artillery, and also that they were the only ones that managed to keep from getting captured. They had been running and walking now for nearly twenty-four hours straight, and they were completely exhausted. When they got in our woods they just fell on the ground and went to sleep without even digging a hole.

This night seemed to go by exceptionally slowly, and it was the coldest one we had had so far. We all tried to doze off now and then, but it was no use. It was too cold to sleep. It was too cold to do anything. About 4:00 in the morning it started to snow, and it kept getting heavier all the time. By the time it was daylight, there was a real snow storm on. There wasn't much of a wind, but the snow was coming down so heavily that you couldn't see over a hundred yards in front of you. Our colonel in charge said that this was the chance we had been waiting for. Now we could start moving in the daylight, and the krauts wouldn't be able to see us. We had close to two hundred men in our little group now, and soon we were headed west again on the first road we came to. We thought we would keep going until we ran into something. By noon we were still going, and we had not seen any signs of any Germans or any Americans. But all of a sudden the snow quit falling. We didn't dare stay on the road any longer, and we didn't want to take the chance of getting caught in another town. We came upon a huge chateau, just a few hundred feet from the road, so we moved in and took the place over. There were no civilians around anyplace, so we weren't able to get any information as to whether the Germans had been there or not. We were now back in Belgium, and all of the civilians had been fleeing with the Americans rather than be captured by the Germans again. We stayed in this old chateau for the remainder of the day and the next night. During the night, we could hear a lot of small-arms fire in the distance. This meant that there were other GIs still resisting the Germans close to us. Our colonel sent out a patrol to contact them, and they reported back that these GIs needed help desperately.

By dawn we were on our way to help them. We had had no food since the couple bites of bologna the day before, and our stomachs were aching. We soon got to the town they were in, and once more our men started to dig in positions around the town. This time the Germans weren't attacking yet. They were dug in on a hillside about three-quarters of a mile from our town, and the only action there was the exchange of small-arms fire between our troops and theirs. I went back to my old job as a messenger for our first sergeant, and we organized ourselves as best we could.

We stayed in this town until about noon the following day. Several waves of Germans hit our position on the edge of town during this time, but our troops repelled all of them. On one attack, our men captured about ten krauts, and they were brought into the town for questioning. The guys we were helping in the town still had a radio set with them, and they were constantly trying to contact some of our troops in the rear to see if there was any help headed in our direction. Several times they were able to contact other outfits, but each time they would contact one, they would always report that their opposition was too great and they were pulling out for the rear. There seemed to be no help coming from anywhere. We ourselves had now retreated about thirty miles since the first day of the attack, and it looked like the only thing we could do was start retreating again. Finally, our radio men contacted some tank outfit, and they said they would come and help us. They ran out of gas before they ever got to us, though, and they were caught helplessly by some attacking krauts. During the forenoon of this second day, two of our men in the holes at the edge of town shot themselves through the foot. They said it had happened accidentally, but our officers knew better. These guys just couldn't take it any longer, so they figured if they shot themselves, the medics would see to it that they got safely to the rear. Had they known that they would be left in the town when we started to retreat again at noon, I'm sure they would have pointed their guns in some other direction.

Yes, by noon of this day, we were once more on the retreat. The Germans had pulled up with heavy forces and tanks to the edge of our town. Our officers knew it was useless for our few men to try to hold against them as they started to attack, and we all moved into the thick woods behind the town. I have no idea as to how far we walked, but I know that by this time the morale of our remaining men was very low. Everyone was hungry and tired and cold. Whenever two or three of us got together, we would always find ourselves talking about one subject: whether or not we should give ourselves up or not the next time we were attacked. For the past week, we had only had a few bites to eat, and our stomachs ached. We had been beaten every time we had met the krauts, and they seemed to be getting more powerful all of the time. We knew of no help coming from the rear, and we thought that the American lines must have crumbled throughout all of Europe. We thought the Germans were winning the war.

About this time our officers decided that they would try retreating as we had learned while training in the States. This was known as rear-guard action. It meant that as we retreated, our officers would leave about twelve men at each big crossroad we came to. These men were to stay at this spot and hold up the Germans for as long as they could—or until they ran out of ammunition. This would give the main body of our group more time in which to get back. It meant certain death or capture for the men left behind though.

We started retreating on the roads once again, and the officers started to leave a few men at each crossroad. By the time we got to another crossroad, it was Company B's turn to leave twelve men. Frankie, Quimby, and I were three of the twelve men ordered to stay behind. We were scared, and as we watched the rest of the guys head down the road, we were wishing we could be going with them. Soon they were out of sight, and we were left to our fate. We started digging holes with our helmets, but the ground was frozen, and we couldn't make much progress. We felt helpless, and we all had lumps in our throats. The longer we stayed there, the more nervous we got. We tried to figure out how in the devil twelve GIs armed with only rifles could hold up a whole German army. There seemed to be no answer, and our only hope was that no Germans would come up our road. We must have stayed here about two hours without seeing or hearing anything. Suddenly, we spotted a half-track coming down the road to our right. It was coming very fast, and we got ourselves into position to do the job we had been left to do. As it got near to us, we saw that it was an American half-track, but to play safe, we kept our rifles pointed toward it. The driver spotted us as he came to our crossroad, and he waved his arm. He stopped and he had five GIs with him. Three of them had been wounded badly and were lying in the back. He told us which outfit they were with, and that the Germans had just attacked them about two miles down the road. They said that most of their men had been captured, but they had got away and were headed for the rear as fast as possible. They told us that we were crazy if we stayed here and waited for them to attack us, but we had been ordered to stay here, so we stayed. They took off again, and it wasn't long until they were out of sight also. We didn't have to wait long, and we heard many vehicles coming down the same road as the half-track had just come.

As they got closer, we could see that it was the Germans that were coming this time. We could see a long column of German trucks, headed by three huge tanks. Each of the trucks was loaded with German infantrymen. They were out to lick the Americans. The closer they got the more scared we got. The rumble from the tanks and trucks got louder and louder. When they got about five hundred yards from us, the lead tank spotted us and opened up with its machine gun. Our rifles were useless against the tanks. We were soon driven from the crossroad and into the woods again. We retreated until we spotted a small town at the foot of the hill in back of us. We could see no activity in the town, but we spotted a couple of Jeeps standing by one of the buildings. We ran into the town and up to the building where we saw the Jeeps.

Inside we found four GIs who were waiting and were in the same boat as we were. They knew the Germans were coming, but they didn't know which way to retreat in order to get away from them. We told them about the long column of krauts that we had just seen coming in this direction and we all decided to get out of town, before we were caught. By this time, we were getting desperate. We decided we would keep running as long as we had any breath left in us. As we came out of the building, we once more spotted the same long column of tanks and trucks. They were headed directly for our little town. The twelve of us ran for the woods on the far side of the town, and the rest of the GIs jumped in their Jeep and headed out of town in the same direction on the road. Once more the tanks stopped and started to fire at us as we ran from the town. This time they scored some hits. Two of our guys were hit, and they fell face-first into the snow. As soon as we were in the woods the krauts pulled into the town. We kept running because we knew that they were at our heels. I ran into a branch once and lost my helmet, but I didn't take time to stop and pick it up because every second counted. I remember Frankie ran into another branch once and hooked his jacket. He gave one tug and kept going. The whole back of his jacket got left hanging on the branch, and all he had left was the front and two sleeves. We must have run for an hour steady, and then we were so exhausted that we all stopped, threw ourselves on the ground, and rested. Our lungs ached from lack of wind.

By now it was dark again, and as we lay there, we suddenly realized that it was Christmas Eve. We didn't have the slightest idea where we were, and none of us seemed to care whether it was Christmas Eve or not. All we knew was that it was cold, and we wanted something to eat. We lay there for about a half an hour, then we decided we would try once more to see if we could find our way out of this mess. We started walking. I had a compass that we could see at night, so we set our course due west. We walked for about an hour and we came to a river about a hundred yards wide. By now it was 9:00 at night. There was a full moon out, and there were millions of stars overhead. On the far side of the river it was all open country with no trees. We could see a road running parallel with the river about two hundred yards on the other side of the river. It was cold, but the river was still running. There was just a little ice near each bank. We knew we had to get across the river, but we could see no bridge, so we stopped again to figure out our next move.

As we stood there, we saw about twenty sharp flashes in the hills about three or four miles directly in front of us. A few seconds later, we heard a bunch of shells screaming over our heads and crash in the woods about a half mile behind us. We looked at each other, and a big smile broke on our faces all at the same time. These shells were American—we could tell by the sound. Did this mean that the Americans had stopped the Germans and were attacking back again? Did it? Were we only a few miles from the American lines again? Were we? We slapped each other on the back, and our hopes of getting back again had been raised sky high. As we stood there, we saw more and more flashes, and more and more of our shells whistled over our heads. Now we knew for sure that these were Americans coming in our direction. We couldn't wait to get to them. We jumped into the river and waded across the icy stream. Lucky for us, it wasn't deep. The water came to about our knees, and it ran into our shoes, but we didn't care. The Americans were coming!

We were soon on the bank on the far side, and as we walked, the icy water squished in our shoes. We started going down the road on the far side of the river, headed for the hills where we had seen the flashes from our artillery guns. We hadn't gone far when we came to a small house and barn along the side of the road. We could see a light in the house shining through a crack in the door, and we rushed up to it hoping that maybe we would run into some more GIs. One of our guys ran up to the house while the rest of us hid in the barn. He walked into the house, and all was quiet. Soon he came back to the barn and told us to come in. He said that there were three Belgian civilians in the house, and they would tell us what they knew about the movements around the area during the past day.

As soon as we were all in there, they all started to talk at once. We couldn't understand much of what they were trying to tell us, but we understood enough so that we found out that the Germans had captured all of this ground and they were dug in, in the woods and hills all around. They said that the Germans had been going by in trucks for two days straight now, and they had seen hundreds of American prisoners being taken to the German rear by German guards. They said that there had been heavy fighting going on between the Americans and Germans all during this past day a few miles away. They also told us that they didn't think we would have much of a chance getting over to the American lines because there were thousands of Germans all over the place. With this information we decided that we would have to figure out some pretty clever schemes if we were going to get back without getting captured.

One of the Belgians asked us if we were hungry, and we all shook our heads. She went down in her basement and brought up two loaves of dark bread and a small tub of butter. We sliced the bread, put big hunks of butter on it, and had a real feast. We ate until the bread was all gone. There were about ten of us in the house, and we figured our chances of getting back were mighty slim. The bread and butter had tasted so good that each of us pulled out our billfold and emptied every cent we had on the table in the house. We told them that that was our pay for the food. In a few minutes, we were out of the house and on our way once again.

We had gone just a few yards down the road, when we heard a Jeep coming from behind us. We jumped into the ditch, but the Jeep stopped when it got to us. The driver had spotted us in the moonlight. We were very much surprised to find there were two GIs driving the Jeep. We thought the Germans had taken over these roads. These two GIs were in the same boat as we were. Their outfit had been retreating for the past week as we had been doing. They didn't know where they were going, but they wanted to get back to the American lines.

As we were standing there talking, an American armored car pulled up with five more GIs in it. They told us to climb on. The armored car went first, and I got into the Jeep and found Lt. Mayer Goldstein was in the front of the Jeep. He had become our company commander on December 16 when Captain Deck was killed. Mayer had been wounded in both legs earlier in the day. Another Jeep pulled up, and Frankie and Warren Quimby got into it. Our three vehicles started down the road, but we didn't get very far when we ran into a long column of American tanks and armored vehicles. The lead tank had run into a strong German roadblock ahead, and everything was held up. Suddenly, the armored vehicle we were following pulled around the side of the tanks and turned off on a side road to our left. The Jeep Frankie and Warren Quimby were in passed our Jeep and got in behind the armored vehicle, and the three of us started off on our own. We went for about a mile when we came to a small town. There was no road around the town, and we knew we would have to go through it.

The armored car in the lead speeded up to about forty miles an hour and headed into the town with our other two Jeeps following. As we came to the first house, we saw a German half-track standing alongside of the house and a kraut guard standing in front of the house. As we drove by, his head made a quick turn, and when we were passing, we saw him run into the house. We didn't see anyone else until we got to the last house on the other end of the town. Here was another guard, and as we drove past, he ran back into the house also. By now it was about midnight, and we were going full speed ahead. About a mile down the road, the armored car in the lead ran into a German roadblock. It caught a blast from an antitank gun, and I believe all of the fellows aboard were killed. The Jeep Frankie and Quimby were in managed to stop, and everyone jumped into a ditch filled with water to get out of the fire from the Germans at the roadblock. The kraut machine guns kept firing, and soon they started tossing hand grenades into the ditch where they were lying. One of the grenades landed alongside Quimby and ripped off one of his legs. Frankie said he tried to help him as best he could. A few minutes later a bunch of krauts rushed them and captured the ones who were still living.

The story of the guys in the Jeep I was in was a little different. When we saw all the trouble the other two vehicles ahead had run into, our driver threw the Jeep into reverse and started to back up the crest of the hill we had just come up. Just as we were almost over the hill, a machine gun burst hit us, and our driver was killed. The rest of us made a dive for the ditch and jumped up and headed for some woods about a hundred yards from the road. There were about eight of us running, and the krauts opened up on us. Two of the guys were hit, but we all made it into the woods, including Lt. Mayer Goldstein, who had been wounded in both legs earlier in the day.

We made a lot of noise as we tried to get farther back into the woods. We stopped for a minute, and we could hear a group of Germans come running up the road where our Jeep was. They fired into the woods, but we all lay down and covered ourselves with snow. We were as still as could be, and we listened as the Germans talked a hundred yards away. They called into the woods and told us to come out with our hands up, but we lay still. Finally, the Germans started to walk back down the road and disappeared. We slowly worked our way deeper into the woods. Lieutenant Goldstein's legs had turned stiff, and it was hard for him to walk. One of the guys had been hit in the neck, and it was bleeding very badly. His left arm was limp, and his jacket was covered with blood. He told us he thought he could make it alright if we didn't go too fast. The third guy had been hit in the seat. He said he could make it alright if he didn't sit down anyplace.

Next we checked to see what guns we had left. We had two rifles. The rest of the guys had all lost their guns when we jumped from the Jeep a few minutes before. I was the only one that had a compass, so we set our direction for due west again. We had to walk slowly, and we tried to help the three wounded guys as much as we could. We must have walked for about an hour through the woods, and the going was rough. We could find no trails anywhere, and by this time, our three wounded guys were almost exhausted. The lieutenant's legs had turned stiff from the wounds, and two of our guys had to drag him between them in order to keep him with us. The kid that was shot in the neck kept falling down all the time, and he was getting awfully weak from loss of blood. Each time we would stop to rest, the blood would drip from his limp arm, and the snow became stained with blood.

About 4:00 in the morning, we finally came to another road. We looked down the road and spotted another small town about a half mile away. We knew that we couldn't keep going like this much longer, so we decided to head for the town. We decided that if there were krauts in the town, we would give ourselves up. With this thought in mind, we headed slowly down the road for the town. The moon was still shining brightly, and we knew that if there was anyone in the town, they would see us coming. We got to within a hundred yards of the first building in the town, and we stopped to see if we could hear any noises from the town. Everything was still. We started slowly ahead again. Suddenly, right in front of us a voice in the still night yelled, "Halt!" We froze in our tracks. We could not see anyone, anyplace. Then the same voice yelled, "Who the hell are you?" We hollered, "Americans!" Then the voice said, "One of you come forward to be recognized." One of our guys walked up and saw a guy step from the shadow of the house. It was a GI. It was hard to believe our eyes, but it was true. We had reached the American lines. We all rushed up to him and started to ask him a hundred questions. He said he was with the 82nd Airborne Division, and they had just captured this town about three hours before. There were about a thousand paratroopers in the town, and they were getting ready to start attacking in the direction we had just come from. They were going to start their attack at daybreak.

As soon as we got in the town, the paratroopers loaded our three wounded guys in an ambulance and headed for an aid station with them. The five of us that were left were taken to a house where the officers of this outfit had their command post. The officers said that they wanted us to help them, if we could. They unfolded a bunch of maps on a table and asked us to point out all the places we had seen heavy forces of Germans during the last couple of days. They said they needed this information so that they would know where to concentrate their forces when they started their attack in a couple of hours. We put a bunch of marks on their maps, but don't imagine they used them once they started. When we finished, they loaded us in a Jeep and hauled us back to their kitchen crew. Here we were fed the biggest meal you would ever want to lay your eyes on—and we really ate. It was now early morning of Christmas Day, and the paratroopers left the town and started their attack into the woods ahead. The five of us jumped in a truck that was going to the rear for supplies and we set out to try to find the rest of our 28th Infantry Division.

It took about a week for us to get organized again. Thousands of green replacements were hauled into our town and assigned to our outfit. We also had to get all new equipment because the Germans had captured nearly all of our artillery pieces, machine guns, et cetera. As soon as we had everything we needed, we started to train with our new replacements. We knew that we would soon be called forward again to help counterattack in the bulge.

On January 5 our orders came. We had now been off of the line for nearly two weeks, and the First Army figured that we should be pretty well rested up again by now. We were ordered to move forward and help in the attack. We now had everything we needed except for a kitchen outfit. . . . So, we had to live on cold rations.

None of us were in very good spirits as we started going forward again. We were in no hurry to get up there: every day that we could stay off of the line was another day that we would be sure of living. The trucks hauled us up to within about ten miles from the lines again, and as it started to get dark, we once more found ourselves walking in two columns down the road headed for the front. We had hilly country to go through, and our progress was slow. We were to be ready to start our attack at 7:00 the next morning, January 6. Our objective was to capture the town of Spineux, Belgium. The only information we had about the town was that we would have to attack through some woods for about five miles before reaching it. We were told that there were heavy German forces dug in throughout these woods and that we would probably meet a lot of resistance when we got to the town itself.

The night was another cold one, but there was a bright moon out. We kept moving steadily down the road with very few rests. About midnight, we found ourselves with only about two more miles to go, so we knew that we would probably be able to get a little rest before we shoved off in the attack at daybreak. Suddenly, over our heads we heard a loud roar. We looked up, and two German planes had spotted our column moving on the road. They came at us one behind the other, and when they were directly over us, we heard a bunch of loud whistles. Both planes were dropping many antipersonnel bombs on us. We all made a dive for the ditch, and luck was with us again. The planes had misjudged, and all of their bombs landed and exploded in an open field about two hundred yards to our left. None of us were hit, and we were soon on our way again.

When we got to our jumping-off point, we all lay down in the woods and waited for daybreak. About a half hour before it was light, we started forward on the attack. Our 112th Infantry Regiment acted as one body, and we shot many spearheads into the woods ahead. It didn't take long and we could hear the familiar sound of the German machine guns firing in our direction again. We ran into many German strong points, but our officers would send patrols on each one, and the krauts started to retreat. This was the first time that most of us in the 112th Regiment had ever seen the Germans back up, and it did us a lot of good. We began to think that maybe the Germans weren't the super race we thought they were. This time, we had them on the run, and we were following close behind. Even though most of our men were green troops, we kept ourselves organized beautifully. We kept constant contact with each other, and we were suffering very few casualties. Our medics were on the ball, and our wounded were always taken care of as best possible.

By three o'clock in the afternoon, we were almost up to the town. Our company had captured about twenty krauts, and we sent them to the rear with a couple of our guys. Everything went fine until about four o'clock. We were still advancing slowly, but we found ourselves fighting in awfully thick woods.

There was an awful lot of brush, and we could only see for a short distance. About this time, some of our new men started to get scared, and they got "trigger-happy." In other words, they started to shoot at anything they saw move in front of them. Some of these new men shot and wounded or killed about five of our own men.

Soon it started to get dark, and we weren't quite to the town yet. Our officer in charge decided that we should stop and dig in for the night. He said that we could attack the town the next day. Our company gathered together, and each of us started to dig a hole to spend the night in. One of the guys in our company had just captured a kraut, so he gave him his shovel and made him dig a hole big enough for our guys to get in. He sat and ate a box of K-rations while the kraut dug his hole. It wasn't long until it was dark again. It was cloudy this night, and there was no moon. We figured we had chased all of the krauts back into the town of Spineux, so there wouldn't be anything for us to worry about this night.

All was quiet until about midnight. Then we suddenly realized that we had underestimated the krauts. The crazy fools left the town and started attacking back into our woods. I guess we all felt like a bunch of stupid jackasses. We had had them on the run all day, but now we had stopped and given them time to reorganize. They were after us this time. It wasn't long until our whole company was surrounded and small-arms fire was coming in on us from every direction. We immediately began to spread out, but as they saw us moving, we drew more and more fire. Many of our guys were hit. We formed a big circle, and the battle was on. It kept up for about an hour, and then slowly the German guns quit firing. They must have withdrawn back to the town again, because by 3 a.m. all was quiet. I was in a hole with one of our new men, and this was his first night of combat. He was scared to death, and I was trying to make believe that this was old stuff and that I wasn't scared a bit. Suddenly, we heard someone walking in the brush in front of us, and we heard a voice call out "Hello." We spotted the figure of a man walking toward us. We couldn't tell whether it was a kraut or one of our men. Suddenly, the kid I was with rose up and fired, and the man fell to the ground. As daylight finally came and we could see the color of his uniform, we could tell that it was a kraut, and he lay less than thirty feet from our hole. As it got light and we could see all around our company, we counted over thirty dead krauts that our men had shot during the night.

Soon we were on our way once again for our objective, Spineux, Belgium. By noon, we were all in our positions around the town. We could see many German soldiers moving around in the town, and they hadn't spotted us moving up on them. Our big battle was soon to begin.

Our officers radioed back to our artillery and told them to shell the town heavily for twelve minutes. We had to get across an open field about 250 yards wide before we could get to the first building of the town. Our officers told us that when the artillery had been shelling for eleven minutes, we were all to leave the woods at once and head for the town. This would get us up just as the shelling stopped, and we would be able to get the krauts before they had time to get out of their holes.

Just as the shelling started, the order came for us to fix bayonets and prepare to charge. As each minute ticked by, our hearts beat louder and louder, for at the end of the eleven minutes, we knew we would be in the open and on our own. The end of the eleven minutes came, and we found ourselves racing across the open field toward the town. This time we were all screaming like a bunch of wild Indians. We were firing our rifles and Tommy guns in every direction. The shelling stopped, and we hit the town and made our way from house to house. During the first half hour the krauts gave us a bad time. They were firing at us from windows, down steps, and cellars, but their resistance slowed up as we progressed, and by dark the town was ours. We had captured over two hundred Germans, including six officers. It took us a long time to search the prisoners, and we all collected a big supply of souvenirs. It was here that I got my first German pistol, a beautiful P38 with a leather holster and two clips of ammo. This had been the height of my ambition since we entered combat. I also got myself a razor off of one of the prisoners, which I used for many years. I had lost my razor on the first day of the breakthrough a month before, and I hadn't shaved since. Bill Kleeman led our attack with his Tommy gun. He was the first man in Company B to enter Spineux.

After we were through searching all of the prisoners, we gathered up all of their wounded and made the Germans carry them to one building. By now it was dark again, and our officers said we would spend the night in Spineux. We split up in bunches of about five guys each and went into the basements of the houses. Our bunch happened to get in a basement that had been used as the German command post. There was a stove that was still going well, and it had a big kettle on top of it. We lifted the cover, and there before our eyes were two chickens being boiled in water. These krauts had been making some supper just before we started our attack. We tested the meat, and it was well done. We each broke off a piece and stared eating. It wasn't long until the chicken was gone. Our stomachs were full, the basement was warm, and the five of us settled down for a good bull session. We had a couple of candles burning on a table, and we were in Home Sweet Home. About ten o'clock that night, two of us decided we would go upstairs with our flashlight and see if we could find any more souvenirs lying around in any of the rooms. We left all of our guns in the basement and started searching every drawer in every room. When we got to the fourth room, we opened up the door and flashed our light inside.

I was holding the flashlight and what I saw made my hair stand on end. Our mouths dropped wide open. There on the floor in front of us sat two kraut soldiers. Whoever had searched this house earlier in the evening had missed them, and we had been sitting in their basement eating their chicken. We had no guns with us, so we just kept the flashlight beam on them. They slowly got up and they raised their arms over their heads. Their rifles were lying over in a corner, and they had just been sitting there waiting for someone to find them. We got them down in the basement, and after we finished searching them, we took them to the same building where the other prisoners were being held.

The next day our Company B was relieved in Spineux by Company B, 424th Infantry Regiment, 106th Infantry Division. We left with our prisoners and returned to our battalion headquarters. We made stretchers for the wounded, and the German soldiers carried all of them, both theirs and ours.

This was the last combat action we saw in the Bulge. Our 28th Infantry Division was now ordered to a rest area in France. We traveled by truck and spent the next few days living with French families in the town where we reorganized. We got our kitchen crew organized again and were fed three meals a day. We started to prepare ourselves for the next combat mission we would be assigned to, which would be fighting with the French First Army in the Colmar area.

—*From the files of the U.S. Army Military History Institute*

Lionel P. Adda
D Company, 393rd Infantry Regiment, 99th
Infantry Division

The 99th Infantry Division arrived in Western Europe in November 1944 and was assigned to the quiet Ardennes sector as a place to gain some limited combat experience before being deployed to a more active area of the front. In a span of a couple of days, Lionel Adda quickly gained more combat experience than he ever had hoped for.

OF ALL MY WORLD WAR II MEMORIES, those of the first few days of the Battle of the Bulge remain the most vivid. On December 16, our positions, which were in a densely wooded area, abutted the international highway at the Belgian-German frontier. Immediately in front was a ditch paralleling the two-lane macadam highway, and beyond there was a cultivated field which offered a field of fire of between 100 and 150 yards. The terrain then dropped off, and the edge of the field was our horizon. By walking about 100 yards to our right, however, we could see the dragon-teeth tank traps beyond the pillboxes of the Siegfried Line.

I was on sentry duty from 4:00 to 6:00 on the morning of December 16. Toward the end of my watch, I saw that the horizon was brightly lit, as if by searchlights. On other occasions there had been some illumination of the sky at night in the direction of the enemy, but it had never been as bright as on this night. I became concerned and considered calling Staff Sergeant Enloe, our platoon sergeant, whose sleeping hole was in the first squad's area. I hesitated, however, since Sergeant Enloe was a very deep sleeper, and when I had called him on another occasion, I had found it difficult to wake him up. In the meantime I heard conversation about 100 or 150 feet to my right; perhaps with a better view the sentries could discern the reason for the light. On my left, however, all was quiet. Finally, I decided to waken my relief a little early, and for a few minutes we wondered about the light on the horizon. I then entered my sleeping hole, but I recall sensing that this morning there was something wrong. In addition to the light, perhaps subconsciously, the warnings which we had been given recently were contributing to my uneasy feeling. About a week earlier we had been visited by an officer who urged us to improve our fighting holes so that we "would be able to live and fight in them for days, if necessary." Then came the engineers, who installed trip wires and flares in front of our guns.

I had just taken off my boots when the first shell struck. We had had some minor harassing fire before, so I was not concerned, but the volume of fire increased rapidly. There were tree bursts, and shrapnel was entering the small opening of my sleeping hole. I put on my boots and was outside seconds after the shelling stopped. My fighting hole was on the other side of the 1st Squad machine gun, so I dropped into the nearest foxhole, which turned out to be Sergeant Enloe's. (He occupied mine during the ensuing fight.)

By the time I reached the hole, the 1st Squad gun had started to fire and the 2nd Squad gun began shortly thereafter. The bright light, which would have silhouetted the attacking Germans coming over the rise, was gone, and I had difficulty picking out targets. Tracers and one or two flares revealed bodies crawling toward us, and I was firing my carbine more rapidly than I had ever done before. I noticed that the 1st Squad gun on my right was firing effectively, while the 2nd Squad gun on my left was firing a little high.

Suddenly, I heard a shout in German a few yards in front of me. I recognized the last word—"Hitler"! Then there were two sharp explosions one or two yards to my right—hand grenades—followed by a burst of burp-gun fire. The bullets dislodged dirt and stones in front of my hole, and they struck me painfully in the face. It occurred to me that I might be exposing myself too much. The fighting hole was well built, narrow, relatively deep, and with a firing step. However, Enloe was significantly shorter than me, so I had to crouch in a narrow space in order to place my weapon at the level of the top of the hole.

Directly in front of me, about fifteen yards away, a German soldier raised his head and threw away his rifle. I called out instinctively, *"Kamerad, kommen sie hier."* (Friend, come here.) Sergeant Enloe ordered everyone to hold his fire, and the soldier rose and walked toward me, crossed the highway, and stumbled through the ditch. He was a handsome young man, not more than eighteen, wearing a snow cape, and with a faint smile of relief on his face. His eyes never left my face or the carbine I had trained on him. One of the B Company sergeants had him stand with legs apart against a tree and relieved him of his grenades. The soldier, fearing that he would be shot, began to cry. He would probably have been the first German I would have had to face in hand-to-hand combat if the enemy had crossed the highway. A rifleman was assigned to bring him to B Company headquarters. There may have been German penetration some distance to our left, along the path to headquarters, and I was told later that both men were killed on the way back.

Shortly after this, the burp (submachine) gunner, probably the officer who earlier had tried to exhort his men, tossed away his weapon, tentatively raised his head, and slowly began to get up. Several rifle shots were fired, and he dropped to the ground and did not move again.

All was quiet the rest of the day. At about four in the afternoon we received word from the right that a German attack might be developing. I recall Sergeant Enloe's words to me as

75

we prepared to fight again: "Good hunting," he said, as calmly as if we were starting out on a pheasant hunt in Pennsylvania. But there was steel in his eyes. The attack never materialized. (Sergeant Enloe received a battlefield commission, was transferred to a rifle company, and was killed in action some weeks later while leading an attack on German positions. He was a cool, intelligent, and very courageous soldier.)

The night seemed endless. All of us were on high alert. German patrols were operating in our rear. An occasional burst of automatic weapon fire into the ground, designed, I suppose, to draw our fire, revealed in the flashes Germans as close as fifty yards behind us. To our front I began thinking that I saw in the misty darkness some of the bodies move. Our squad sergeant said I was seeing ghosts. However, as dawn came, one could see that at least three bodies had vanished, including the burp gunner who had tried to surrender. Perhaps both of us were right about what I had seen.

We were immensely relieved to have passed through the pre-dawn and dawn without another attack, but at about 8:00 we were told that our position was untenable. We fell straight back, reached a dirt road just in time to see a group of mortar men pulling out with a Jeep and trailer loaded with ammunition, and continued further on to what appeared to be a headquarters area. There was something of a clearing and a dirt road. Many of the trees had been cut down, and the troops had actually built tiny log cabins for themselves.

Quite surprisingly, all was calm and quiet the rest of the day and that night, although again we did not sleep. I had the impression that perhaps we were being shielded by some unit, conceivably one that had been in reserve. I don't recall our even setting up a defense line or perimeter.

Next morning we were told that the Germans were deploying large patrols, up to a hundred men, and that they were attacking scattered units such as ours. We started to leave the clearing for the woods. The machine gun was moved to the edge of the clearing and was trained on the road. My squad sergeant sent me back for more ammunition. Just as I picked up two boxes, I saw and heard coming down the road a large group of smiling Germans, herding and prodding in front of them some of our soldiers. The GIs were being forced to shout, "Surrender, Americans." I recognized some of the members of one of our mortar platoons. Still carrying the ammunition, I ran back to the gun just as some of the men were moving into the woods.

Then began a very strange fifteen hours. We moved along a barely discernible path in the forest, led by an officer whom I did not recognize. He was understandably thoughtful and somber and looked at a map frequently. At one place we left the forest and crossed an open field in groups of two or three, running as fast as we could, and reentered the field. Occasionally we would stop, and immediately we would begin digging in. We had no shovels, and because of the tree roots we made little progress. At one point we were told that we would make a stand where we were; however, we remained there for only about one hour. The situation was eerie—there was no sound of fighting anywhere nearby, the forest was enveloped in mist, and we had no idea where we were or where we were going.

The day wore on, and with the mist it was becoming dark early. We emerged from the forest and entered a very large cleared area sloping upward. We came to a dirt road, passed a burned-out Jeep, and then saw far ahead up the hill the barely discernible outlines of a building. The second gunner and I began to argue about the name of the town we were approaching. We were stopped by a burst of automatic weapon fire—the tracers passed far over our heads. Although the ground was saturated from the runoff of the melting snow, we began digging in. Our squad sergeant called us and said we were turning back. We had been at the head of the column; when I turned around I was surprised at the number of men behind us—perhaps as many as seventy-five. In their midst there was a tall, strongly built German prisoner. He was turning his head, glancing quickly and anxiously, obviously looking for a chance to escape. The rear of the column moved into a draw or ravine which ran at roughly a right angle to the direction in which we had been moving. The approaching darkness, the gloomy aspect of the draw, and the stress of the past three days suddenly began to affect me. I began to feel that this would be my last day alive, and that I would not see another dawn.

Although we were moving through the draw in increasing darkness, the cloudy sky was reflecting fires that were burning not far off. To this illumination was added the occasional glow of rockets passing overhead. We were obviously near areas of combat.

At one spot there was some small-arms fire. I looked across the draw and saw, in the dim light, paper or wooden targets in human form—this had been a practice range, but now the shooting was apparently being directed from the target area to the other side. The draw narrowed somewhat, and we came under artillery fire. There was at least one air burst; later I speculated that perhaps we had been shelled by our own artillery. In dropping to the ground, I knocked off my helmet, and the machine gun I was carrying at the time hit me on the back of the head. I am sure I would have felt more pain if my adrenalin level had not been so high. We rushed through the narrows, heading none of us knew where. A soldier approached me begging for help. He had been struck in the throat by shrapnel, could scarcely speak, and smelled of blood. I could only offer encouragement, urging him to keep moving. He turned to someone else. I learned later that he did not make it.

The group began to move more slowly. We were emerging from the draw, and the light from the bright orange sky revealed that an orderly column was being formed. I recognized the voice of a sergeant from one of the rifle companies, encouraging us and urging us to keep moving. We had reached American lines. We had survived to fight another day.

—*The* Bulge Bugle, *November 1990*

Jerry C. Hrbek
428th Military Police Escort Guards, 99th Infantry Division

Military policemen have always played an important role within the U.S. Army in being responsible for captured enemy prisoners. Jerry Hrbek shows how even in the heat of combat, there is still a place for a little bit of humanity when dealing with your opponents.

THERE WERE EIGHT OF US HOLED UP IN AN OLD FARMHOUSE in the village of Berg, northeast of the towns of Bullingen and Butgenbach, with nineteen Jerry prisoners. We had been waiting there for two days for some personnel from G-2 (military intelligence) to come and interrogate them.

About 4 p.m. on December 15, 1944, a carryall (truck) came down the first road in front of the house with five sergeants aboard. There were three master sergeants and two staff sergeants. They set up a table in the cellar in preparation for doing what they had to do. They were dressed in formal GI fashion, ribbons and all. We all looked like bums compared to them. To me they looked out of place and not someone who would be anywhere near the front.

One of them officiated behind the so-called desk. There were three of us in the room with them—Sergeant James, Richardson, and myself. "Okay, soldier, bring them in one at a time." The first prisoner came in, stood in front of the table, and came to attention, clicking his heels. The sergeant asked him what outfit he was in. He clicked his heels again and said "Fifth Panzers." He was dismissed, and the second was brought in.

They went through the same procedure with him, also the third and fourth man. When the fifth came up, he was asked the same question, only his answer was the 6th Panzers. The sergeant behind the table looked up from his writing and asked him again. He got the same answer. Slowly the sergeant stood up and stood there about thirty seconds looking at the man. His open hand shot out and with a thunderous slap he hit the Jerry right across the face. I was standing about four feet to the left of the prisoner. The incident happened so fast and totally took me by surprise. Inside I was mad as all hell. I pushed the Jerry aside, pulled back the bolt on the Thompson gun I was carrying and stood there pointing it at the sergeant. "You ever pull that on any of our prisoners and I'll make you a part of that wall behind you," I calmly told him. I watched him turn white with rage. One of the other sergeants said, "Hold it, soldier, what the hell do you think you're doing?" Sergeant James had been standing behind me, leaning up against the stone wall, his right foot propped up on the wall behind him. He stepped to the table and spoke to the sergeant: "You heard what he said, and that goes for all of you. You don't hit any of our prisoners." There was total silence. He backed up slowly and went back to his place at the wall. The sergeant behind the table was clearly shook up and, I believe, embarrassed in front of the others.

The next two prisoners were out of the 5th Panzers, and eight and nine were out of the 6th. When they were finished, six of the nineteen were with the 6th Panzer Division. The sergeant behind the desk came up to me and said, "They'll hear about this at division, soldier." I looked at him, and I was still pissed off. "Tell them for me also that we've been getting prisoners from the Sixth Panzer for the past three weeks, one here, two there." He made some comment that "it couldn't be, the Sixth Panzers were in Holland." I replied, "That's G-2's problem, we just bring them in for you, and we intend to stay alive."

My duty that night was at the front door of the farmhouse. About fifty feet away, sitting at the base of a tree and at the edge of the road, I could see Tommy Tompkins in silhouette. Tom was five feet one inch tall and had more ass than a herd of buffalo. He was from Oklahoma.

The night was crisp and clear, and time slipped by fast. It slips by fast when you run out of things to think about, and ever since the Normandy invasion I had already thought about home over ten billion times.

During the night and toward dawn, I was hearing things I didn't like. The door I was leaning against was being pushed out, and Sergeant James stepped outside. "How's it going, Yankee," he said—he being from Georgia and myself a New Yorker. "I don't know, Sarge, listen up for a while." We stood there in total silence and then the thum, thop, thum hit our ears. "Theirs or ours?" I asked. He didn't say a word. He turned and disappeared through the door.

About ten minutes later the door opened again, and Sgt. James said, "We've got to get out. The Jerries broke through and are coming straight for us." By now it was light. He waved to Tom, who came running, and they disappeared behind the door again. Tom came back out carrying a .30-caliber machine gun. He was busying himself out in the middle of the road. Johnson, Richard, and Doc Ward started filing the Jerries in a formation of fours. Everything went like clockwork. Tom had his barricade all ready to stop the panzers out in the middle of the road. The prisoners were ready to go. I turned to look back at the house. Sergeant James and Corporal Whitehead were helping a wounded prisoner up to the column. I looked at the man; he was jaundiced, and part of his face was missing. I looked at Sergeant James and Whitey, but got no answer. The prisoner was about twenty years old.

When Sergeant James saw Tom and his barricade, he said, "What the hell do you think you're going to stop with that, Tom?" Tom looked up at him from his sitting position behind the gun and said, "I've had it. This is as far as they go. No more, this is the end." It was sadly and frustratingly comical. The sarge looked down at him and said, "Tom, get that equipment into the weapons carrier (truck) and move it fast!" Tom got the message real fast. He had it all set up in the back of the weapons carrier in nothing flat.

A Jeep pulled up kicking the dirt off the road. Lieutenant Wilson of the divisional MPs and two non-coms told us to get out fast. Their Jeep had a mounted .30-caliber machine gun. They swung the vehicle around and took off. Someone said, "Nice guys, you would think they would stay with us."

The weapons carrier was in the lead, with Ack driving. Sergeant James was standing on the seat next to him, Tom in the back. Doc Ward and Corporal Whitehead ("Whitey") were on the right side of the column of prisoners, Richardson and Johnson on the left, and yours truly taking the rear. We got about a mile from the road. The sergeant decided to take to a huge, open field on our right because of a knocked out railroad bridge crossing the road in front of us. The abutments on either side of the road were at least one hundred feet in the air.

The field was about the size of five or six football fields. A dirt road ran right down the center of the field. We got to the approximate center of the field when two of the Jerry prisoners at the rear of the column were talking excitedly to each other. The wounded man walked about fifteen feet behind them, and I was behind him. Those two guys were getting me nervous. I yelled at them, *"Mach schnell!"* (Make it fast!). One of them pointed at the tree line behind us. I did a quick look and my heart almost quit. A half a dozen Tiger tanks were coming out of the woods, and hundreds of soldiers were pouring out on the field. They were about two hundred yards away. We were behind enemy lines, which was bad enough, but this seemed ridiculous. I yelled at Sergeant James, who was standing on the passenger side of the weapons carrier facing the whole scene, and he acknowledged my pointing. I pointed the Thompson at the two who were by now enjoying our predicament. When I yelled at them, they closed up a bit. The wounded man was farther back than before. I yelled to the two clowns and motioned them to get hold of him and take him along.

Two planes broke the tree lines and dropped to the field, preparing to strafe us. I yelled at the sarge, pointing. He turned and jumped off the vehicle, running down the road waving his arms, frantically trying to wave them off. He had immediately recognized them as ours. They couldn't have been fifty feet above the field, one behind the other. Sarge succeeded in his endeavor. The first one passed over our heads and started to climb. He got about fifty yards past us and about a hundred feet in the air when he blew up in a black blast of smoke and fell in a belly flop onto the field. I had a difficult moment deciding what to watch: the planes above us, the tanks at the edge of the tree lines, or the prisoners. I believe we were all hypnotized, prisoners as well as captors alike. The second plane almost ran into the first when the first exploded. The second pilot maneuvered to the right in a half roll straight up and was gone. To this day I believe they were Thunderbolts.

The column kept moving, and no one shot at us, I believe because they saw we had prisoners. We reached the end of the field, crossed the railroad tracks, went down an embankment, and straight up a hill of about forty degrees. The hill was about two hundred feet in length. Halfway up, I saw a sergeant lying on his back. He was yelling in both German and English, "*Schnell, schnell,* hurry, hurry," he said. "Keep them moving, son. Keep moving, don't give us away." Then I noted the hill was full of men dug in, big guns, 90mm, pointing downhill. My God, the Jerry army following us will catch hell.

We got to the top of the hill and ran the prisoners the next hundred yards to a road. Two 6x6s (trucks) were coming down the road, both with Red Cross markings. I tried flagging the first one down, but he was moving too fast. I stepped a little into the road and waved. The second one stopped. The driver asked, "What's up?" The wounded Jerry was standing next to me. "You carrying wounded?" "Yes," he answered. Looking at the wounded man, the driver made a remark to the effect, "Hell, he won't make it. Look, if the guys in the back will have him, it's up to them." I went on the back of the truck with the prisoner and pulled back the tarp, the vehicle had no tailgate. The men inside were all wounded, bandaged, only temporary stuff by the medics. I looked at the nearest man to me and asked if they would mind taking this one with them, pointing to the prisoner. "What say, you guys?" he addressed about a dozen wounded GIs. They looked at him and in unison waved him in. With my fractured German I turned to him and said "You're going to a *krankenhaus*" (hospital). He lifted his arm to my shoulder and said, "*Danke, danke, Amerikaner.*" (Thank you, thank you, American.). We helped him into the vehicle. I gave the driver the on-the-double sign. He waved back and took off. We hitched rides on different vehicles and walked, ran, anything, just to get to Elsenborn. We got shelled twice, but no one, prisoners or anyone, in our outfit was hurt.

—*The* Bulge Bugle, *May 1994*

Jim Forsythe
A Company, 1st Infantry Regiment, 106th Infantry Division

The overrunning of the combat-inexperienced 106th Infantry Division by the German forces invading the Ardennes resulted in one of the worst defeats ever inflicted on an American army division, with at least seven thousand GIs marching into POW camps. Jim Forsythe recalls his capture and time in a German POW camp and his eventual return home.

I WAS ASSIGNED AS A RUNNER IN COMPANY A, 1st Infantry Regiment, 424th Battalion of the 106th Infantry Division. We GIs were scattered sparsely in a holding action for a couple of weeks before December 16, 1944, and were almost at leisure, with little or no action for several days. We were billeted in the village of Lommersweiller in various houses that had a spare room and issued only forty rounds of ammunition for our rifles. At this time, we did not anticipate a battle, and forty rounds appeared to be more than adequate. We were informed that ammunition was being rationed because there was a strike on the East Coast and the dock workers would not load ships. They wanted better working conditions. They should have seen our working conditions.

On or about December 10, 1944, we began to hear distant rumbling similar to a thunder storm or distant tornado. About December 12 we could distinguish that a great amount of military equipment was moving. There were no airplanes flying. The weather was overcast with light rain and heavy fog. We could distinguish engines running and tank tracks squeaking.

We the GIs attempted to inform our superiors that possibly the Germans were assembling lots of tanks and equipment within a few miles of our location. Our squad sergeant informed us that it could either be American or German movement; however, it was not our place to worry since the war was basically over. Anyway, the brass knew what they were doing and that we would be told when and what to do. However, in a few hours we were ordered to get onto trucks immediately and were driven to Wintersfelt, unloaded, and dispersed along a fence at a location known as Schnee-Eifel. We were under heavy rifle, mortar, and artillery fire immediately, and I had no chance to dig in. We had no cover other than trying to stay just below the slope of the ridge in front of us.

In the early evening of December 16, in black darkness, German tanks followed by infantry started passing through the village. As ordered by our squad sergeant, we fired at the tanks and infantry. Our forty rounds of ammunition were gone within a few minutes. Most of our squad was killed within the first few minutes of the battle. Five survivors, including the company commander, Captain Cashion, slipped into a root cellar and spent most of the night listening to a continuous line of German tanks passing within a few feet of our location.

In the early hours of the morning December 17, our company commander, Captain Cashion, lunged outside with his arms waving over his head and yelled, "Officer, officer" and surrendered to the Germans. One of our comrades, John Barouche understood German. He said our captain told the Germans there were more Americans in the root cellar. He was indeed a traitor to hopefully save his own skin. I have since learned that I should not judge what a person, even yourself, will do under life-threatening circumstances. Captain Cashion's actions probably had little or no effect on the immediate results.

About daylight the Germans ordered us to come out or that a tank would fire into the root cellar. Someone opened the door, and there were several SS troops and a tank with the muzzle pointed into the root cellar.

The four of us stepped outside the root cellar and surrendered to the SS troops, who quickly searched us. The one that searched me was polite. The first thing he did was to take two cigarettes from a package of four in my coat pocket. He put one in his mouth and one in my mouth, lit both our cigarettes, and put the remaining two cigarettes in my pocket. I didn't habitually smoke at the time. He spoke good English and told me to put my arms down and that if I behaved I would not be harmed. I found the SS troops to be very professional soldiers. They did not blatantly mistreat us. Their rules became very simple: do exactly as they ordered you to do, or be shot. They took the four of us to a big barn in the village. There were possibly twenty other GIs in the barn and several wounded GIs lying down around the barn and nearby. By dark there were possibly one hundred GI prisoners held in the barn where we spent the night. A few attempted to escape and were shot. A terrible battle continued in the area all through the night.

On December 18, many of the prisoners were assembled outside the barn. There were possibly two hundred Americans in the barnyard, most of them dead. The Germans went around the downed Americans, probing with bayonets, and any and all that flinched or moved were shot in the head with pistols. It was extremely difficult to see and hear the young men, who were wounded and could not walk, beg for their lives, when approached by a German soldier with pistol drawn for the purpose of executing the young men simply because they could not walk and keep up with the other prisoners. I mentally suffered for many years after the war by remembering those young men begging to be allowed to live. And yes, most of them cried and called for their mothers.

The German soldiers were very efficient at executions. Possibly, the pistol shot was more available, as most German soldiers wore a pistol. This was perhaps less expensive and more prestigious for the executioner than a rifle shot. I am sure that the German executioner may have not enjoyed performing this dirty task. The Germans were so efficient that they did not care to allow the wounded Americans to live and require transportation and medical attention. Instant death was a more efficient method. Possibly if any of the German executioners survived the war, they too must have lived with the cries of those executed young men in their ears every time they tried to rest.

We were formed in a column of four and started walking, I assumed toward Germany. All wounded prisoners that became too tired or limp from fatigue or wounds were shot in the head.

We marched all day without food or water and were kept overnight in a big barn. On December 19, we again were marched all day and stopped three times to be interrogated. The first interrogating officer was extremely polite at first. He explained how necessary it was for them to win the war quickly, to stop all the bloodshed. He suggested that the German troops at the front were without adequate clothing and politely explained that he must therefore relieve me of my rain coat and top coat. Most of us GIs were dressed in wool pants and shirts, field jackets, top coats, a rain coat, and combat boots. We were marched for a couple of hours and then interrogated again. This time the interrogating officer began very politely, asking for military information, but he rapidly became furious, screaming at the top of his voice, demanding that we, "the useless ones," give up our combat boots for his loyal troops at the front. About this time, curdling screams were heard. I was told that if I did not comply with his orders, the next station of interrogation would find methods that would make me gladly comply. I now believe that the screaming was performed by a German just to scare the hell out of us and hopefully get more information from us. I gave up my combat boots and was supplied with wooden shoes. I was more fortunate than most since the majority of the prisoners lost their boots and got no wooden shoes. Later, when I was in Stalag 12A, I was able to trade a silver name bracelet that I had in the crotch of my underwear for a pair of dilapidated hobnail shoes. We were marched again to another interrogation, where remaining coats and shoes as well as watches and jewelry were confiscated.

The Germans had prepared for a long war. They had dehydrated carrots, including the tops intended for animal food; it looked like alfalfa hay. They also made bread consisting of some grain and mostly wood byproducts. Each loaf was dated, but the bread would last indefinitely. I have eaten bread that was ten years old. We had now gone over three days and nights without food or water. The Germans gave us some green soup made from the dehydrated carrots and a half slice of bread. The soup had the same effect as the old fashioned "black drought" used for total bowel evacuation. We were marched to a train station and loaded fifty into each thirty-foot freight car. The cars had no toilet facilities, food, or drinking water. We were locked in the cars for three days and nights. Unfortunately, the green soup we ate before being loaded into the cars was not acceptable to our stomachs, and we all came down with severe dysentery. With standing room only and no toilet facilities, most of the GIs were down on the floor wallowing in the filth. At the end of three days and nights, many were dead, and the ones that were alive were very sick. We were removed from the freight cars and marched a short distance to a very large camp, an interrogation, qualification, and distribution center known as Stalag 12A, located at Lemberg, Germany. Incidentally, I still have my German POW dog tags.

There were Russians in the camp who had been prisoners for a long period of time and were relatively established. They made a kettle of soup from some unknown ingredients and were able to give each of us about half a cup of the concoction. After being without a scrap of food or water for over four days, this concoction was a life-saving meal. That evening the English prisoners were able to provide the new prisoners with a cup of tea. Before this time, I had heard Englishmen speak of "having tea." Most GIs thought this was a near feminine thing to do. I take this opportunity to apologize to the English. They were formidable in combat, and having tea is an elegant thing to do. From this experience I learned to appreciate a hot cup of tea. We were given a thin, small blanket. The bunks were three tiers high, running the length of the building, with a one-by-six-inch frame around the entire wood deck. The deck was about five feet wide. A six-foot man could not lie straight out. We were stacked like sardines, belly to back, very tight for the length of the bunk. Fortunately, there was some body heat generated. Unfortunately, you could not avoid contact with the filth of dysentery from others. By now, most of the men had bleeding dysentery. We would lie on one side or the other, very compact. When somebody could not tolerate the pain of bones against boards, the word would be passed down the line, and we would all do a sitting twist to turn over on the other side.

Some attempt was made to keep the same nationals in like compounds. The French nationals were treated very well. They had adequate warm clothing and lots of food, the food being supplied by the American Red Cross, shipped to France from the United States, and then transported from

France to the German compounds by the French-operated Red Cross American Lend-Lease trucks. The trucks were driven by civilian Frenchmen. The Americans were treated less fortunately: some Red Cross food parcels were delivered to the American compound, only to be confiscated by the Germans. Some small portions were issued to Americans who worked in the factories of war production.

The Russians were treated like dogs. However, they were accustomed to a very rough and tough life in the Russian military. They survived reasonably well. The English and Australians were similar to the Russians in their toughness. The Italians, Indians, Pakistanis, and Persians were totally treated as subhuman. The French, Americans, English, and Aussies were not often or purposely abused. The Italians, Indians, Pakistanis, and Persians were continuously and repeatedly beat up, bayoneted, and abused.

At this camp there were guards from all levels of German society. The SS were highly professional. They rarely abused anybody. If you obeyed the rules, they treated you somewhat reasonably. You fractured the rules, they simply and without expression shot you in the head. The German youth were highly indoctrinated, hated all but Germans, and enjoyed abusing any and all nationals. There was the old guard, consisting of older or wounded military and veterans of World War I. They had no stomach for the German cause, and some were very considerate of the prisoners. In all of the stalags that I was in, there were no Jews: they had been sent directly to the gas chambers.

I have no documentation of the names of the camps or proximity to a city. We knew the camps more by number than by name. We were not interested in documentation, as we did not expect that we would live to get out. Your life expectancy was possibly a week, the length of time that you could live with acute dysentery. I was in a total of thirteen camps; I do not remember all the names.

I distinctly remember being in Lemberg for a few weeks. The camp was built adjacent to a large electric plant. On Christmas Eve 1944, the English attempted to bomb the power plant with 2,000-pound bombs. Because the stalag was adjacent to the power plant and had no identification as a POW camp, it suffered more damage from the bombing than was done to the power plant. Many prisoners were killed. I remember the earth rolling from the concussion of the big bombs similarly to swells on the ocean. I was on the floor one second, and seconds later was thrown against the ceiling. Later, I learned that the bombs did the most damage to the officers' section of the camp and that Captain Cashion was killed in that bombing raid.

While in camp, we could see the dogfights overhead. The Germans had excellent fighter planes, including jets. The American bombers with their fighter escorts would arrive in great numbers. At this stage in the war, most of the German pilots were aces, due to having been in and surviving many dog fights. The German jet planes were not very efficient and could not carry enough fuel for a prolonged flight. However, they would take off and fly through the American squadrons and have a turkey shoot in a very few minutes. Their jets would rip several American planes to shreds, and the air would be littered with the American plane parts, parachutes, and bodies of the American crewmen. It took considerable time after the turkey shoot for all the debris to fall to the ground. Much debris would fall into the prison compound. On one occasion an American pilot parachuted and landed in our POW camp. It was very unfortunate for the pilot; however, it was good news for us prisoners. It was good to see a healthy, well-fed American. The Germans only gave us the news that they wanted us to have: usually, biased propaganda. The American pilot enlightened us to the actual events of the war.

The Germans had a field day when President Roosevelt died. They told us prisoners that he was the only strong leader that the Americans had, and now that he was no longer leading the country, Germany with its great leader would win the war for certain, and quickly. By now, most of the German war machinery and factories were bombed out, and Roosevelt had ceased sending large squadrons of four-engine bombers over Germany, to avoid the loss of civilian life and property not directly war related. The Germans were very aware of Roosevelt's compassion for not bombing cities where civilians were likely to be killed. They were setting up factories and military headquarters in beautiful resort cities. I remember being on a work trip and walking through Zerbst, a most beautiful resort city. There were thousands of German tanks and other fighting equipment throughout the city.

Within two weeks after President Truman became president, the sky was filled with very large squadrons of four-engine bombers. They bombed each and every available target, including Zerbst. There was not one building standing in Zerbst after a heavy bombardment. President Truman's attitude was that if we must fight, let's fight to win. Also while in the prison camps every day we could see the V1 and V2 missiles flying to the west toward England. Also, the long-range rockets, which were not known to us, were fired toward the American lines in a continuous roar.

The Germans had a better trained military and equipment than the Allies. The only reasons we won the war were our reason for fighting and the dedication and courage of our young men. The tactics of the Allies was that the Western Front would hold fast while the Eastern Front would push. The purpose was to have the Germans moving their equipment to the east to stop the thrust, getting them out in the open for the Allied planes to pick off, exhausting their inadequate fuel supply and wearing down their old equipment. Then the Allies reversed the procedure, going from west to east and cutting the Germans to pieces. Unfortunately, the Germans were moving most of us prisoners away from the front to avoid having us recaptured. Therefore, we were walking across Germany from east to west, then from west to east most of the time.

We would sometimes work on farms and be kept in barns or other outbuildings. I was fortunate that most of the time I had guards that allowed you to pick up small potatoes and other farm produce to eat. Sometimes they allowed one or two prisoners to go outside the barn and make soup in the farmer's wash kettle. We burned potatoes in open fire to make charcoal, and we would eat the charcoal to retard dysentery. The ones that got severe dysentery and lay down usually died within three days. The ones who had courage enough to stay on their feet, exercise, and eat some charcoal may have sometimes lived with the condition.

In some of the camps we built little kriegie burners. They were like small forges. We built them mostly out of tin cans with a fan and a crank made from a welding rod or other stiff wire to turn the fan. You could boil a few potatoes or a little soup with a handful of wood chips. You could not survive on the vile food that the Germans issued; you had to be industrious enough to supplement your food with anything you could come up with and by any and all means.

I remember an occasion where a Russian detail of men was sent out to a factory to perform some work. Apparently the Germans discovered that one of the Russians had stolen a tool from the job site. Early that evening the Germans turned a search dog loose in the Russian compound, intending that the dog would find the guilty person. The dog was never seen again. The story is that the Russians butchered the dog and had a feast. There were no rats, cats, or dogs in or around the compound; they were all considered a delicacy. The occupants were near death from starvation and would eat anything.

I have no use for thieves and liars. However, I and most other prisoners were reduced to stealing anything we could use. When I was out on a work detail, I stole anything useful that I could hide under my clothes and bring into camp. At times I came into the camp with potatoes in my pants legs. You learned which guards would not perform a detailed search when you returned to camp and would take a bribe or turn their head and allow small, harmless items to be brought in.

About a year before I was captured, I was a real physical specimen, weighing in at 178 pounds, and was six feet tall, with a twenty-nine-inch waist and a forty-eight-inch chest. I had flawless teeth and was extremely strong. I was one of those kids that could lift the end of a truck or car. I was never defeated in any and all styles of wrestling, from college rules to no-rules full-contact fighting. Due to my experience and ability in the martial arts, I was extensively trained in the air force for special commando services where courage and knowledge were required. When I was liberated and transported to Rheims, France, where I spent a month in the hospital, I weighed only 108 pounds and had extreme dysentery, scurvy, lice, acute arthritis, bed sores on my shoulders, hips, and back, considerable tooth decay, and frostbitten feet. I had survived only by courage and determination. In prison I never had a change of clothes, a toothbrush, or a bath for five months and seventeen days.

At Rheims some of the American cooks actually cried at seeing the wretched condition of us ex-prisoners. They had all the wonderful food to treat us in grand fashion. However, they knew that our stomachs had shrunk, and if given all the food we could eat, we would have foundered and killed ourselves. They had to feed us a very little and increase the ration very slowly until we were capable of eating regularly. Those young men on all occasions gave it all to assist, help, or save a life of a countryman without considering his own danger. At the hospital in Rheims just after our liberation from prison, we would get two or three in each bed, as we were accustomed to cuddling while in prison to attempt to keep warm. None of the camps were heated, and the temperature was usually below zero. It appeared quite strange to the people who had not been prisoners.

A smaller soldier carrying a severely wounded man on his back was asked if he was too heavy. The soldier replied that he's not heavy, he's my buddy. Nothing was too heavy or too dangerous when it came to helping a wounded buddy.

After a month in the Rheims hospital, I was standing in line for hours to board a military transport plane to the United States. I became unstable and fell to the ground. I was placed back into the hospital for a few days and then sent by truck to the coast of France, where I boarded an LST ship for a trip of twenty-two days back to New York. The LST, a very small, flat-bottomed ship, was well supplied with food. We liberated prisoners enjoyed the food and keeping warm, and the treatment and care of the crew of the ship was as if it had been a five-star hotel.

At New York they gave us a homecoming dinner, any food we could think of, and then sent us by bus, train, et cetera, to our various locations. My homecoming dinner as I most desired was steak, ice cream, and milk. I was put on a train for a two-day trip to Paragould, Arkansas, the closest station to home. Midway of the trip, a conductor from Cincinnati, Ohio, took me home with him to stay overnight with his family, rather than sleep in the train station. I believe the conductor may have lost a son in the war and that possibly he enjoyed my stay at his house as much as I did. Then the next day I boarded a train to continue to Paragould, Arkansas, a few miles from my home at Leachville. A neighbor that I knew before going into the service, Hatley Robins, stopped to give me a ride. Hatley had been in Paragould overnight with his mistress. He told me of his great achievements of eating enough aspirin to appear to have a heart murmur and beat the draft and confided that he had made lots of money during the war by buying and selling rationed farm equipment. Hatley dropped me off at my home.

My parents went into a state of shock and disbelief. They had not yet received news of my release. The only news they received was from an English girl I dated a few times while in London. Alice knew how to get news from the War Department, and she learned that I was missing in action. She wrote to my parents to tell them the bad news that I was missing in action. They eventually received information that I was alive and a POW. With no further news, they had given up hope and assumed that I was dead.

Seven days at home and then to the army-navy hospital in Hot Springs, Arkansas, for thirty days' restoration before being discharged, and I finally went home for good.

Richard DeGraw
Battery D, 634th Antiaircraft Artillery/
Automatic Weapons (AAA/AW) Battalion

Allied air superiority kept American ground forces relatively free of enemy air attacks during the campaign in Western Europe, but there always remained a need for ground-based antiaircraft units in the U.S. Army. Richard DeGraw, a member of one such unit, speaks of his capture in the Ardennes and time in German captivity.

I WAS TAKEN PRISONER OF WAR WITH THIS BATTERY on December 20, 1944, during the Battle of the Bulge. On or about December 18, 1944, the battery commander had all Bofors (40mm aircraft guns) and half-tracks brought to a bivouac area on a hill. During this time we became completely surrounded by the enemy. To defend ourselves, we used our air-cooled .50-caliber machine guns, which were mounted on half-track vehicles; small arms; hand grenades; and bazookas, but we could not hold back the German assault. Our positions were under heavy field artillery fire all hours of the day and night.

The battery commander tried to get the battery out of the encirclement. However, all roads and fields were under heavy German fire, and escape became impossible. As we saw the German tanks come into sight, we were forced to hoist a flag of surrender, or the complete battery would have been annihilated. The bivouac area was set up in the woods. This provided very good camouflage for the battery during our last hours of freedom. Prior to our surrender we destroyed our trucks, guns, and half-tracks. We left nothing for the Germans to use.

The first thing the Germans did to us after we surrendered was to separate the privates from the noncoms, and the noncoms from the officers. With this task completed, we were forced on a march behind the German lines. We walked three days during which we had rain and snow. At night we were given shelter in barns, churches, and houses. We would be assembled in groups of twenty or twenty-five men, and the guards were posted outside of the buildings.

Each day the German guards would tell us that we were going to ride on a train, but it wasn't until the third day that we were loaded into railroad box cars. During the three-day march and the one-day train ride, we did not wash or shave, and our rations of food consisted of three boiled potatoes and a cup of terrible coffee each day. Never were we given any drinking water.

During our train ride, we were sealed in the box car and were not allowed out of the car even when the train was not moving, not even to go to the toilet. We used our helmets as toilets.

While we were on the train, American planes strafed it, killing about six of the American prisoners of war. When the train reached its destination—I do not know where—the dead Americans were piled on the station platform, and we never found out where they were buried. We disembarked at this station and started an eight- or nine-day forced or death march. During the march, several of the men collapsed, and we never heard of them again. Another soldier and I carried Pvt. John A. Dilcomyn in order to keep him from falling out of the ranks during the march. John did make it to Stalag 4B but was never heard from after that.

We billeted at Stalag 4B for several days and then we were taken by truck for about fourteen miles to Moosburg, Germany, where we spent our time until we were liberated by the American army. There were about seventy or eighty men shipped to this town, and they came from several different outfits that the Germans had overrun during the Battle of the Bulge.

We were billeted in what I believe was a school building. We were allowed a cold shower and shave once a week. Our bunks were triple-deckers with wooden slats six or eight inches apart, with no mattress and only one blanket. We used our shoes for a pillow.

No time was allowed to enjoy recreational activities, not even listening to a radio. There were electric lights in the building, but they were never turned on; there was heat in the building, but we were never warm.

The food at this prison camp was poor, and the portions were small. One-sixth of a loaf of potato bread was served with a bowl of watered soup and a cup of coffee. We went out in the fields to work on the railroad, digging up the tracks, and sometimes we dug up turnips. We would eat them raw and dirty. When I was taken prisoner I weighed 170 pounds. When I was liberated I weighed 89 pounds.

Our work detail was removing rails and ties from the German railroads so that the advancing American army could not use the railroad. We would pile the rails and ties next to the road bed, but because of our poor health, we were unable to do much work in a given day. Talk about blessings in disguise.

During our captivity we always had Sunday off from work, and we would just sit around and talk about what we would do when we got home. I always wanted to own my own diner, having had enough of raw turnips. I never knew anyone that gave up hope of going home.

We were never given new clothing, and I still had on the same clothing when I was liberated 118 days after I was taken prisoner. We were issued rags for socks and would fold them around our feet something like you would fold a baby's diaper. This was very uncomfortable to say the least.

During our imprisonment, only one Red Cross package was divided among seven men—no tobacco in it. The German guards had taken out the cigarettes and smoked them. A Red Cross package should have been issued once a week. We only had the one. I guess the Germans kept the rest for themselves.

Even though we were never physically abused, we were mentally abused. The lack of proper food and living conditions took its toll on our health.

During the month of April, 1945, we had no idea that the American army was so close to the town that we were being held prisoner in. The guards spoke very little English, and as I said before, we had no radio. We never heard any artillery or small arms fired prior to seeing the Americans. We were taken out to work on the railroad in the morning, and the guards told us by nightfall we would be liberated.

We were brought back to the school building at about 11:30 a.m. We were given our ration of water-soup and bread and told we could stay outside the building and wait to be liberated. About mid-afternoon we could see our tanks and infantry coming across the field. The tank hit the fence and ran it down. We were free at last.

The Americans gave us food, water, cigarettes, candy, and toilet articles on the day we were liberated. We stayed in Mühlberg that night, and the following day we were transported to the American air base in Germany where we received new clothing and ate steaks, chops, and drank milkshakes. We stayed at the air base for about fourteen days.

From the air base in Germany we flew on a C-47 to France. When we landed, we were loaded on a liberty ship and set sail for New York Harbor, and from there we went to Camp Kilmer in New Jersey. I was given a sixty-day leave from Kilmer with orders to report to Fort Knox, Kentucky, where I was assigned to guard German POWs. *Was this on purpose—now I'm guarding them?*

I stayed there until I received my discharge on November 8, 1945.

—The Bulge Bugle, *August 2000*

Kenneth G. Myers
394th Medical Detachment, 99th Infantry Division

A small part of the German plans to break through the American-held Ardennes included the use of German troops dressed as GIs. These German commando teams operating behind American lines caused soldiers like Kenneth Myers to think anybody could be the enemy.

I WAS TWENTY YEARS OLD WHEN I WAS DRAFTED. After basic training at Camp Van Dorn, Mississippi, we went on maneuvers through Mississippi, Lousiana, and Texas. Then we were shipped overseas with the 394th Medical Detachment for the 99th Infantry Division.

We were stationed at Hunningen, where I drove a truck for the medics. One day I checked my gas tank and noticed that it was below the half-full mark. I went to the motor pool and asked Sergeant Seninsky for gas. He told me we had no gas. I said, "I will go to the service company and get some." When I got to the service company, I found that they had none. I told Lieutenant Wartonbee that I would go and get some if he wanted me to. He seemed surprised that I would be willing to do that, but I assured him that I would be glad to do it. He said, "OK, but the red crosses will have to come off your truck before you go." I told him that was no problem, and he gave me a map. He said, "Follow this, and don't go by the signs on the road." I started out on the trip, watching each crossing and marking it as I crossed it.

When I got to the gas depot, the Red Ball Express trucks were coming in. Each truck had only one layer of five-gallon gas cans. I got one driver to back up to my truck and started in the front to stock it to the top of the truck racks. I unloaded five trucks into this one I was driving and started back.

When I got to the gate, the guard stopped me and said, "What are you doing?" I said, "We need gas, and I'm going to the front lines." He said, "With all that gas, what do you think will happen if it is hit with a shell or a land mine?" I said, "Not much more than if it was just one layer. Please just let me go." He said, "You will never make it." I said, "Never is a long time."

He stepped back and I started out. Even with the heavy load I was carrying, I had no trouble except trying to miss the large holes in the road. When I got back to the service company, I went in and told Lieutenant Wartonbee I had the gas. He came out to the truck, I threw the flap up over the top of the truck, and he said, "Hell's fire, Myers, how did you get all that gas on that truck?" I said, "I loaded it from the Red Ball trucks—you can have all of it, but the last layer, that's mine."

I took it back to our motor pool, and we filled all our Jeeps. There were twelve cans left across the front of the truck. We covered them with full field packs and other equipment we were hauling.

The next morning the major called me and said, "I want you to take some money to the Red Cross." I got in the truck and went to the aid station. We loaded four or five bags on the truck, and the major told me where to go, and I was on my way.

I got to the town, and there was a courtyard with a twenty-five-foot-high wall with a big arch to drive through and a large planter in the middle. The planter was about twenty feet wide and thirty-five feet long. As I went through the arch, I had to back up and turn sharper in order to get past the planter. I saw the Red Cross up in the corner of the courtyard. I drove around the end of the planter and down along the wall. Backing up to the loading platform, I got out, jumped up on the back dual tire, grabbed the rack off the truck, and walked along the bed of the truck. When I got to the opening, there was just room to squeeze through. A soldier was standing at the opening with an M1 rifle in a vertical position. I said, "Move, so I can get in." He just stood like a statue, so I said, "Move, so I can get in." He still didn't move, so I pushed him out of the way and went in. I said, "I have the money for the 99th Infantry Division; what do you want me to do with it?" A soldier sitting in the back of the desk told one of the other soldiers to help me unload it, which he did. I said,

"Do you want me to sign anything?" He said, "No." So I went back to the soldier at the opening and told him I wanted out. When he didn't move, I took him by the arm and moved him aside and went out, stepped on the tire, jumped to the ground, and got in the truck. As I was leaving, I noticed along the side of the planter a big bus with the top cut off about four inches below the seat tops. It looked weird, and I stopped and looked at it for a few seconds, and then went on. I got to the crossroad and a Jeep went by. He was really flying. He said, "Come on."

I got back to the town and was parking my truck between a large manure pile and the house, but then I decided to park it in back of the house. I walked up to the aid station. When I went in, everyone turned pale. The major said, "Myers, where did you take that money?" I said, "To the Red Cross, where you told me to take it." He said, "You are lying to me." I said, "No sir, I am not." I then told him what the town looked like and described the big courtyard with the planter and told him where the Red Cross was located. He said, "That town was taken before you left here." I said, "Thanks a lot!" Then everything came to mind—the soldier at the back of the truck, I now realized, was a German instead of an American. The floor inside the building was covered with splattered blood, and there were scrapes all over the front of the counter. To the right was a large pile with an old field tent covering it. It had cobwebs and mud all over it. I never suspected a thing because all the soldiers had American uniforms. They all looked clean, and I never thought of them all being Germans. They all had M1 rifles. The only clue that anything was wrong was the blood on the floor. But, after all, it was the Red Cross building, so I didn't question that. I felt that my guardian angel had surely protected me during that trip.

The next morning was December 16. I looked out, and the Germans were coming across the field. I went up to the aid station and said, "What are we doing here? The Germans are only a couple of hundred feet away and headed in this direction." The major said, "Myers, you are crazy." I said, "It would do you good to come and look for yourself." He looked out and then told me to go down and see the colonel. I went to the colonel and asked him the same question: "What are we doing here?" He said we were supposed to hold, no matter what it cost. I went back and told the major, and he sent us back to the colonel. When we got there, an announcement came over the radio that we were surrounded. The colonel jumped up, grabbed some stuff from his desk, and said, "Everyone for himself, and the hell with the rest of them."

I got the truck and went by the aid station. If he had been a few seconds later, we could have had a truckload of Germans. They stood on the banks along the road and didn't even fire a shot.

We got back to Mürringen and soon got a call for the medics. Another medic, Lanier, and I went out and found two men. One was lying face down in the snow. I said, "This is the fellow down here we need," and Lanier said, "Yes, this other fellow is dead." When he said that, I looked at the other fellow. He lifted his head. We went back and rolled him over. Snow and ice was all frozen to his face. I took my scissors and cut the snow from his nose and mouth so he could breathe. We carried him back, and when we took him to the aid station, the major said, "Take him to the morgue." I backed out of the room and said to Lanier, "We will put him in this other room and we'll take care of him." The major found out and told us we were wasting our time.

The soldier had been hit in the head with shrapnel and a part of his skull was turned like a flap, but connected on both sides. It was tight, and we worked around it and got his brains back in his head. Then we moved him from Mürringen to the

B Company clearing station, which had been evacuated. We kept our badly injured patient in the air raid station with us.

Around midnight we were told that we were going to make a break for it at 2 a.m. We loaded all the wounded on the truck and got orders from the major to leave our injured friend. He said he was going to die anyway. But we got him on the truck and transported him to a hospital.

On our way out that night, we fought the 2nd Infantry Division. They thought we were the Germans, and we were told to leave our vehicles and walk. We walked down the road about a mile, and then they said, "Go back." We were like a drove of cattle, not knowing where to go. I got back to the truck I was driving and asked the wounded if they were all right. They said they were, but the weapons carrier two cars back was hit and blown to pieces. I looked back, and it looked as if a man was sitting in the vehicle behind it. I went back, and it was a full field pack with a helmet sitting on it. I started back to my truck, and a German opened up with a burp gun.

I put one hand over my face and the other over my heart and fell in a ditch. He came up over the hill and across the road where I was lying and dropped his knee down by my side. My heart sounded like someone was beating on it with an anvil, it seemed so loud. I lay there, and he kept shooting. I realized later that he was shooting at wheat stalks that were on the hill.

After a while he gasped and fell backwards. I stayed there for a while in fear that if I got up I would be shot. Finally, I crawled away and came out where our infantrymen were standing. I said, "Do you know where I was a minute ago?" I told them I was lying underneath the German who was shooting up on the hill. One of the infantrymen told me that when the bright light went off, he could see the guy and shot him. I didn't see the bright light because I had my face buried in the snow.

We stayed around until nearly daylight, and they sent a patrol and found that we were Americans instead of Germans. So they let us through, and we took the wounded to the hospital. When we arrived, I told the colonel if they were going to do anything for this fellow with the head wound, they had better do it quickly. Then we went back and carried in another soldier. When we went back into the hospital, there were six people working on him, rubbing him and giving him shots.

We were sent to shower and change clothes and eat. When I came back later, I went in to see how he was getting along. I asked him how he was doing, and he said, "I fell out of bed and I have a headache."

He was sent back to the States, and I thought that was the last time I would see him.

After Mürringen, we went to Aachen and got replacements and went back up to Elsenborn Ridge. I went out to get oil for our lights. When I got to the ammunition dump, I went down into an air raid shelter. As I got there, a liaison officer called for white phosphorus. The colonel came on the walkie-talkie and said it was against the Geneva Convention. The liaison officer said, "Who is fighting with it? We have eight German tanks coming straight at us." So the colonel gave him white phosphorus, the Americans fired one mortar, and the liaison officer said, "You have it zeroed in—pour it on." Then the whole sky filled up with shooting fire, all colors of the rainbow, and it melted those tanks down over the tracks. I got the oil for our lights, and returned to the aid station.

Two nights later, I was asked to take my truck and go back to get the mail. We had not gotten any mail for two weeks. I said, "That truck is too big, and with no load on it, it won't have much traction in the snow and ice. If you will give me the shop truck, I will go." So they gave me the shop truck, and

Tomat said, "I will go with you." I was glad for the company, so we started out.

We had no lights, but there was enough shell fire that the road was well lit for us. Sometimes we would have to stop, but it was never very long until the shell fire would again light the way for us.

When we got to where we were to pick up the mail, there was so much that the back of the truck was stuffed with mail. Then we started back. When we got to the long grade uphill to Elsenborn, I said to Tomat, "Look on the left ridge. There is a patrol coming toward us." We kept looking, and when we got up to where they were, men were lying in the ditches on both sides of the road. I kept driving as fast as I could, which was fifteen to twenty-five miles per hour. We had a BAR on the side of the truck, a .50-caliber machine gun on the roof with a belt of ammunition for it, and Tomat had an M1 rifle, but not one of the soldiers got up. Tomat kept looking back as we passed through them with no trouble. The angels were with us again.

There were many memorable experiences. But back to our friend who "fell out of bed." He was a driver for Service Company 394 at the time of his terrible head injury. His name is George Serkedakis. After the war ended and I came back home, I took up my plumbing trade. I met and worked for Serkedakis' sister and kept in touch with him through her. About nine years later, I was driving down 18th Street in Washington, D.C., when I came to a red light I looked over in the car next to me, and there, to my surprise, was Serkedakis. I tapped my horn and said, "Serkey!" We parked in a nearby parking lot and talked for hours! He told me that he had been conscious and had heard the major tell us to take him to the morgue. He also heard me say, "We will put him in the next room and we'll take care of him."

He has a metal plate in his head where the shrapnel hit him, but fifty years later we are both alive and exchanging war stories. Serkedakis lives about five miles from my home, and we get together often.

—*The* Bulge Bugle, *November 1999*

2 | THE AMERICANS FIGHT BACK

Edgar E. Bredbenner Jr.
B Company, 318th Infantry Regiment, 80th Infantry Division

Edgar Bredbenner remembers that being wounded meant the long battle to survival was just beginning during the Battle of the Bulge.

THIS WAS A DAY I WILL NEVER FORGET, and it was probably the longest day in my life. The 80th Infantry Division had moved up from central France to join the Third U.S. Corps, along with the 26th Infantry Division and the 4th Armored Division, to attack the southern portion of the Bulge area. It was a long, cold ride in open trucks with no blankets or overcoats, and we spent almost two days without stopping. At that time we had about fifteen or sixteen men in our squads, and we attacked Ettelbruck, Luxembourg, on December 22, 1944. We fought there for three days, losing many men, all officers, and all of our automatic weapons. This attack was called off because of the cost in men, and on Christmas Eve we again loaded on open trucks to join the 4th Armored Division in their attack into Bastogne, Belgium. This was another long, cold night.

Early on Christmas morning we moved out and were immediately fired upon. A burst of burp gun hit me in the neck and ear, took off my helmet, and shredded the towel wrapped around my neck. Medics patched me up, and we continued through the thick woods deep on the right flank. Tanks were on the road on our left, but we could not hear them; the air was so heavy and the snow swirling about.

We had sniper fire from the rear, the right flank, and from the front. Artillery fire and mortars shattered the trees about us, but we kept moving forward into the attack, losing many more men. About 1 p.m. a tree burst hit me in the thigh and opened my leg up. A medic patched me up, gave me sulfa powder and morphine, and said to hike back to the aid station, which was five miles. No stretcher bearers were getting through the waist-deep snows, and the enemy had closed in behind our lines. Three of us started back, but without our weapons. One man had his heel shot away, and the other had been hit in the back, and none of us were bleeding, it was so damp and cold and in the deep snows. We found wounded men who had been shot and killed by snipers while trying to get to the aid station, and their equipment gone.

The medics had no blankets for the wounded. We had no overcoats, shoe pacs, or any of the needed camouflage clothing. If wounded, you walked out; if you stayed, you froze to death. No fires were allowed, and we saw no buildings at any time.

After a P-47 sprayed us with machine gun fire, we reached the aid station about dark. We were checked out and placed in ambulances to travel to an air-evac hospital near the French-Belgian-Luxembourg borders. We were told we would be flown to England and probably to the United States. We all fell asleep in the warm ambulance, and all of us had severe pain from frozen feet and legs, and did they ever sting. We were placed on stretchers and put aboard the plane after a change of bandages. About five hundred feet up, three German fighters fired a short burst and hit the plane. But we were lucky. They evidently saw the air strip lights and realized that this was a medical area and flew off. One engine was out, the plane was on fire, some of the men and nurses were wounded or killed, and the copilot was out of commission. The pilot was wounded but brought the plane around, and we landed back on the air strip. We were back mobile again and helped remove the dead and wounded. Ten minutes later the plane exploded. I was moved to an operating area, and I sat in a chair while a doctor gave me seven shots of Novocain and opened up my thigh to the bone. I sat there and watched him. Today, I probably would have passed out! We never got to England.

—*The* Bulge Bugle, *May 1998*

Ralph Schip
18th Cavalry Reconnaissance Squadron

The 18th Cavalry Reconnaissance Squadron was attached to the 2nd Infantry Division in October 1944 and formed part of the 14th Cavalry Group tasked with guarding the Losheim Gap. It was there that the German Fifth and Sixth Panzer Armies would attack. Ralph Schip recalls one small incident during the Battle of the Bulge.

THE OVERALL TENOR OF EXPERIENCES DURING A PERIOD of combat can often be encapsulated in the recounting of a very short-term, specific experience, which by its intensity can be vividly recalled in fine detail, even after forty-five years.

The title of this vignette, if it needs one, is "The Night Mickey Did *Not* Get Shot."

Troop E was a compact, close-knit group, a fighting machine of very diverse men who had been fine-tuned by our leader, Capt. "Pappy" Meadows.

Our M8 assault guns were veritable mechanized armories, when consideration is given to all the extra armament we managed to acquire by devious means. The assigned equipment consisted of a 75mm howitzer, .50-caliber machine gun, bazooka, rifles, and grenades of all types. In addition to all this, each GI had his own personal preferences as to what was needed to do the job at hand. My extra weapon and pride and joy was a Thompson submachine gun, the old "Chicago Typewriter," complete with Cutts-compensator and the whole show—none of those crazy "grease-gun" plumbers' friends for me!

I did have to be content with ammunition clips rather than the original-style drum. Possibly the Chicago hood who turned the particular gun in for the war effort forgot to include this drum. Anyway, it was a considerable comfort to be able to hose-down an area at night when some unidentified noise or movement, real or imagined, came within the short range of the .45 slugs. I believe the statute of limitations has run its course, and I could not now be prosecuted, but I'm not ready yet to admit exactly how I acquired this unauthorized weapon.

Anyhow, to make a short story long, one of the accepted functions of mechanized cavalry was to act as rear guard when such was needed. To this end, we were assigned the duty of entrenching at a road intersection while a large number of vehicles and personnel of an armored division task force withdrew and formed a new defense line farther to the west. It was then our assigned duty to interdict and delay the onrushing krauts, emboldened by victory, schnapps, and whatever else was drunk.

It is a major understatement to say that it was considerably unnerving to watch all this armor and heavy equipment proceeding away from the direction of battle. Unfortunately, such were the fates of combat. Finally, about dusk, the last vehicle had rumbled by, leaving only our compact, close-knit, fighting machine to greet and entertain the krauts whenever they elected to make their move.

At dusk, it was decided that no one was to move at night. Also, we concluded that the Germans would answer a verbal challenge by a potato-masher (hand grenade) into the open tank turret or a burst of burp-gun fire. Accordingly, we decided that the orders of the night were to fire first and ask only afterward.

Ground fog hung close to the snow-covered ground. The thick, icy fog alternately lifted and settled, creating all sorts of imagined movement to whomever was on watch. During the bone-chilling cold and spine-tingling suspense of a very long night, I was seated on the tank commander's seat in the open turret, wrapped in three GI blankets while on my duty shift, with my trusty Thompson to my right and below on a shelf. About 3 a.m., as the fog lifted ever so slightly, a lone figure suddenly materialized close in front of me. I reached frantically for the Thompson, but the carrying strap caught on a latch or projection, and I was running out of time to deal with the moving figure. This left the only viable action of a verbal challenge, "Who's there?"

From out of the mist materialized a hoarse whisper, "It's me, Mickey. What time is it?"

I never did ask Mickey why he left his foxhole at such great risk to find out what time it was. Nor did I ever tell him how very close he came to being a statistic and how narrow the margin was between vividly remembered experience and grim tragedy. The very next morning I removed both the stock and carrying strap and thereafter fired the Thompson from the hip.

Oh, Mickey, if you are still out there, here's the story, much too late. Also, if you have not yet purchased a watch, maybe it's time to give some serious thought to such a purchase, and "don't leave home without it." Your very life may depend on it.

—*The* Bulge Bugle, *May 1992*

Marino M. Michetti
B Company, 508th Parachute Infantry Regiment,
82nd Airborne Division

The 82nd Airborne Division was in reserve while resting in Rheims, France, when the German Ardennes Offensive began and was quickly rushed to help plug the gap in the American lines. Marino Michetti explains what he and his unit did to stop the German advance.

AT DAWN ON DECEMBER 16, 1944, APPROXIMATELY TWELVE enemy divisions pushed through the lightly held Ardennes in Belgium. Three American divisions, the 28th Infantry, the newly committed 106th Infantry, and the 7th Armored, were trying to hold on a pathetically thin line. The Ardennes had seemed the least likely spot for a German counterattack because of the unlikely success of a lightning thrust with armor through the thickly wooded area and rutted roads.

At 2000 hours on December 17, the 508th Parachute Infantry Regiment, still attached to the 82nd Airborne Division, was alerted for immediate movement to Belgium. That night we spent in parking personal belongings, drawing weapons from supply, and getting set for our move early in the morning. By 0900 on December 18, the 508th, loaded in huge tractor-trailer trucks (Red Ball Express), joined the division convoy as it left Sissonne, France, and headed for Werbomont, a small village in Belgium.

At 1800 on December 19, twelve hours after the regiment had arrived at Werbomont, we got orders to move to Chevron, two miles east. We made this move on foot. Here we could not dig down too far because we hit water after digging a foot in the snow. Marching in the snow-covered road, we met soldiers and tanks of troops moving to the rear. I did not know where we were going except to meet the Germans where these other soldiers had run into a hell of a lot of them.

In the afternoon on December 20, the regiment was alerted for another move. We still had not made any contact with the enemy. The 504th and 505th Parachute Infantry Regiments had already met the enemy to the east at Haute Bodeux. Due to a shortage in transportation, the entire regiment could not make the ten-mile trip by truck and still be in position by dawn. I was in the group making an all-night road march.

By first light on December 21, despite the fact that no one had any sleep, the regiment, still out of contact with the enemy, was tactically disposed along Thier-du-Mont, a ridge a thousand yards south of the Belgian village of Goronne. Jeep patrols moved constantly across the front, searching for the first signs of the approaching Germans. The entire 82nd had changed position and now was pushed out like a long finger into the middle of the north side of the wedge the enemy had driven into the American lines. At the tip of this finger was the 508th, supported by the 319th Glider Field Artillery Battalion.

Behind us, we had a small house for our CP. Later that afternoon, on my way to get some K-rations, I passed a building full of large bags of GI bread. I saw a plane flying low, one of our fighter planes. The next thing I knew, the plane began strafing the ground next to the building. I just fell to the ground.

That evening, parachutes were dropped out of the sky, over our heads. I later learned that the Germans dropped three hundred of these chutes. Everyone that had a weapon must have opened fire, including myself, on what we thought were German paratroopers. These parachutes were found to have been holding dummies, to see where we had our firepower.

On XVIII Airborne Corps' order, the 82nd Airborne Division withdrew, beginning at 2100 hours on Christmas Eve, blowing bridges and sowing mines. The 504th Regiment established positions to the right of the 508th Regiment. The 505th Regiment pulled back and dug in on the high ground west of Trois-Ponts, linking on the left with the 30th Infantry Division. The 508th Regiment, deployed near Vielsalm, was attacked in force—and, skillfully fighting off several aggressive 9th Panzer Division armored task forces, pulled back to take positions on the right of the 505th Regiment.

With a covering force of one platoon per rifle company, it was a different story. Now that less than one-third of the regiment was holding the same ground, contact was nearly impossible. The early evening was quiet enough for the men on the ridge, but at 2300 the fireworks began. Artillery began falling in the 1st Battalion area, and B Company sustained a few casualties. Shortly after the artillery barrage reached its fullest intensity, the Germans shortened the range and substituted smoke for high explosive. With the river and both banks shrouded by smoke, the advance regiments of the Germans made a crossing. In the B Company platoon, all was quiet. Suddenly, the shriek of a Jerry whistle was heard, and several Germans seemed to rise suddenly out of the snow and smoke. B Company's machine guns split the enemy formation with bands of steel, and the troopers held.

The reason for this penetration was to bring relief to the units surrounded in the initial fighting in the counterattack. Elements of the 7th Armored and 106th and 28th Infantry Divisions were fighting in a perimeter a few miles southeast of the 82nd Division. Any elements which could reach the banks of the Salm River would be evacuated to the rear through the escape channel for regrouping.

In the 3rd Battalion area, a five-man Jeep patrol led by my corporal, Robert Mangers, of the S2 Section, said in a radio message back to battalion headquarters, "Tanks rolling by, fifty yards apart. Two columns of *panzergrenadiers* (German motorized infantry) are marching down the road at close inter-val." At 0900 on December 23, Corporal Mangers transmitted his last message. He was not heard of again and was picked up on the morning report as missing in action.

In the 2nd Battalion area, enemy armor was moving northeast toward the regimental area and attacked the town of Salmchâteau, several miles in front of the battalion posi-tion. A heavy volume of fire was directed on the Germans from the commanding ground of Thier-du-Mont ridge. One tank, a Mark III, was KOed in front of D Company. F Company was west of D Company near the village of Comte.

In the 1st Battalion area, our mortar squad was on Thier-du-Mont ridge. I had carried six rounds of 60mm mortars on top of my full field equipment. We were north of Rencheux, where we had taken defensive positions. C Company was north of us, and A Company to our south. Some other GIs had dug my foxhole for me and the other three men in our squad. I could look down on the Germans who were on the other side of the river. We could see some distance to the east. In the after-noon, we set up our mortar behind our foxholes, one trooper with the base plate and another with the tube. A corporal, our squad leader, directed our fire into the Germans. Fifteen hun-dred yards was not too far away—we were out of rifle range. I could see little barrages explode when the mortars hit, and the Germans ran for cover. The corporal was the only one that knew anything about the mortar. I had previously been with the 782nd Airborne Ordnance Company, where I handled all the ammunition used by the division.

About midnight, I heard shouting and noise—a group of Americans and Germans were in an open area behind us, on the ridge. I asked the trooper in the foxhole to my left, "What should we do?" I remember us getting out of the foxholes with our hands behind our heads! My whole world seemed to have crumbled around me. What would my friends think of me now? I really felt ashamed! I was seeing flashes of my childhood, when I saw the white lights from the tracers in the burp-gun firing at me! The Germans were all around us. The Germans huddled us in with a small group of other prisoners, prodding us with their rifles. They had come up on the ridge behind us.

I was back at the house we had used for our CP, only this time the Germans were using it to interrogate the prisoners they had taken. I had to take everything out of my jump pants pockets. I had quite a collection because we had just received some Christmas mail before we left Sissonne, France. I remember some nice, white handkerchief someone had sent me. Pocketknife, fountain pen, three packs of cigarettes, five packs of some razor blades, wallet with some English money (four one-pound notes) and two one-dollar bills. I remember having bread and coffee with the Germans at daylight, Christmas morning—"Merry Christmas."

Farther south, in the vicinity of the bridge, A Company's covering force, Lieutenant Lamm's platoons, straddled the road from Vielsalm to Goronne, a few hundred yards west of the bridge. The main weight of the German attack fell upon the twenty-four A Company men. After visiting all his squad positions, Lieutenant Lamm returned to his CP to dispatch a runner to Capt. Benjamin Delamater, commander of the 1st Battalion covering force. I never got the word to pull back.

The platoons from all three battalions reported to Lieutenant Colonel Stanley, covering force commander, and the seven-mile trek to the new positions began. By 0800 on Christmas morning, the entire regiment was assembled in new positions. Although the whole regiment did not participate, the delaying action of this covering force was one of the best pieces of fighting in the 508th Parachute Infantry's history.

—*The* Bulge Bugle, *August 1992*

Bruce C. Clark
Combat Command B, 7th Armored Division

Originally, the main goal of Combat Command B of the 7th Armored Division was to provide escape corridors for the beleaguered regiment of the 106th Infantry Division. Brigadier General Bruce C. Clark took it upon himself to expand his responsibilities to delay the German advance through the Ardennes.

BEFORE WE CROSSED THE ENGLISH CHANNEL IN 1944, a senior American general, in addressing his commanders, said: "Once you have reached a certain line or have taken a piece of ground, you will not give it up without my personal permission."

At the time, I felt that such a rule in tactics was rigid and probably dangerous. If my understanding is correct, the original rules of fisticuffs of boxing required each contestant to "toe the line" drawn across the center of the ring. He lost if he failed to keep his position. The Marquis of Queensberry established new rules, which are in effect today, which eliminated the toe-the-line requirement and put mobility into prize fighting. The tactics of boxing were thus changed.

After I was handed the command of the Saint-Vith area in the early afternoon of December 17, 1944, I hastily estimated the situation. I had been brigadier general just ten days. My military future and that of my command was very important to me. It did not look hopeful.

I tried to develop in my mind what it was that the German commander was required to accomplish in what appeared to me to be an all-out desperate operation. I felt that punching a hole through the Ardennes was not his mission. Neither was the capture of Saint-Vith or Vielsalm or establishing a bridgehead across the Salm River. These could well be steps in his operation, but Hitler's gamble had to be for decisive stakes.

121

Decisive objectives were far to my rear and toward the English Channel. With these ideas in mind and without any orders but to "go up to Saint-Vith, contact General Jones of the 106th Division, and if he needs help, give it to him," I felt that I must fight a flexible delaying action and not let my command and associated units become decisively engaged.

I disposed my command, as it arrived piecemeal, to provide such a defense. I established a base of fire with dug-in direct weapons using a tank destroyer company, which had recently been issued 90mm-gun TDs (M36s).

I established a mobile counterattack force of part of a battalion of tanks, concealed near and behind Saint-Vith. It was used to counterattack whenever the Germans established a dangerous situation, but then only to sweep the enemy and return to its rendezvous for further orders.

A rather weak defensive line resisted the Germans. The troops on this line were engineers, armored infantry, and reconnaissance units. They took a terrific beating. Some of the most heroic fighting of the Battle of the Bulge took place in these units. Their deeds have never been adequately recorded nor awarded. These are the unsung heroes of the U.S. Army's greatest battle. Several company-sized units were reduced to one-third of their original strength in four or five days of fighting. Still, I had to pull back on occasion to keep them from being cut off and destroyed.

Once, during the battle, I was asked: "When you counterattack and restore your line, why do you withdraw your counterattacking force instead of staying there and holding?" My response was something like this: "This terrain is not worth a nickel an acre to me. In my tactics I am giving up about a kilometer a day under enormous pressure, but my force is intact, and I am in control of it. A few kilometers' advance cannot be of any substantial value to my German opponent. He must, I believe, advance many kilometers and very quickly if he is to accomplish his mission. The 7th Armored Division is preventing him from doing that. We are winning, he is losing."

My division commander understood that concept perfectly. General Montgomery understood it. Fortunately, he supported this concept, even to the extent of overriding the orders of his subordinates.

In 1964, when Gen. Hasso von Manteuffel and I spent several days together at Saint-Vith discussing the battle at length, I learned for the first time what the German concept of the operation was. I repeat it from these discussions and other discussions with Gen. Heinrich Freiherr von Lüttwitz, who commanded the "secondary effort" of the operation.

> For the German Plan to be successful, three things had to happen:
> a. The German attack had to be a surprise.
> b. The weather had to be such as to prevent strikes by Allied aircraft on the German columns coming through the Ardennes.
> c. The progress of the German main effort through and beyond Saint-Vith must be rapid and not delayed.

The defensive and delaying concept used at Saint-Vith prevented the third requirement of the German operation from happening until the American troops in the rear area could be positioned to handle the situation later.

On December 22, 1964, at a press conference in Watertown, New York, General Von Manteuffel stated, "On the evening of 24 December 1944, I recommended to Hitler's adjutant that the German army give up the attack and return to the West Wall." He stated that the reason for this recommendation was the time his Fifth Panzer Army had lost in the Saint-Vith area.

Recently, in a question-and-answer period after I had talked on the Battle of Saint-Vith, a college ROTC student said, "General, what is the principal job of a general in the conduct of such a battle as Saint-Vith?" My answer was, "It is to prevent the confusion from becoming disorganized."

—*U.S. Army Combined Arms Research Library*

Gus Theodore
103rd Antiaircraft Artillery (AAA) Battalion, 1st Infantry Division

The 1st Infantry Division formed part of V Corps, which also included the 2nd, 9th, and 99th Infantry Divisions. These four American divisions formed a strong barrier that restricted and straitjacketed the northern shoulder of the German salient in the Ardennes. Gus Theodore remembers certain events during the fighting.

I WAS WITH THE 103RD ANTIAIRCRAFT ARTILLERY BATTALION, which was attached to the famous 1st Infantry Division—the Big Red One—our outfit protecting the infantry and artillery in our area. The 1st Infantry Division made the invasion in North Africa and Sicily. I was a young replacement and joined the outfit in England in 1943. The division made the invasion on Easy Red Beach (Omaha). A lot of the boys got killed going in. We were a little late landing in our LST because they had trouble establishing a beachhead.

After we came into Normandy, we pushed through Saint-Lo, France, and fought our way through other towns, the Hürtgen Forest, the Siegfried Line, and captured Aachen, Germany. This was the first German city to fall to the Americans. We then got pulled off the front lines for a rest.

A Belgian family let us stay in their house, so we parked our artillery piece and the truck in their yard. We thought that the division would be headed back home for training purposes, and I thought that would be a good deal for us: only in combat for seven months and then heading home to train others. As fate would have it, no such luck.

While we were staying with the Belgian family, a USO show was going to be held in Eupen, Belgium, and we were told that one man from each gun section could go to the show. My ammo man, Marshall Wilcox, was the lucky guy that got to go. He came back kind of early, and we asked him why. He said German artillery was shelling the area, even though they weren't supposed to be that close.

Marlene Dietrich from the USO and all the generals in the front row started leaving for their outfits. We didn't know it at the time, but the Germans had busted through the 99th and 106th Divisions, so we had to go and plug up the hole.

Our gun section and half-track with four .50-caliber machine guns got into a convoy moving up with the field artillery. A lieutenant from the artillery was leading us, but I don't think that he was too smart. He led us deep into German lines until he figured out that he had made a wrong turn. We pulled a U-turn and backtracked to what was called the Elsenborn Ridge. We stayed there most of the time.

We had Germans in front and to the right of us most of the time during the Battle of the Bulge. All the outfits hung tough and didn't let the Germans get by us. To the south and west of us were Bastogne and Malmédy, and the troops in those areas held as well.

In Malmédy, the Germans captured almost one hundred American artillery troops, marched them into a field, and shot them. The field was covered in snow. Ira Bonnet, from Monson, who was lost, crept up through the snow and witnessed the shooting. Only one or two survived, and this event became known as the Malmédy Massacre. After this, we didn't show any mercy for the Germans.

The weather was cold and snowy. We starved, froze, and got shot at. It was so cold—about below zero without the chill factor—and about two feet of snow. My mother sent me a package with cookies, two pairs of ski stockings, and a whole salami in it. The salami had mold all over the outside skin, but we were so hungry it didn't matter. I took my bayonet and cut off the slimy skin. The meat looked good, so I sliced it up for me and the boys in the gun section. Believe me, it was delicious. I bet the Germans smelled the aroma and got jealous of us.

The stockings were a life saver. When we crawled in our holes at night, we slept with all our clothes on; jacket, overcoat, two pairs of GI socks, and the stockings that my mother had sent to me. I didn't have any shoes, just overshoes. The stockings that my mother sent to me saved my feet from freezing.

On December 25, Christmas Day, the Germans threw about fifty planes against us. I was the loader and trigger man on our gun. I said more "Hail Marys" and "Our Fathers" than the pope probably says in a month. There is an old saying that there are no atheists in a foxhole.

We hit one German plane, and the pilot bailed out, and most everyone in the area shot at him. I didn't shoot at him with my rifle because I had a change of heart. The others that shot at him were probably mad about the Malmédy Massacre. The poor German was my age, nineteen years old. I had a piece of his parachute, but I threw it away—I didn't want that kind of souvenir.

About three days later, I was cleaning some of the snow away from around the gun pit when the Germans were shooting their 88mm artillery shells at us. Most of the shells were going over our heads, so I said to the guys in the gun pit, "It's about time headquarters got shot at instead of us."

I spoke too soon. One shell fell short and landed about twenty or thirty feet away from us. Good thing it hit over me, because most of the shrapnel from a shell goes forward. I got hit from a piece of the shrapnel that sent me flying. I landed in the snow, and my buddies patched me up and sent me to a hospital. The shrapnel that hit me was a big piece because it didn't penetrate into me but ripped my shirt and shoulder. They took me to a hospital and sent me back to my gun site the next day. I was very lucky, or my prayers helped me and defended me for a while. I came back to the gun crew and finished off the Bulge and made it into Czechoslovakia when the war ended.

—*The* Bulge Bugle, *February 1999*

Dustin M. Aughenbaugh
C Company, 55th Armored Engineer Battalion, Combat Command B, 10th Armored Division

The 10th Armored Division formed that part of Patton's Third Army that attacked into the southern flank of the German Ardennes Offensive. Dustin Aughenbaugh was an engineer who helped to clear the way for his division's advance.

COMPANY C, 55TH ARMORED ENGINEER BATTALION, Combat Command B (CCB), 10th Armored Division, was part of General Patton's Third Army advancing in the vicinity of the Saar-Moselle Triangle prior to December 16, 1944. As the divisional engineers, it was our job, with the help of infantry and/or recon units, to see that our armored columns could bypass or breach obstacles in the armored attack; at least that is what I had been trained and taught at the Engineer School at Fort Belvoir, Virginia, and at the 10th Armored Division training facility at Camp Gordon, Georgia. We held pretty much to that type of action.

During the early afternoon of the December 16, while our tank column was advancing in the Ardennes, we were suddenly pulled out of an attack and started moving north toward Luxembourg. That morning we had heard that something big was happening north of our position, so sudden changes like this were normal. I asked the lieutenant, a tank commander, what was happening; he replied, "Don't know, we were just ordered to move north; it looks like we are heading to Luxembourg." He suggested I go back to the half-track and take it easy for awhile. Generally, one or two of us engineers rode with the lead tanks during an advance. Besides, I felt a helluva lot safer up there than in the half-track. We traveled the rest of the day and all night, with an occasional stop along the way, and to add to the problem, it was a bitter, cold, and snowy day.

We arrived in the Bastogne area on December 17, about thirty-six hours before the main elements of the 101st Airborne began to arrive on December 19. Combat Command B, commanded by Colonel Roberts, consisted of three tank columns totaling about seventy tanks and 3,500 men, with about eighteen units of the 609th Tank Destroyer Battalion, our own mobile artillery, armored infantry, AAA, and other supporting units. As I understand, when the 101st Airborne arrived on December 19, CCB was then attached to General McAuliffe's command of the 101st Airborne.

Our armored columns, known as Desobry's Column, took up positions and prepared to defend the approaches to Noville, which was about three miles (or more) north of Bastogne. The other two columns, known as Cherry and O'Hare, took up offensive positions to the east at Longvilly and Wardin. This way we established a main line of defense for the area, and about this same time, enemy tank fire started falling near our positions. You could see the German tanks moving over the ridge through the fog and blowing snow. Fortunately, they were either Mark IVs or Panthers, but you had to keep your head down, and on that frozen ground it was difficult. Our TDs with their 76mm rifles did a very accurate job that first day. As I remember, with high German initial losses, it forced them to withdraw back over the ridge. I did not see many enemy ground troops with their armor in that attack; however, the krauts were laying down a lot of machine gun and small-arms fire, which made preparing the MLD almost impossible. Most of our work was done after dark on the night of December 17. I was a demolition man, so at night we kept busy with preparing obstacles and, mostly, laying mines, all of which made life a little exciting. Our six-pound mines were so ineffective, they couldn't blow dirt off of the enemy tank tracks, so we engineers and a few armored artillery would generally try to stack the mines or add six pounds of TNT to the mine to make them as effective as the krauts' teller mines: that is, if we had time to dig the holes or rig them with prime cord.

On December 19, our (Desobry's) tank column pulled back west of Noville to form part of the Bastogne circle on the north and east side of that town. In the process of withdrawing to the MLD, Lieutenant Colonel Desobry and most of the command post were wounded and taken prisoner. About this same time, the men of the 101st were moving in with our tank teams to help secure the circle around Bastogne. It was years later that I learned that at the same time, CCB of the 9th Armored Division was providing armor on the west and south sides of the Bastogne circle. To me, it was just another area. I did not know I was in Belgium, let alone the town name, which meant nothing to me. Of course, later on, while in the hospital, I heard about this big battle of the war, and I didn't know I was even involved.

I had been wounded by machine gun fire in early November during the Metz offensive, and after escaping from the convalescent hospital, I managed to return to my unit just two weeks prior to the Bulge. Then, on the night of December 20, I was wounded with shrapnel, so I remember very little of the battle conditions after that night; but I do remember that first clear day when all of our planes were overhead, making us feel good.

General McAuliffe later paid us a great compliment when he said, "It always seems regrettable to me that CCB of the 10th Armored Division didn't get the credit it deserved in the Battle of the Bastogne. The 10th Armored Division was in there the day before we were and had some very hard fighting. We would never have been able to get into Bastogne if it had not been for the defensive fighting . . . of the 10th Armored Division."

—*The* Bulge Bugle, *August 1998*

Albert N. Garland
L Company, 334th Infantry Regiment, 84th Infantry Division

The 84th Infantry Division formed part of the American Ninth Army, based north of the Ardennes, and was transferred to the First Army a few days after the German attack began. The battle-tested 334th Infantry Regiment, which Albert Garland belonged to, was the first into Belgium and held its place in the front lines with heavy artillery support.

ON THE MORNING OF DECEMBER 20, 1944, I was a first lieutenant commanding Company L, 334th Infantry Regiment, 84th Infantry Division. For the past month, we had been in almost continuous action as part of the U.S. XIII Corps, Ninth U.S. Army, in and around the north German towns of Prummern, Beeck, Wurm, and Lindern. (For part of that month, we were under the operational control of the British XXX Corps, then commanded by Lt. Gen. Brian Horrocks.) Our primary objective from the beginning was the Roer River, and we were getting close to it despite strong German resistance and miserable conditions.

I had been told the previous evening that our battalion—the 3rd Battalion—was being pulled out of the lines for a short stay at the division's rest center at Eygelshoven, a small Dutch town that lay just across the border some ten to twelve miles from our present location. I had also been told that my mess crew and its equipment was going there right after it had delivered a hot breakfast on the 20th, and that I could expect a number of two-and-a-half-ton trucks to reach me shortly after the mess crew departed. These trucks would take my company to Eygelshoven, at which time I would release them to their parent unit. (If I remember correctly, these trucks belonged to a quartermaster truck company, one of several such units then supporting the division.)

My mess crew arrived with our hot breakfast early on December 20 and left about an hour later. The mess sergeant and I talked about his going to Eygelshoven, and he promised he would have a good meal ready for us when we got there about noon.

At about 0900 the trucks arrived, and I soon had the company loaded and ready to go. As we pulled out to become part of the battalion's convoy, my soldiers were in good spirits, thinking ahead to several days in warm, dry billets among a civilian populace that really seemed to care for them.

We did not reach Eygelshoven that morning. We did get there eventually, but much later: February 1945. I did not know at the time, but shortly after we started out, the battalion commander received orders to head for Aachen, which lay in the opposite direction.

When we reached Aachen, we were told we were going to Belgium, but where in Belgium no one seemed to know. Why we were going was another unanswered question. My main concern was for my mess crew. I kept wondering if the mess sergeant had been told about the change in plans, and whether I would ever see my cooks again.

I don't think anyone in the convoy that day had any idea of the extent of the German breakthrough, or what steps were being taken to counter it. We found out much later that we had followed the 7th Armored Division, another Ninth Army unit, to Belgium. We did run across some of that division's rear-echelon units but never encountered any of its combat elements.

We paused for a short break in Liège, where I had to turn over to the MPs a truckload of my soldiers who were designated to serve as guides along the way to our final destination. We still did not know where that was, and I screamed and hollered about giving up my soldiers, but lost the argument. With the way things were going, and with so little information, I feared I would never see those men again: the same fear I had about my mess crew. The soldiers did get to me in the next few days, seemingly none the worse for their experiences.

From Liège we headed almost due south and reached the town of Marche early in the evening. It seems to me that we traveled almost 130 miles. We were ordered off the trucks and into defensive positions on the outskirts of the town. We had no maps of the area, we did not know where the Germans were, and we did not know what we were expected to do. We knew there were other U.S. units around but did not know where they were. A 7th Armored Division aid station was just closing down and leaving, but the medical personnel could tell us little about the situation.

Two days later my company was defending a three-mile front that ran from one small Belgian town, Marenne, to another equally small one, Menil. We weren't sure who was on our left, but a sister company was on our right, across a small valley, in the town of Verdenne. It, too, had a wide front to defend.

I kept one platoon in town with me, plus a platoon of tank destroyers that had been sent up by someone in the rear. My other two rifle platoons occupied strong points along a wooded ridge that ran almost to Menil. They used foot patrols to keep in touch with each other, with me, and eventually with a U.S. unit that appeared in Menil. We also had wire communications with each other, but we could communicate with battalion headquarters only by radio.

We did know we had one heck of a lot of artillery in support and were told to call for it on the slightest German provocation. That we did, in a big way, even when one German force broke through the Verdenne defenders and circled to our rear. There it stayed in a wooded area about a thousand yards away until the day after Christmas. Actually, that German unit's advance had been halted by our battalion's reserve company and by other companies from the regiment that had been fed into the fight. The only thing we knew for certain, however, was that we were to stay where we were as long as we could.

We received a welcome surprise early on December 26 when our mess crew arrived with a Christmas dinner, which featured turkey and all the trimmings. (Well, almost all of them!) My mess sergeant told me he had been trying to get in touch with me for several days, but had not been able to do so. He had finally found a back road into Marenne that skirted the German force in our rear, and had received permission from battalion to try to get to us with some hot food. He and his crew were a most welcome sight, and the platoon carrying parties were soon on their way to pick up their share of the food.

Unfortunately, before we could distribute the food, and before the carrying parties arrived, the leader of the platoon I had kept in town told me that the German force that had been in our rear was now coming in our direction, down the valley between Marenne and Verdenne. It was still early in the morning, and he told me that while he could not make out the German vehicles, he was sure, from the sound of their engines and the noise their tracks were making, that they were headed for our town.

I instructed him to pull his daisy chains (antitank mines tied together) across the street (there was only one in town), and I alerted the tank destroyer platoon leader to get his vehicles cranked up to take on the approaching German armor. From what information I had, I assumed we still had some time before the Germans came in. It was a sizeable force headed our way. I knew because we had been dueling with those people for the past several days.

I was sadly mistaken about how much time we had; I had no sooner finished talking with the tank destroyer commander than the lead German vehicles were coming down the street. Apparently, my platoon had not been able to place its mines across the roadway, and the tank destroyers were now practically helpless since each was in a separate building and not prepared to fight.

Our few bazooka rounds bounced harmlessly off the side of the lead German tank, which was a monster, so I did the only thing I could; I called for an artillery concentration right on top of us. Fortunately, we had plotted just such a concentration, thinking we might need it at a future date. I had some difficulty convincing the artillery liaison officer at battalion headquarters that I knew what I was doing, but he finally approved the shoot.

I managed to get word to my other two platoons as to what was happening in Marenne, and told the farthest one out to alert the U.S. unit it had made contact with in Menil. I ordered the nearest one to take up positions on the west edge of town, where it might pick off any German stragglers, but I warned the platoon leader about the concentration that was about to come in. Those of us still in town headed for cellars.

I don't know how many artillery battalions fired that concentration for us, but there must have been quite a few. Any German soldiers and vehicles that did not see their end in Marenne fled the town, only to be mopped up by my two platoons and the unit in Menil. Unfortunately, I think we took the second stories off most of the houses in Marenne and deposited them in the street. But I came up out of my cellar grinning from ear to ear and very happy to be alive. So were the few men I still had with me, including the mess crew, none of whom had ever been through anything like this. To our sorrow, though, we saw that a German tank had flattened the trailer that held our Christmas dinner.

My company was relieved several days later, and we moved to a reserve position, strangely enough in what was left of Verdenne, the town just across the valley, although it took us several days and lots of walking in what seemed to be circles to get there. Still later, beginning on January 3, 1945, in a driving blizzard, our battalion was committed as part of a large U.S. counterattacking force (the VII Corps) to close the bulge the Germans had driven in our lines. Three days later, I was lying in a roadside ditch, trying to hide from the effects of a German artillery bombardment that was shredding the tops of the trees that bordered the ditch and covered the surrounding hills and valleys. My radio operator, just behind me, tugged on one of my boots. When I turned toward him, he motioned that I had a call on the radio, which was on the battalion command net. I inched back to him, reached for the mike, and gave my call sign. Our battalion S1 was on the other end. He said he just wanted to let me know that Headquarters First

Army had just approved a battlefield promotion to captain for me, effective January 4. Rather sarcastically, I suppose, I accepted the news, which was the last thing I needed to hear at the time, and asked him to get me a set of captain's bars for when and if I ever got out of that ditch alive!

We took part in the rest of the so-called Battle of the Bulge and ended our stint in Belgium in late January in the small town of Beho. In early February, we finally made it to Eygleshoven and those warm, dry billets. And for those of us who were left—there weren't many—it was good to be home.

—*From the files of the U.S. Army Military History Institute*

Allan H. Stein
F Company, 508th Parachute Infantry Regiment, 82nd Airborne Division

It was originally intended that both the 82nd and 101st Airborne Division defend the area around Bastogne. However, on the morning of December 18, the 82nd was diverted northward to Werbomont, Belgium, to help stop a German armored thrust. Allan Stein recalls a certain incident during that time.

A THIRD OF OUR COMPANY WAS STATIONED near Rheims, France. A third were on R&R in England, and a third were in hospitals or gone. I was to go on R&R December 17.

About 7:30 p.m. the company commander called us in. We were to mount up: we were going into Belgium. A crisis seemed to have happened. We loaded up in open-bodied trucks and with full speed ahead, headed off for a place called the Ardennes. I had just received a package from home with four cartons of cigarettes. Where the hell did you put four cartons with the other stuff we had? Naturally, I somehow lost my gas mask. The container was a very nice place for all those little oddities one takes with one.

It was a miserable, cold trip. We passed through towns where already the people were on the move. "The Germans are coming."

I was carrying the new folding bazooka. I had never fired it for effect and was hoping to do so as soon as we hit our base. I don't know how long we traveled, but we passed through Malmédy and Saint-Vith and unloaded in Bastogne. Orders were that the Screaming Eagles (the 101st Airborne Division) were to hold Bastogne, and we were headed up toward the northern part of the Bulge.

I asked if I could try out the bazooka but was told that we didn't know who was around us. I was struck by the desolation and emptiness of the towns; burned-out buildings and barns; black holes where shells had hit. In the miserable cold, we didn't see anything or anyone for the first few days.

On the 24th we moved up to a hill and dug in. You could hardly break through the ground to dig a foxhole. I remember finally lying down and covering myself with my shelter half. I don't know how long I lay there, but it was getting so warm and comfortable. The sergeant woke me up. I was covered with snow. I think that if he had not found me, I would have become one of the frozen statues that we saw. I went on a patrol, my first one, with two others. Following the book, we crawled, stooped, and heard what sounded like tank engines. We came back and reported. That night we were ordered off the hill by the command of the British Second Army, which we were attached to.

On the 24th we dug into a field. That night, what seemed like an entire German battalion hit our positions. Our entire line opened up in continuous fire until we were down to a few clips. Cans of loose ammo were brought to us to reload our clips. At that time I thought it was the proper time to try my bazooka. I aimed it at where our outpost had been. I fired it, and "bam," it hit a tree. I was reloading the bazooka when I thought someone had hit me in the face. When my ear started bleeding, I realized that I had been hit by shrapnel.

The next day we were ordered to move out. It was discovered that my tree burst had broken up a platoon of Germans getting ready to hit our position. Their bodies were punctured by wood and shrapnel. The bazooka worked. The field in front of us was filled with the frozen bodies of dead and dying Germans. On the way out they mortared our positions. I heard them coming in. I hit the snow and heard a thump. I closed my eyes and figured, Stein, you've had it. God must have been watching. I looked to my left and saw a dud mortar (round) about three feet away from my head.

I think the most bizarre memories were of the frozen, dead bodies being tossed into trucks like cord wood. And even today, on a cold December night, I look up at the moon and wonder and thank God I'm still around to remember.

Oh yes! My four cartons of cigarettes were wet and of no value. I also wonder, what if I had gotten to Paris with those four cartons? They were worth a fortune. But better the cigarettes than me.

—*The* Bulge Bugle, *August 1991*

John Brush
30th Infantry Division

The 30th Infantry Division was resting in the neighborhood of Aachen, Germany, after hard fighting in the Roer River sector when the call came for it to be sent to the Ardennes to stop the German advance. John Brush was an engineer who describes his part in stopping Kampfgruppe (Battle Group) Peiper.

ON OCTOBER 27, 1944, THE 30TH INFANTRY DIVISION established a rest center on the outskirts of Kerkrade, Holland, in the buildings of Rolduc College, founded in 1106 A.D. and ranked as the oldest educational institution in the Netherlands. Most of the buildings were constructed in the eighteenth and nineteenth centuries.

The rest center was operated to accommodate one combat infantry battalion at a time. It was an outstanding success in restoring a sense of well-being to cold, weary, and muddy men. Provided were beds with linens, hot showers, captured chinaware, and silverware, to do away with the need of mess kits. Also available were tailor and barber services, writing facilities, legal aid, and Special Services entertainment. My squad was sent here on the day it opened to help with the maintenance and other duties.

Two of us were assigned to the officers' mess, a really soft setup. We had to be in the serving room about thirty minutes before meals. The food came up from the kitchen on a dumbwaiter. We put the food on plates, and another fellow served the tables. This was almost identical to the job I was assigned on the ship coming overseas. As the dishes were emptied, we stacked them, sent them downstairs to be washed, cleaned off the tables, and set them up for the next meal. Then we were through until the next meal, to enjoy all of the facilities, movies, shows, whatever. It was interesting to be able to explore the old buildings outside of the areas being used, from their cellars to the attics. There were some classrooms in the attics and one art room. I visited that room several times to use the materials available for sketches, some of which I still have.

I had a case of the "GIs" (diarrhea) about the second week there that lasted a day or two and left me weak. December 16 was the beginning of the end of our easy life, although we did not know it when the day started. On the 16th we could hear the steady rumble of tanks and trucks on the main highway all day. Rumors were flying, but nothing was known about what was going on. Some of the troops at the rest center were pulling out. Our squad was alerted that evening to be ready to go on short notice. We packed quickly and then waited. The next day, Sunday, December 17, the 30th Division was transferred to another corps command and given orders to move south at 11:15 a.m. By 4:30 p.m., most parts of the division were rolling south on the main highway nearby. We joined the rest of our unit as it came through in a continuous column heading south in heavy traffic. There also was considerable horse and wagon traffic going the other way as civilians fled the Germans. We stopped numerous times during the night, sometimes because of traffic tie-ups, sometimes because of air raids by the German Luftwaffe, whose planes were active all night.

We arrived in Malmédy, Belgium, the morning of December 18. Our unit set up headquarters in a paper mill, which had been used previously as a replacement center for troops moving to the front in this area prior to the German offensive. The mill had been abandoned or deserted suddenly, from the looks of things. There were signs that breakfast had been interrupted, with some food partially eaten left on the tables. Clothes, equipment, and even rifles were scattered everywhere or left by cots. It even looked as if some of the men left only half dressed, going out in the cold without necessary articles like coats and, in a few cases, even shoes.

In the room of the supply sergeant, also gone, the medic and I made an interesting find. Underneath two cots, in cardboard boxes, was a hoard of cigarettes in ten-to-a-pack-size boxes that were supposed to be handed out to the replacements as they came through the depot. They were mostly Lucky Strikes and Camels, which meant that the supply sergeant held out the most popular brands—the easiest to sell on the black market—and distributed less-liked brands. In all, we got over one thousand of these half packs, and neither of us smoked. We promptly stored them in the tool boxes on our truck. As a result of this find, we became the most popular and well-liked fellows in the outfit.

Our platoon got their cigarettes free whenever they wanted any, and we had lots of offers to buy or swap from the smokers who never had enough nicotine. There wasn't much around to swap for right then. Nearly everyone got to pick up new out-fits from the supply room and discarded or kept the old stuff as they wished. German pistols, usually popular trade items, were not so popular at the time because Germans reportedly treated prisoners roughly if they caught them with German weapons. At least for now, the guns were a drag on the market for frontline outfits. I had had a Walther P38 but had already gotten rid of it, probably at the rest center.

We rested during the day, and that evening we went to the front to lay mines and put up barbed wire. We went west out of Malmédy then south through the forested hills toward Stavelot. Along the highway in the forest, we passed a huge supply dump that was being evacuated. The men loading the boxes said that they would probably have to burn a lot of the supplies, so our two trucks each picked up several boxes of extra rations. Further along the highway, we came to a gasoline dump that the Germans would dearly like to have; in fact, they were counting on several of these dumps for the gas supplies that they would need.

Below us in Stavelot, elements of the 117th Infantry Regiment were fighting the Germans who were across the Amblève River from the 117th and another force of Germans to the west who had already crossed the river and had swung back to keep the vital Amblève River Bridge open. All after-noon we waited at a house overlooking the town for a chance to move in with explosives to blow the bridge. The 117th occupied some buildings on the west side close to the bridge, and the Germans were in a building just across the bridge and beside the road. It was probably only a hundred feet between the lines. Heavy small-arms fire and mortar and artillery fire coming over the bridge made it impossible to get on the bridge in daylight or to even get a good look at it up close.

After dark a group of about ten of us was selected to blow the bridge, and we drove within two blocks of it by staying off the road that led directly to it. At a pre-set time, our movement forward was to be covered by close artillery fire of smoke shells and proximity shells. This support, we later found out, was one of the first times a new fuse for the artillery proximity shell was used. It went off when the shell got within a pre-set distance of any object. This airburst was the worst kind to be under. At the time, however, we did not know how they were timing these bursts so close to the ground, but we sure could appreciate how they were making the Germans keep under cover.

By the time the artillery was to start its shelling, we had moved our pile of explosives up to the nearest building to the bridge on our side. We were short of regular TNT, having only a couple of fifty-pound boxes; but, we had plenty of antitank mines, with five eleven-pound mines per box. They also contained TNT. There were two boxes for each of us to carry to the center of the first span of the bridge and a couple of extra boxes. We were ready with about twenty-four boxes, mines, and TNT when the artillery barrage began. That was our signal to move.

In what seemed a long interval of time but was probably only a few minutes, we finally stacked the last box on the bridge. On my second trip I stepped on a loose piece of corrugated roofing blown off some building. The racket was loud, but very fortunately for us, at the bridge approach, a shell burst at the same time, covering up the sound and keeping the Germans from detecting us. I was one of the "lucky" ones who made three trips.

With all the explosives now in place, we moved back to safety around the first corner and inside a building and sat against a wall to wait for the sergeant to connect the wires to the detonator and set off the pile of explosives. A loud boom announced that the charge had gone off okay, and in a couple of minutes, when the smoke and dust had settled, word came back that the first arch span had vanished.

The loss of this bridge was a big blow to the Germans, who already had a heavily armored force to the west of the bridge. Now their supply line was cut. We were later awarded the Bronze Star medal for that action but spent the rest of the night laying a minefield along the river at the south edge of town.

Other incidents I recall, although not the exact day it occurred, involved the commander of the 82nd Airborne Division, Gen. James M. Gavin. I was among a small group of engineers with an infantry column advancing along a country road. The advance stalled when we came upon a German Tiger tank that pinned down the lead men. Further back, we rested in a ditch while a bazooka team tried to work its way around to the tank's rear unobserved. A general walked up with a squad of paratroopers and demanded to know why the infantry was letting one tank hold them up. Without waiting to be told what was under way, he got out in the middle of the road and began firing his M1 rifle at the tank. The Germans could not see that it was a general standing there, but the sight of one man firing uselessly at them in this manner made them suspect he was trying to cover something else. Instead of firing at General Gavin, they started turning the tank's turret around looking for trouble elsewhere. They spotted the bazooka team and blasted them with their 88mm cannon. The general probably got a medal for his outstanding bravery, but most of the witnesses on the scene that day felt that the German tank chose the wrong target.

Our platoon was next sent to guard a small road across the valley from La Gleize, where a heavy German armored force was stopped. This was the same German panzer group that had passed over the bridge at Stavelot before we blew it up. La Gleize was a small village south of Roanne. We were to dig in at a farmhouse to cover a small country road. When we moved in, our heaviest weapon was a .50-caliber machine gun, of which I was the main operator. We fixed a daisy chain, a string of tank mines on a rope that theoretically was supposed to be pulled across the road from our foxhole just before a tank got to it and too close to see it. These mines would blow the track off a tank and disable it from moving, probably blocking the road for any vehicles behind. It could most likely still fire its guns.

We were within sight of the Germans across the valley at La Gleize, about a mile away or maybe a little less. With binoculars we could see them moving around the houses during the day, as I'm sure they could see us. At night we could hear tanks start their engines, move around, and then stop. Some were in the town and some nearer us but concealed in the woods below us. By carefully looking through the binoculars, we could usually pick out several tanks visible between buildings and sticking out a little from behind a building.

It was getting much colder at night. It got down to two degrees above zero one night. Most of us slept in the barn during the day with only a light guard out since we could see over the open farmlands for at least one-half mile to the nearest patch of woods. At night everyone went on guard in our line of foxholes. These were two-man foxholes, so we could buddy up, with one watching while the other rested and tried to stay down in the hole and cover up enough to keep warm. There was more snow by now, and it was so cold we sat in the foxholes fully dressed and wearing our sleeping bags on top of our overcoats. Even then, comfort didn't usually come until daylight, when we could move around and the temperature warmed up a little. The first heavy snow fell December 21, the day we blew up the bridge.

Each night we expected the Germans to come up the road as they moved around, but what we did not know until later was that they were extremely low on fuel and were trying to conserve their meager supply. They had hoped to capture at least one of the large depots of gasoline the Americans had stored along some of the roads in the area. However, what fuel was not moved was burned to keep it from them. After a couple of days, we were reinforced by an antiaircraft unit with a 90mm antiaircraft cannon and its crew. This action helped our feelings considerably since that gun was more the size needed to handle a tank.

This gun, emplaced behind us about fifty yards, was just over the top of the hill. After setting it up, the crew estimated the range and picked one of the tanks we had pointed out as its first target. They fired a round and missed, corrected the range, and fired a second round that ricocheted off the front of the tank. We could hear the sound of the shell hitting the tank and the following whine of the ricochet, allowing a second or two for the sound to reach us. We cheered the marksmanship of the gun's crew. Five hits with armor-piercing shells apparently failed to penetrate the Tiger Royal's (King Tiger, or Tiger II) twelve-inch sloping frontal armor. They did, however, evidently shake up those inside the tank, because they decided to get behind a building for protection. They backed up and swung around to drive fully under cover. As they maneuvered, the less heavily armored rear was exposed for a brief fatal moment to the 90mm gun crew. Another hit, and we scratched one tank and its crew. We had fully expected the Germans to shoot at us at any time, especially after the AA gun arrived, but they never did.

La Gleize was captured on December 24 by a German armored column with infantry support that came down the road from Spa to La Gleize. This force, as well as the road, was plainly visible to us. Through binoculars we watched the column move into town. As it turned out, the Germans had thirty-nine tanks, seventy half tracks, thirty-three artillery pieces, and thirty other vehicles in and around La Gleize. Many of them were out of gas entirely and had to be abandoned when the strong counterattack came.

The Germans retreated across the river on foot. They had been under heavy artillery fire for a couple of days, not only from the gun behind us, but other positions that were pounding them continually. The main body of the Germans withdrew about 3 a.m. on December 24. The day before was clear for the first time in days, so our planes were out harassing the fleeing Germans. Their tanks and other vehicles were blown up by a rear guard left behind for that purpose.

We moved west on the road a mile or two to join other units of our outfit for the first time to have Christmas dinner and a day's rest. Some of us relaxed by going deer hunting. Deer tracks were plentiful in the snow. We roamed around a hill behind the farm where we had stopped, but we didn't want to stray too far away. My group saw only a rabbit near the end of our hunt. I sat down in the snow, rested my Browning automatic rifle (BAR) on a fence rail, and shot most of a thirty-round clip at the rabbit as it ran untouched up the hill. I had picked up the rifle at the paper mill where we first stopped. I was one of the few in the outfit that had training in a wide assortment of weapons, including the BAR, and thought it a good idea to keep it in the truck as extra firepower if needed.

Our next job was road patching. To obtain crushed rock we went to a quarry west of Spa. On the second trip we were traveling a road along the top of a mountain and out in the open. I was manning the ring-mounted .50 machine gun and watching for planes, which was part of my job. Down in the valley below us, I spotted nine German Messerschmitt fighters coming up out of the valley in our general direction. I shouted the alarm, but everybody else looked and said the planes were British Spitfires. In a very short time, they overtook us, and the first one flashed by with a big swastika on its side. I fired at it as the rest of the guys in the back of our truck and the other two trucks with us were going overboard to hit the ditch without waiting for the trucks to stop. The driver and the noncom up front saw the first German plane as it went by, so all the trucks ground to a quick halt. I also fired at the second plane, which was close enough for me to see the pilot wave. Then I, too, hit the ditch, figuring that the planes still coming our way would strafe us for sure. They flew by without firing a shot, so they must have been looking for more important targets.

January 6, 1945, was a hard day for me. I had the "GIs" again the day before and was feeling weak. An offensive all along the northern edge of the German penetration had begun on the 3rd, and the 117th had pushed into Trois-Ponts. Under the cover of a railroad bridge here, we assembled parts of a pontoon footbridge. We had to carry the parts nearly four hundred yards along a road to a suitable spot to put the sections together and push the span across the Amblève River. There were six men to each assembled section.

The road curved along the river, with its steep banks on our right and the forested mountain rising on our left. As we rounded the curve, we passed five knocked-out American

Sherman tanks dispatched by a German Tiger Royal tank parked at the next bend. It probably sat there and let all five of the American tanks get around the corner before shooting the last one to block the road and then picking off the others one by one. All had neat holes through their armor from the Tiger's 88mm canon. The Tiger's front armor was scarred by armor-piecing shells, one of them even embedded in the armor about five inches deep. The Tiger Royal had been destroyed by a direct hit on the side by a bomb. The turret was blown off, and the frontal armor was split open, which enabled us to see that the tank's front armor was nearly twelve inches thick.

We did this looking after the bridge was completed. There was snow on the ground, and footing was not good. Because of my illness, I was losing my grip on the assembled bridge section I was helping to transport before we were halfway to the site. The carrying pole finally slid right out of my hands. That overloaded the other five men, so one of the fellows that had already reached the river site was sent back to take my place. In a short time the bridge was in place across the stream and secured to the far bank. It was about fifty feet from a light, civilian country bridge that had collapsed under the weight of a German tank. There was also a wrecked German ambulance off the road on our side of the stream. One of our men found a chrome-plated Luger pistol inside the ambulance.

Four of us were left to guard the bridge and stand by until the arrival of the 112th Infantry Regiment of the 28th Infantry Division, who were to pass through our lines and cross over the Amblève on the bridge that we had put in place. I volunteered to stay since I could still shoot if necessary and was not able to complete my other job. That is the way we were able to see so much of the details at this site.

Finally, we saw the approaching relief column of the 28th Infantry Division coming around the bend. We had expected to be fired on all the time, and the shelling was not long in coming after the foot soldiers arrived. Mortar shells began hitting, first higher on the hill, then nearer the road as the range was corrected. Unlike artillery shells, a mortar shell lobbed in slowly and gave no warning sound until it exploded. The firing started just as the 112th Infantry Battalion started across the bridge.

We took cover behind the Tiger tank that was nearby and stayed there until the infantrymen had all crossed. In case a hit or near miss on the bridge should damage it, we would have to do some repairs with the extra parts that were at the site just for that purpose. They made it without any hits too close to the bridge. By the time we started back to the cover of the railroad bridge and got ready to move further to the rear, the 112th was receiving small-arms fire just a few hundred yards past the bridge.

Mortar rounds continued to bracket the road that we had to take back, so we moved along fast and kept low. As we got back to the last curve by the last wrecked American tank, an officer in a Jeep was waiting to see if the 112th had gotten across okay. We gave him the word, then hitched a ride on the Jeep and high-tailed it the last two hundred yards to the railroad bridge at Trois-Ponts. A couple of mortar shells hit on the road well ahead of us, and one just up the hill from us spattered us with a little dirt and rock, but no shell fragments hit anyone. Our artillery and mortars were counter-firing on the Germans now, so in a few minutes the German shelling stopped near us, and we all got into our trucks and moved back to our camp area.

With snow on the roads, a lot of our work was getting trucks, Jeeps, and a few tanks out of ditches when they would skid on the slick surfaces. The winches all of our engineering trucks had on them were great at pulling if there was something solid to tie onto. We moved back to "our" paper mill at Malmédy, but it wasn't the same. The mill had been hit by bombs during several air raids. Visibility was not very good, and the Americans in the rear thought the Germans were holding Malmédy and dropped loads of bombs on the town. The HQ men of our outfit that were there when the raid came escaped injury. They said that there were some casualties in town from the raid but not many.

My squad of engineers left Malmédy on foot on January 14 with a column of the 117th Infantry Regiment. About two miles out of town up the hill was a crossroad village called Baugnez, a tiny settlement. Here we found the group of murdered American GIs, now frozen and buried in the snow, in what later was called the Malmédy Massacre.

According to reports I read after the war, these Americans—over a hundred men—were from a battery of the 285th Field Artillery Observation Battalion. Lieutenant Virgil Lary and a few others managed to survive their wounds and crawl away, but the dead GIs they left behind went undetected until we stumbled across them January 19, 1945. The German group that committed this atrocity on December 17, 1944, was led by Lt. Col. Jochen Peiper.

We continued over the hill southeast on the road to Ligneuville, which was the objective for that day. Ligneuville lay at the bottom of the valley along the Amblève River, our old friend. Most of the way down was through forests on both sides of the road. There was some light-weapon firing up at the head of the column. We were to sweep for mines to clear the road for tanks and trucks that would follow. We found some mines laid before it had snowed, but the mine detector could not pick them all up. A Jeep following slowly along just a little behind us hit one with a roar. Some of the mines were apparently frozen and would not go off until several vehicles had run over them.

The battalion was strung out along the road, mostly in the woods, when a couple of 88s fired on us from somewhere across the valley. We could hear these shells coming, so everyone hit the ditch, trying to make it deeper than it was. This shelling lasted for several minutes until American counter-fire stopped it. Moving again, I saw two fellows who had been hit by shell fragments by the side of the road waiting for a Jeep to take them to the rear. Now we were at the edge of the woods and in sight of the town below us. The first house was about fifty yards from the woods. Then the houses were scattered along the road single file for about a block on each side. Fighting got rough. A squad flushed a couple of Germans from the first farmhouse and then moved on down the street. They quickly set up the infantry HQ in that first building.

We swept the road for mines that far, and then got behind the building to wait until the shooting died down. These infantry units were way under strength, between casualties and frostbite problems. One corporal (acting as staff sergeant) had a platoon of only six men left. A platoon is normally thirty-six men. Other platoons were similarly low in personnel. As we sat there awaiting word to move, one of the infantrymen said to us to just continue talking as we were and not make any sudden moves until one of their men checked something out in the field behind the house. This fellow was crawling up on a slight mound that we could now make out. He got up to it okay and poked in his rifle and up popped a young German sniper. The top had been well hidden, so the sniper could probably have picked off an officer had he waited a while and not been caught. They brought him over to the HQ and started questioning him, rather roughly, too, since only a couple of hours before we had uncovered the grisly sights of the murdered GIs. He was the first German to fall captive that day. He started out with the standard name, rank, and serial number bit but after a few kicks and blows was babbling away to tell all he knew. He was quite young, most likely a teenager, maybe sixteen or so years old.

It was getting late now, and most of the houses had been cleared, so we moved down the street to find a cellar in which to spend the night. As yet, no tanks had gotten down the road to town. All that had tried had hit mines buried in the snow too deep for our detectors to pick up. The next day, dozers of our unit cleared the road of snow, tanks, and mines to open the road into town.

There was still a bridge standing across the river here at Ligneuville, and the infantry unit crossed it the next day. We hit it lucky at this spot since the Germans had only held it lightly. Only one and a half miles away over the hill as the crow flies, very heavy fighting raged for two days around Thirimont. We could hear the battle sounds. Our divisional artillery fired nearly eleven thousand rounds on the 15th, mostly at the Thirimont area. There also was some fighting around us. The Germans launched an attack on the infantry that had crossed the river and tried to get to the bridge and blow it up. With artillery support called in almost on their own heads, the 117th Infantry Regiment group held. The next day the 119th Infantry Regiment passed through our lines, continued to press the Germans, and took Pont without too much trouble. Our HQ was in a hot town for several days. Enemy artillery continued lobbing shells at the bridge area, hoping they might score a direct hit and possibly knock it out.

It was in the woods south of Pont that I had another narrow escape. Another engineer and I and a group of about fifteen infantry riflemen were off scouting a trail through the woods toward Recht that the Germans held. They had roadblocks on both highways covered by artillery and infantry. We were to look for a possible bypass or shortcut. This trail would have been wide enough for a Jeep but probably not a tank. The going was rough, with the two of us changing off every fifteen minutes, breaking trail through the snow, which was at least knee deep and at times drifted even deeper.

Again we were sweeping for mines, and I was in the lead. We were being as quiet as possible, when suddenly a burp gun broke the silence with a long burst. I fell over backwards into the snow because that was the easiest way to hit the ground with the heavy battery pack on my back. We fired no shots. I didn't even carry a gun while using the mine detector. Some snow fell from the evergreen trees around us where the bullets had passed, but in checking we found none of us had been hit. It was just a blind shot through the heavily snow-laden evergreens. This was possibly just a German patrol out like ours, but with the situation as fluid as it was, it could be the lead of a whole regiment. We waited, guns ready, for nearly five minutes. The infantry sergeant in charge said, "Let's fade out to the rear." We started back one at a time, the others covering. Still, there were no more shots. In a few minutes we were all up and covering ground—snow and all—like sixty. Evidently, the Germans had done the same thing, for we had no more contact with them.

Another close shave occurred within a day of this last one. Again, I was carrying a mine detector to help check out a road to be used later. An American tank, disabled by a mine the day before, lay just off the road. We were to work up the road from this spot to a patch of woods ahead. An infantry squad was along for protection. We were only about one hundred feet from the tank, when the sound of an 88 coming in close sent everybody to the deck. I flipped backwards again, and behind me I saw a dome of snow about six feet high. I can't explain the stopped motion that I saw unless I blinked or something to freeze the explosion. The dome was the exploding 88 shell barely twenty feet from me.

Fortunately, most shrapnel fragments are thrown in the direction that the shell is going, and none of them from this particular shell hit me. An infantryman was hit in the leg by one piece, but he was not badly hurt. There were more rounds coming in, and the ground under and behind the tank was soon crowded. A few more rounds and the firing stopped. We moved away from this spot that the Germans evidently were firing on at intervals. On our return we detoured around this spot to get back to our trucks.

On January 19 we moved into Recht, and on January 23 we were within sight of the town of Saint-Vith. The unit we were with did not go into town. This privilege was given to the 7th Armored Division, who had been ordered out of the town a month before. The battle of the Ardennes was over for us.

Sam B. Peters
F Company, 2nd Battalion, 328th Infantry Regiment, 26th Infantry Division

The 26th Infantry Division had first seen combat in October 1944 and had lost almost three thousand men during the bitter fighting in the Lorraine area of France. By December 1944, the division consisted mostly of inexperienced infantry replacements. Sam Peters describes the confusion of battle that so many combat veterans remembered.

ON BEING RELIEVED FROM THE LINE, we were trucked to Metz, France, where we moved into some very ancient French Army barracks. Being near the border with Germany, Metz had always had a strong military base. In addition to the base, there was a string of caves where the soldiers could entrench themselves when attacked. The Germans used these caves very effectively when they were defending against the attacking Americans. There was a very long siege before they could be dislodged.

The barracks we were to occupy were filthy, and the mattresses the Germans left were infected with lice. Most of the American soldiers pitched the mattresses outside to be destroyed and then slept in their bedrolls on the floor. For us, this would be heaven.

Our superior officers had told us that we would be in rest until after the holidays. This seemed logical, since we needed the rest. Many of us needed some new equipment, and we were expecting to get a large number of new recruits from the States. It was felt that we could use time to give the recruits some combat training. We were settling in pretty well. On December 16, I received a cake from Alline which all of the guys in my platoon thought was delicious. The army postal service was great for getting it to me on my birthday.

On my birthday we began to hear rumors about the German breakthrough in Luxembourg and Belgium. The III Corps, composed of the 80th Infantry Division, the 26th Infantry Division, and the 4th Armored Division, were alerted for an immediate move, possibly beginning on the morning of the 18th. According to plans, the 4th Armored would depart first and would have priority on roadways and equipment, since their mission called for a dash up the Arlon Highway to attempt a breakthrough to the besieged 101st Airborne Division in Bastogne.

The 26th Infantry Division was scheduled to follow at 0830 on the 20th, using a different road network, mostly secondary roads. There was some delay due to road congestion and the lack of bridges across the Moselle River at Metz. All but one of the bridges had been destroyed during the long battle for the city. However, all of the 26th Infantry Division units were in place in or around the assembly area at Eischen by 2300 hours. All of the infantry troops slept in foxholes in the freezing cold forest.

The big mission of the regiment was to cross the Sure River and capture Wiltz, which had a road network helping to supply German troops attacking Bastogne. The first action was by the 1st Battalion, which attacked and captured Hostert, which would later become the jumping-off point for Task Force Hamilton.

The battle plan for the 328th Infantry Regiment, Col. Ben Jacobs commanding, called for the three battalions to position themselves on the right flank of the attacking 4th Armored Division. The Germans in this area were attacking in a southwesterly direction. The 1st Battalion was ordered to attack Arsdorf with the 3rd Battalion.

The 2nd Battalion, under Maj. Albert Freidman, was organized into a task force with ack-ack, engineers, tank destroyer units, and tanks attached. The task force would be commanded by Lt. Col. Paul Hamilton and would have the dirtiest job of all, the capture of Eschdorf, which was heavily fortified with both troops and armor.

E Company, commanded by Capt. Vaught Swift, who was later awarded the DSC, went out in front north of Grosbous and ran into strong German forces dug in on the high ground in front of Hierheck, a small village at crossroads leading into Eschdorf. They were pinned down for the rest of the day— December 23.

The next morning, Company F, commanded by Capt. Reed Seeley, replaced E Company. When we tried to advance, we met a large German force on the reverse slope less than a hundred yards away. The Germans were well camouflaged in the snow with white capes. They opened up with a murderous rifle and automatic weapons fire. Captain Seeley and I were directing troops and a tank along the road. The tank was hit by 88 fire, knocking Captain Seeley to the ground, but not seriously hurting him. He was later killed in action. The 88 was destroyed by a bazooka man, Pfc. D. Giouanazoo. When the smoke cleared, a previously unseen Tiger tank trembled nervously for a moment and waddled off down the slope toward Echsdorf and safety. Had he stood in place and fought, we would have been in serious trouble.

Staff Sergeant Joseph Mackin was directing 2nd Platoon troops out of our west flank when he was hit in the head by rifle fire and killed instantly. He was greatly admired and respected by his superior officers and loved by his platoon. He was greatly missed during later operations.

It took F Company all that day to get over the ridge and into Hierheck. E Company was having much the same problem along a parallel road to our left. They were held up by German troops firing from a house on the outskirts of the village. The mortar squad, under Tech. Sgt. Bruce Mannwiller, was able to get heavy fire on the house, and the Germans surrendered. Except for patrols and perimeter defense, our troops spent the early part of Christmas Eve in houses at Hierheck. However, about midnight we received orders to prepare for a night attack on Eschdorf, departing at 0100 on Christmas morning. This would be done with troops who had been on the move since leaving Metz five days before, with very little sleep and no hot food. Many of these men were new replacements received at Metz and were unfamiliar to infantry operations. However, we did have all of the officers and noncoms and, as a whole, the troops performed very well, some exceptionally.

The fighting in Eschdorf was confused and jumbled. For two days and nights, there were both Americans and Germans dodging each other in the streets, buildings, barns and basements. Enemy tanks were racing up and down the town

157

square. Our artillery and mortar fire was knocking down walls and filling the barnyards with rubble. Some of the things that happened in Eschdorf were strictly from Hollywood.

One platoon from F Company commanded by Lt. Myles Gentzkow went in with the first wave of the attack. The men found themselves surrounded by German troops and tanks. They found sanctuary in the basement of a house with a connecting barn. The farmer kept them posted on the movement of the Germans and brought each man a fresh egg and some hot soup. They remained in hiding for thirty hours. Captain Seeley did not know where they were until Staff Sgt. Joseph Feily was able to escape back to the company CP later Christmas night.

My 2nd Platoon, accompanied by Captain Seeley, crossed a small stream and moved into Eschdorf from the west. We were close enough to touch Germans during much of the night. One of the problems of night attacks with infantry troops is the inability to distinguish between friend and foe in the dark. Bumping into people with semiautomatic weapons with drawn bayonets is not a fun way to spend an evening. This became so desperate that Captain Seeley gave the command to withdraw to a house on the road leading into Hierheck. This move was made without casualty, even though we had to cross an open field. The house we occupied was solid masonry, two-story with a basement. There was an American tank by the side of the house, but it had been hit and was not mobile but still occupied. Our men took up position at all the windows, doors, and corners of the house. The Germans finally realized that the house was occupied and began shelling us very heavily from Eschdorf, and the men eventually found it advisable to retreat to the basement.

After sustaining shelling for several hours, the house caught fire and began to burn from the top. It eventually burned to the basement level, which was saved by a heavy concrete ceiling. None of the men were burned in the fire, nor did the basement get very hot. Late in the day, Captain Seeley began to send men back to the battalion headquarters one by one. This necessitated the crossing of the road in front of the house which was under fire and also crawling along the road ditch back to Hierheck. Several men were hit during the process, including me. One of the sergeants was critically hurt and was lying in the ditch where he spent most of the day. We could not move him until dark. Private First Class Paul Hauck, our company runner, crawled out to the wounded man several times, giving him encouragement and refreshment.

E Company made their attack on Eschdorf from the east and had much the same problem as F Company. Its platoons were cut off and disorganized by German troops and tanks. Captain Swift crawled and ran through machine gun fire back to the rear to seek tanks. He brought back two, one of which was immediately destroyed at the crossroads east of town. The other tank disappeared in the conflict. Captain Swift rejoined his troops in houses on the edge of town, where they stayed Christmas day and night. They were relieved the next morning.

The 1st Battalion of the 104th Infantry Regiment came in late Christmas Day and joined Task Force Hamilton in the capture of Eschdorf. They were lined up in front of the task force headquarters at Hierheck as I was placed on a stretcher, strapped to a Jeep, and sent back to an unknown field hospital.

On arriving at the hospital, the nurses dressed my wound and said they had some good news for me. "You will be flying back to the States tomorrow." What wonderful news, but alas, luck failed me. The next morning I was driven to a general hospital in Paris. On arrival, I was examined by a surgeon who advised me that I would have surgery the next morning. They sedated me heavily for a good night's sleep. The next thing I heard was a loud scream. A soldier across the hall was having a leg amputated.

The next morning they operated on my leg. Actually, it was what they call in the army a million-dollar wound: not too bad, but bad enough to keep you out of combat. During the next few weeks, I would spend time in three hospitals in France and one in England.

During the Battle of the Bulge, the 26th Division had 360 men buried in six cemeteries, including 324 who were buried in Luxembourg Cemetery, which is located just outside of Luxembourg City.

—*The* Bulge Bugle, *February 2001*

3 | CHRISTMAS IN THE ARDENNES

Robert M. Bowen
C Company, 401st Glider Infantry Regiment, 101st Airborne Division

The job of the 101st Airborne Division was to hold the town of Bastogne, Belgium, at all costs, as it controlled a number of key roads in the area. Robert Bowen describes his capture by the Germans attempting to capture Bastogne.

DECEMBER 24 AND 25, 1944, WERE FOR ME two of the worst days of my life. The 101st Airborne Division had been surrounded at Bastogne, Belgium, since the night of the 20th, was short of ammunition and supplies, had its hospital captured, and was in danger of being overrun. I was an NCO rifle platoon leader in Company C, 401 Glider Infantry Regiment, and my company was manning roadblocks on the western perimeter of the encircled city near Flamierge. We had repulsed attacks in our sector on the 19th, 20th, and 22nd. On the 23rd the Germans came again early in the morning out of a heavy fog which hung over the bitter-cold, snow-covered hills, wearing snowsuits and with tanks painted white. They were from the 77th Infantry Regiment of the 26th Volksgrenadier Division, fourteen tanks with infantry.

Although the roadblock had a Sherman, a tank destroyer, a half-track, and a 37mm antitank gun, a combination of misfortunes prevented their being much use. The Sherman was knocked out in the first burst of shelling, the antitank gun was frozen in the ground and couldn't be traversed to fire on the enemy armor, and the crew of the half-track vanished. There was little support from division artillery because of an ammunition shortage, but our 81mm mortars were a big help. The division's history devoted two short paragraphs to the action, making it sound like no more than a patrol incident: nothing about the desperation, hopelessness, and drama of the men who fought and died there that day.

I was wounded about 1600 and put in a basement of a house just behind the main line of resistance where the medics had set up an aid station. The roadblock fell just after dark. All the wounded and medics, the crews of the armor, and a few men from Company C were captured, all that remained of the reinforced platoon that held the position.

The prisoners were thoroughly searched, threatened with death, and finally marched to trucks which took them into Saint-Hubert for interrogation. When that was over, they were put in the attic of a nearby house under the guard of young *gefreiters* (privates) with itchy trigger fingers.

We were hustled out of the house early the next morning to a captured American weapons carrier with an attached trailer. A biting wind blew over the chilling snow, piercing our inadequate clothing like a knife. We were hungry, cold, and depressed: hungry because we had been living off of one or two K-rations a day for nearly a week; cold because many of us did not have overcoats, overshoes, gloves or mufflers; and depressed because after fighting debilitating campaigns in Normandy and Holland, with their high casualty rates, this one in Belgium threatened to be the last straw to push us over the edge.

The medics and wounded were put in the weapons carrier (truck) with a guard and driver, the rest somehow jammed in the trailer, and we started down the main street in a northeasterly direction. The town was flooded with German troops and tanks, all going in the direction of Bastogne. Perhaps they were the same ones who would overrun Company C that very night, losing all eighteen tanks and hundreds of panzer and volksgrenadiers in a futile attempt to take the city. Once we left the city, we could see the carnage left by the German offensive: burning villages and wrecked and burning tanks, trucks, and smaller vehicles. Corpses, American and German, bloody, sprawled grotesquely in many instances on whipped snow, ignored by small bands of refugees that wandered about like lost children. In the distance toward Bastogne could be heard the dull explosion of crashing shellfire and the rumble of German artillery. As it was still overcast and foggy, as it had been ever since we got to Belgium, there were no planes in this sector. The wretched ride took hours, with the driver nearly becoming lost despite having a map. The sky began to clear and in the distance could be heard the dull murmur of plane engines.

We came to a small village finally, one that our fighter planes had recently bombed and strafed. Houses were ablaze, walls knocked in by bombs. German soldiers with terror-stricken faces still lay in roadside ditches. Rescuers were going through the houses searching for victims.

The wounded were taken from the weapons carrier and into a field hospital just about the time our planes came back. The Germans shouted, "Jabo! Der Teufel! Der Teufel!"* Every able man rushed outside, firing every weapon available at the screaming, diving, bullet-spitting planes. We in the operating room huddled on the floor as bullets splintered the walls, happy in one way that the weather had cleared but sad in another, that one of those .50-caliber bullets could kill us.

* Jabo is a German contraction of jagdbomber (fighter-bomber).

After being treated, the wounded were taken to a nearby barn which held the rest of the POWs plus some other Americans who had been picked up along the way. The floor was ankle deep in wet, urine-soaked straw and cow manure. Soon more POWs were brought in, air corps men who had just been shot down in supply runs over Bastogne. Once more everyone was interrogated and returned to the barn, which by now was so crowded that it looked like a Tokyo subway train. The guards took several men to a nearby kitchen, and they returned with two kettles of steaming noodle soup. As only the airborne guys had any eating utensils, the ever-present spoon, these were passed around, and everyone got something to eat. Then the guards told us through one of the POWs who spoke a little German that straw was available to put on the floor for sleeping. That was impossible. There was hardly room to stand without bumping into someone. Most of us sat or stood all night.

Christmas Day was dismal for us. Cold, tired, and hungry, we were led from the barn and lined up in a column on the road with five German guards toting machine pistols. We walked all morning on the icy road, frosty breath preceding us. We passed more wrecked vehicles, one an ambulance full of corpses and on fire. Cars sometimes littered the road, and the POWs were made to drag them to the ditches. Feeling quite superior, some of the guards made the prisoners carry their bulky rucksacks.

A stocky, middle-aged guard with a broad face walked just by my side. He had gotten a ration of fried chicken, and as he walked along he waved pieces under my nose, saying "Das ist gut, ja?" Then he would take a bite. His contemptuous conduct didn't last long. Suddenly, the sound of plane motors came over nearby trees. "Jabo," the guards screamed. We dove for the ditches, all but my taunting guard, as the P-47s skimmed the treetops on the right and came barreling toward us with guns blazing. The ditches were shallow, not deep enough to hide our bodies. Even though I buried myself in the snow, I could follow the paths of the .50-caliber shells as they raced across the field and hit the road, showering us with debris and sparks. The planes were past in an instant, made a wide arc, and were back again. A brave medic got to his knees and waved his arms as more bullets tore up the road. It worked. The planes leveled off and left.

I was shaking all over. The bullets had barely missed my head as they tracked across the road. The taunting guard lay in a widening pool of blood, the chicken leg still grasped in his hand. Technical Sergeant Bonner, one of the medics who came up to help the wounded at our road block, was down, a bullet through his hip. It was serious. The guards reorganized us, threatening us with their machine pistols. Bringing the dead and wounded along, we started off once again, but didn't get far. Another flight of P-47s spotted us and came barreling for the road. We scattered like pins in a bowling alley. The planes made two passes and left. Perhaps they recognized our uniforms or were after better targets. We started off again, more wary than ever. Soon a small village came into sight.

The POWs were taken to a building which must have been the headquarters for a Nazi party unit because it was so filled with photos, flags, and other propaganda material. Our medics immediately tended the wounded, but Technical Sergeant Bonner was beyond their limited facilities. They begged the guards to have him removed to a local hospital. The guards refused at first, but later recanted. We were served a meal, a box of dried-up apples, two per man. We sat quietly on the hardwood flooring, nibbling at the apples and watching Bonner in his agony.

It was close to dark when the guards came and took away the wounded. The hospital was a makeshift affair, a convent which had been converted to handle wounded until they could be moved to the rear. Straw pallets on the floor served as beds,

165

and there were gray woolen blankets for covers. I was put in a room with a dozen or so Germans, all of whom had been operated on for frostbite and frozen limbs. Most were in great pain. I was put between two Waffen SS troopers who, at first, eyed me with hatred in their eyes. However, after a while one became friendly and even offered me a stub of a cigarette from a small metal box he carried in a shirt pocket. He spoke no English and I no German, so communication was rough. I did learn that he was an antitank gunner and destroyed several American tanks before a shell hit his gun and killed everyone but him.

Catholic sisters acted as nurses, helping the doctors and serving meals. On Christmas evening everyone got a bowl of steaming stew, and later the sister gave everyone a piece of chocolate. Somewhere down the hall, I could hear feminine voices singing Christmas carols. Even though they were in German, the music was familiar. While they sang the beautiful songs, Technical Sergeant Bonner died. He came to save us at the road block. He died in the effort. Perhaps there was some correlation between his death and the Christmas story.

—*The* Bulge Bugle, *November 1993*

Morris W. Powell
Combat Command A (CCA), 7th Armored Division Headquarters

The 7th Armored Division played an important role in the delaying action fought at the Belgian town of Saint-Vith, which threw the German advance in the Ardennes off schedule. Morris Powell recounts his experiences during an enemy attack on the small village he was stationed in with his unit.

I WAS A DRIVER FOR THE S2 SECTION of CCA. My vehicle was a half-track, which became my home for about eight or nine months. There also were a Jeep and a crew of eight men.

After a whirlwind ride across France with Patton's Third Army, some six hundred miles in twenty-one days (as I read later in books and material I have collected), it came to a sudden halt near the Moselle River. As I understand, the Germans were stiffening resistance on all fronts. It was decided that we were needed to support the British Army to the north. We changed our direction and moved north. We did know that we were in Holland. After some tough campaigns in that sector, things seemed to quiet down for a while. From what I have read, it seemed the Allied armies were preparing for a push into the heart of Germany. But the Germans had other ideas about the deal. We were alerted to be prepared to move about eight o'clock one night. We didn't know where, but I could sense that something was going on. We moved most of the night; it was stop and go all night. I found out later that we had to fight our way into place, which was now becoming the well-known Battle of the Bulge.

One thing we did know was that the weather was changing. Winter was on us, and I don't think everyone expected a winter campaign. We had training in Louisiana, the California desert, and Fort Benning, Georgia, but not for what we were about to face. I think my feet became cold that night and stayed that way for the next two months. Being from Texas, we don't have too much snow, but I saw enough to do me a lifetime.

We pulled into a small village that night, and with a lot of confusion, we set up guard. A few hours later we were on the move again. We were traveling down a narrow road, with fir trees on each side, and we couldn't see more than twenty feet. This might have been a pretty sight with the snow, but this was scary. Someone said they heard tanks, and the major said, "What kind?" Then he said, "Have your bazooka ready." We had seen lots of action across France, blown out equipment, cities, dead animals, and all that goes with combat, but never anything compared to this suspense.

The time was sometime in December, and it was cold. I think Christmas was probably the last thing on our mind at this time. A few days elapsed, and I don't think anyone was getting too much sleep, and the cold never quit. I remember pulling into this small village early one morning, which was December 24—Christmas Eve. One of the natives told us we could use one of his buildings to warm in. It had a stove and was a welcoming sight. This was not exactly the type of Christmas I was dreaming of. But it was snowing, and we knew it would be white.

A word about our half-track and crew: before we left England, we had modified the inside. We were equipped with lots of radios, one .50-caliber machine gun, one .30-caliber machine gun, bazooka, grenades and everyone's personal weapon. This was for our own protection, as S2 had other purposes, such as interrogating prisoners and obtaining information. We had installed our own box that we called our ice box. We put all our rations, goodies, or anything we had in this box. The radio operator was the keeper of this box. We had a major, head of this section, and he shared everything just the same as his men. I can't say enough for the officers and men of this outfit. They were the kind you wanted around you in a situation like we were in.

About two hours later we mounted up to move. It was slow, but we came into another small village—Manhay, Belgium, I think. We spread out, parked our vehicles, and based up, which always came first, no matter what. Take care of your vehicle and yourself later. This always paid off. Never head in; always back in. Never be where you can't move out. As night came on, I remember it being very bright and visibility was good. The moon had come through. I always think about this place—all those pretty dairy cows. We had noticed them when we came in; the barns were full.

We waited for more orders, and we noticed it was deathly quiet—only the distant sound of a German machine gun, better known as "Ripsaw." I later learned that we were to attack the next morning. There was a ridge out there a ways, where the enemy was, but until this day I believe they were closer. We began looking around for a place to bed down and settled on a building close by.

No sooner than we lay down, all Hell broke loose. Big shells started falling everywhere. Someone said, "What is that?" We knew it wasn't us because it was incoming "mail." About this time we were alerted to be ready to move as quickly as possible. We rushed to our half-track, which was facing the road. By this time it seemed the whole town was on fire with bursting shells. Then we heard a terrible noise to our right and knew it was a big tank at full throttle. In the turmoil, vehicles were gathering on the road about fifty yards away. This was our escape route. There was a big flash and collision and the largest tank I think I had ever seen, and the gun, I presume it was an 88mm, as long as a telegraph pole. A Jeep had pulled up with two people, and it vanished under this monster. The collision and flash was the monster crashing into a light American tank. I didn't know the sergeant that came running out of there, but he was frantically saying, "Tiger Royal." On our drive across France I don't remember tanks that large. I had heard they weighed around seventy tons—not all that fast, but a lot of crushing power. I had the opportunity to examine one later on. The Germans were good with the 88mm. They could bounce it off the road into the bottom of a vehicle. I did venture to take a look for the men in the Jeep. Luckily they had jumped out. The order came to move out onto this road. So we did slowly. It was stop and go the rest of the night, with a killer crew of suicidal Germans out there. We seemed like sitting ducks. There was something burning ahead. It was one of our Jeeps that was a victim of that 88. There was confusion on that road that night, and a good many were killed or wounded. We lost a major from the S3 section, and a man or two that I never heard of again.

We pulled back to the same area that we were at that morning. We knew it would be warm, if it were still empty. To our surprise, there was someone in it. After exchange of passwords it turned out to be an artillery unit. This was their kitchen crew, set up, preparing Christmas dinner. They made us feel at home with hot coffee. To me this was Christmas— smelling that turkey and all those goodies cooking.

We grabbed maybe an hour or so of sleep and waited to see what Christmas Day would be. It was an exciting day. The artillery had set up, and those guns must have been hub to hub. It was a deafening roar for several hours. Our kitchen truck came up, and everyone had a turkey dinner. The air force did its thing on the suicide tanks, I understand, and I heard they leveled Manhay. I always think about those pretty cows because I know they had no place to go.

This was my Christmas 1944, but I am thankful for surviving it. It is hard to believe the things that night: men a long way from home on a cold night, combat, cooking turkey, and everyone doing his little part. I am proud to have been a part of it and a part of the unit I served with.

—*The* Bulge Bugle, *November 1993*

Henry W. Stluka
K Company, 109th Infantry Regiment, 28th Infantry Division

The 28th Infantry Division was a rebuilt unit by mid-December with many replacements who had not seen combat before. Henry Stluka describes one small incident with his unit during the Battle of the Bulge and the Christmas Eve dinner that followed.

ON THE MORNING OF DECEMBER 24, 1944, K Company entrucked to battalion assembly area near Moestroff, where we had been for R&R on the 16th when the Germans attacked. K Company had just finished ten days of hell. We had met the powerful German counteroffensive, driving off powerful enemy attacks, infiltrations, and encirclements. But our new mission was to clear out a patch of woods near Moestroff and take the woods. We secured the left flank of the 10th Armored Division.

That night one platoon was left on outposts around Moestroff and one squad was sent on a patrol into Bettendorf, occupied by the Germans. We were to observe the enemy. I was selected to go with the patrol as the radio man and report to the company commander, Capt. Edward L. Peer, every fifteen minutes from the time we left.

We had to descend a very steep hill, walking along a road that was frozen and coated with ice. I slipped and fell on my back with the radio strapped to my back. There was a loud noise—a volley of German artillery came in to our right. We had to cross the river to get into Bettendorf, Luxembourg. There was only one bridge, and our artillery was shelling the river bank and the bridge to keep the Germans from crossing into our territory.

We lost radio contact with company headquarters because of the low elevation. I became concerned when I could not communicate to the company. Captain Peer had said, "If we don't hear from you every fifteen minutes, we know you and the squad were captured."

The town was quiet except for our artillery shells exploding. Members of our squad entered a vacant house and paired up to go into the area to find the Germans and determine how many enemy were in Bettendorf. We occupied three vacant houses. All civilians moved out.

171

I tried desperately to reach company headquarters by going into the attic and punching a hole in the roof with my rifle barrel. The radio antenna was stuck through the roof—still no contact.

My BAR man was with me to guard the "radio man." He suggested we go outside to the top of the hill we had seen while looking through the window in the attic. I told the BAR man that would be suicide because the Germans would spot us in the moonlight when we reached the top of the ice-covered hill. The BAR man stated that he had the Browning automatic rifle to take care of any German soldiers, and besides, the Germans would think we were two of their own, since no one would be stupid enough to expose themselves to the enemy. We went through the streets to the very top of the hill and stuck out like a sore thumb.

Sure enough it worked! I sent a message to Captain Peer and gave him the location of where the enemy was encamped. The artilleryman came on, and I gave him the location of the enemy also. I stayed on and then very effectively corrected our artillery on the enemy positions.

Captain Peer told me to get off the hill and return when we felt it was safe to get out. At this point the BAR man said, "We will get the Silver Star for this!" I told him that this was part of our job, but we may get the Bronze Star.

Hastily, the BAR man and I moved back to the first line of houses, where we saw smoke and live cinders coming out of the smokestack. Some of the fellows found a meat market with steaks in the meat cooler. The house had frying pans and firewood stoves to fry the steaks on.

This was a good Christmas Eve meal—along with K rations. We left about 4:30 a.m. on the morning of the 25th. When we joined the company in the woods, we were trucked out and set up positions in the hills overlooking Moestroff.

About 11:30 a.m., two Jeeps arrived, loaded with insulated food containers filled with baked turkey, dressing, cranberries, hot coffee, and for dessert a big, delicious red apple. Boy, what a delicious dinner that tasted, and it reminded me of those good old home-cooked meals. The large, delicious red apple—the first I had eaten since I left the States—made up for the anxiety on the hill.

—*The* Bulge Bugle, *February 1999*

Roswell N. Wert
1st Battalion Headquarters, 104th Infantry Regiment, 28th Infantry Division

Roswell Wert describes the length to which Americans would go to celebrate Christmas with all the trappings during the Battle of the Bulge.

DURING CHRISTMAS EVE DAY AT ESCHDORF, Luxembourg, I decided that no matter where we would wind up that night, we were going to have a Christmas tree! So someplace along the road . . . I jumped off the back of the squad truck and cut a small evergreen tree. It couldn't have been more than two feet tall, if that. I stuck it on the 57mm gun that we towed, and it rode with us the rest of the day.

That night our 3rd Squad was fortunate enough to have a roof over our heads. We set up the gun across the street from an abandoned wayside inn. It was small; the Germans called it a "Gast Haus." We parked the truck behind the small building, the only one on this road, but I recall there were farm buildings close by, and near a chicken house.

I'm getting ahead of myself.

We went inside. There were kerosene lights that we lit after making sure all the windows were light-tight. There were no civilians and very little food, but the place had not been hit

173

by shell fire and it was dry! We looked around and found the accommodations well suited to our tastes: a large table with plenty of chairs, cupboards, small kitchen, bedrooms, and all the comforts of home.

The fellows brought in their gear after posting a guard on the gun and outside the door. I brought in our little evergreen, and I think it was Jim Treadway, who held the reputation of finding anything, who found a box of Christmas tree ornaments—a box of small silver balls. He either found a stand or fashioned one out of something. So, we set up our little tree, decorated with silver balls. Now, Treadway was a coal miner from, I believe, West Virginia. He said he was also a farmer and that there were chickens across the road in that chicken coop. From somewhere he produced an empty potato sack, volunteered me as his helper, and the two of us headed out the door in quest of Christmas dinner.

Well, we silently made our way to the chicken coop, and as I stood outside "holding the bag," so to speak, Treadway disappeared into the hen house, and there was nothing but silence for what seemed to be an hour. . . . Visualize, if you will, me standing in the snow on a cold, foggy night, no weapon, holding an empty potato sack.

Suddenly, I heard a racket that would have alerted anyone for miles! A lot of squawking and flapping! Treadway had made contact! Out the door flew something—I quickly grabbed it and pushed it in the bag, then another one!—in the bag with that one too. And then Treadway made his appearance. "Let's get out of here before we wake up Hitler!" he said, back to the Gast Haus with our dinner.

What he had done was grope around in the dark, and when he found what he thought was a chicken, grabbed it by the neck, gave it a few sharp spins to break its neck, and flung it out the door to my waiting arms and potato sack. What he didn't discover until we got back was that he had captured what looked like two roosters!!

But we were hungry, and although some of the guys had gone to sleep, we boiled those birds for hours and found some canned green peas, and that was our dinner.

Later that night a tank parked alongside the building, and we listened to some Christmas music on the tank radio courtesy of the Germans. That was our Christmas Eve night as I remember it.

—*The* Bulge Bugle, *November 1993*

Lionel P. Adda
D Company, 393rd Infantry Regiment, 99th Infantry Division

Lionel Adda describes his gloomy Christmas in his snow-covered foxhole during the Battle of the Bulge and the lives risked to celebrate it.

ALTHOUGH MY CHRISTMAS DAY, 1944, was not unusual in either a good or a bad sense, I still remember most of it vividly.

Our unit was moved a day or two earlier from one position on Elsenborn Ridge to another. I had started to dig a new fighting and sleeping hole, and as I awoke I knew I would have a day of work ahead. I remember watching, from the heights of the ridge, a pale sun rising over the battered steeple of the church of Krinkelt. In spite of the circumstances, that sight gave me a feeling of comfort and peace. I was grateful also that this morning, German artillery was silent and that I had survived the fighting of the past week.

It was not very cold, the dark brown earth was fairly soft, and my digging was progressing well. Suddenly, as I looked up, I saw two GIs, tense and with bloodshot eyes, carrying two cans. One of them thrust a small, almost-cold turkey leg into my hand, and the other handed me two slices of white bread and a couple of pieces of hard candy. This was my Christmas dinner. As I crouched in my still fairly shallow hole and started to eat the turkey before it turned stone cold, 88mm shells began falling around us. Almost choking on that first bite, I realized that the Germans were watching those two poor soldiers and harassing them with artillery fire as they delivered our meals. The barrage was short.

When the shooting stopped I looked up, and the men were gone. A few minutes later I heard shells exploding perhaps fifty yards away; undoubtedly, the German gunners were zeroing in on the two men as they moved from position to position. It seemed almost criminal to me that the lives of soldiers could be jeopardized for such an almost meaningless gesture, perhaps so that some quartermaster officer could report to his superior that every man in his sector had turkey on Christmas Day. (I would have preferred one of my K-rations anyway.)

I remained concerned about protecting myself from artillery, so I worked on my position all day. A few days later, with the help of a sergeant, I was able to salvage a door from the only nearby building. I covered the sleeping portion of my hole with it and then piled dirt on top of it. Shortly thereafter, as I was asleep, a shell struck the corner of the hole, the explosion splitting the door and partially collapsing the cover. My ears rang for a week, but the cover probably saved me from serious injury or worse.

That night, as I saw and heard the signs of battle raging miles to our rear, I again felt a sense of gratitude. At least on this day, Christmas Day, the war had passed us by.

—*The* Bulge Bugle, *November 1993*

Charles A. Bodnar
Antitank Company, 47th Infantry Regiment, 9th Infantry Division

The 9th Infantry Division helped to cover the northern flank of the 99th Infantry Division during the Battle of the Bulge. Charles Bodar shares a heartwarming story about his Christmas in the Ardennes.

RUMORS FILTERED DOWN TO US ABOUT A "local" breakthrough to our south. Through stragglers and the grapevine, we were told that the enemy had broken through the American defenses in the Ardennes Forest on the cold morning of December 16. After hasty reconnaissance, we moved eastward, bucking retreating rear echelon units.

It was almost nightfall the following day when the road became ghostly silent, and our column stopped. A Jeep pulled up before us with our regimental commander. Approaching our captain, he said, "They're out there somewhere in or around the town of Monschau, Stark, go find them." Being the lead company, our platoon set out in skirmish form to make contract with the enemy.

Monschau was nestled between mountains, split in the middle by the Roer River. Without incident, we continued onward on narrow, picturesque streets about a mile to the opposite end, when our patrols reported enemy activity ahead. A hasty defensive perimeter was formed, and we were lucky enough to be able to occupy an old homestead housing an elderly couple. I noticed a couple of pictures of German soldiers on a dresser and asked the elderly woman who they were. "Mein soehne," she said. She picked up the two pictures, pointing to one, then the other, giving me each one's name and age. She looked at me and asked, "Wie alt bist du?" I gave my age with my fingers, the same as her oldest son. She looked at

177

me sadly and shook her head, then headed for the cellar with her husband.

The house being situated to defend a main road crossing over a bridge, we set our machine gun behind a stone wall, placing barbed wire entanglements in the bridge. A very confused and dreary report of the German breakthrough was relayed down to us. If the enemy succeeded in its effort, we were told, it would split the Allied Armies, and the American sector would be pushed back to France. Emphasis was put on holding back the northern hinge of the enemy offensive, which by this time we had nicknamed "The Bulge," at all costs, to prevent the capture of the seaport of Antwerp in Belgium.

Dampness began to crystallize on the branches and vegetation which sparkled in the bright yellow, greenish light of our flares. We draped our arms over the machine gun mechanism to keep the frost from freezing it shut in the penetrating cold. Objects in the darkness moved before us in ghostlike forms, advancing from the far side of the bridge. The barbed wire slowed their movements, and our front exploded along our positions as rifle fire and heavy weapons became increasingly rapid, mingled with the cry for "medic." Explosions ripped our line and front positions; the whole area on our side of the river was a cauldron of death. The desire for survival activated our machine gun to spitting fire, as forms on the bridge crumpled and fell over each other in the barbed wire entanglement. The enemy abandoned their casualties and scrambled back across the bridge, leaving us to concentrate elsewhere. Hostile, determined shelling resumed into our defensive line, and the dim light of flares revealed enemy troops filtering over the river. Our supporting howitzers and mortars sent geysers of mud and water skyward from the river banks, but the determined enemy kept slowly advancing toward us, while our guns blew the bridge apart. This eternity of a nightmare continued until all concept of time was lost, and only the instinct of survival was left. Their attack finally subsided as we held our ground and the first flicker of daylight approached with the cries of the dying and wounded mingled with occasional rounds of harassing fire from both sides.

The weather began to change, the fog was disappearing, but the atmosphere was replaced with a cold, crisp snow by the seventh day. Activity at our line was patrolling and intermittent artillery harassment from both sides. We saw our air force active once again, which helped keep enemy big guns quiet during the day.

The old homestead of the aged couple was half destroyed by enemy artillery, but the couple escaped injury huddled in their cellar. Mayhem continued on and off for six days, with only a respite now and then for each side to lick their wounds. It was days and nights of unparalleled terror, each side determined to accomplish its own purpose.

It was December 24, and a hot meal awaited us at our old homestead. In groups we came to have a turkey dinner with dehydrated potatoes, corn, fruit salad, and white bread. Being among the last, I received a generous portion of turkey and vegetables as the cooks made hasty preparations to leave the battle area.

The old couple came out of their cellar and stood gazing at the mess kits full of food we were carrying. Coming face-to-face with them, I stood motionless for a few seconds, then stretched my arms out and offered the food to the woman, saying "*Sie essen*," the best way I knew. She gazed at me sadly and reached for it, saying, "*Danke*." Not understanding, I merely said "Merry Christmas," and gave them both the food and coffee. Retreating to their cellar shelter, she soon returned with the empty mess kit and cup, then holding both my hands said, "*Ich nicht vorgessen sie*." I gave them two cans of hash from my overcoat pocket and said, "*Wiedersehen*."

179

The "Bulge" was eventually eliminated, and after we crossed the Rhine River, enemy resistance weakened. We knew the end of the war was near for the enemy.

More than thirty years past World War II, I was on a nostalgic visit to the areas whose names bring back fears, heartaches, and sufferings endured by friend and foe in the winter of 1944. Almost two kilometers outside of Monschau, I arrived at the home of the elderly couple we occupied during the fighting. It was as if I was approaching it for the first time again with a rifle in hand. To the rear of the house, a very old man and one about my age were talking alongside the river. The younger one approached and asked who I was looking for. I asked if he spoke English, and to my delight he answered, saying, "I little bit, not good." Explaining the purpose of my intrusion, he summoned his father and explained my visit. The old man shook my hand, and held it, looking at my face, not saying a word. He took my arm and led me to the stone wall where our machine gun was positioned thirty-seven years ago. Looking at me and his son, he spoke to the two of us as his son translated for me.

"My father says you were the man that handled the machine gun at this wall."

"How can he recognize me after all these years?" I asked.

There was a slight conversation between the two when the son told me his father remembered me for my curly hair. Three of us were lost in conversation when a frail, old woman with quiet sad eyes, and totally white hair joined us. It was the old man's wife. Her husband explained who I was as she looked at me with a fixed stare that made me uneasy.

"Ask your mother if she remembers me."

Not taking her eyes off me, I detected a little moisture in the eyelids as she put her hand on my left arm, saying something to her son and patting my arm.

"My mother says she has never forgotten the American soldier who gave her and my father his Christmas dinner. You were that soldier."

I couldn't help but give her a slight embrace about the shoulders, at the same time trying not to show any more emotion.

"My mother often spoke of your Christmas meal."

We walked down the road a short distance as I was returning to Monschau, when he said:

"My father also speaks of you as the man behind the gun, the night you held off your enemy when they tried to cross the river. He did not remember you for your curly hair, but the man that might have killed his son." Still looking at me, he continued, "I was on the other side of that bridge."

—*The* Bulge Bugle, *November 1998*

Charles R. Miller
A Company, 290th Infantry Regiment, 75th Infantry Division

The newest large American unit to arrive in Western Europe shortly before the Battle of the Bulge was the combat-inexperienced 75th Infantry Division. Charles Miller recounts his less than perfect Christmas situation during the Battle of the Bulge.

I WAS BORN THREE DAYS AFTER CHRISTMAS, and most of my life my gifts came "Merry Christmas and Happy Birthday!" Well, the "presents" in 1944 will forever color the Christmas season for me.

December 24, 1944, was my first day in combat and my first experience in seeing comrades killed and wounded. My unit, Company A, 290th Infantry Regiment, 75th Infantry Division, arrived in Hoeselt, Belgium, about 1:30

a.m. on December 21. Shortly after midnight on December 22, we were trucked about sixty miles to the Bulge area and took up defensive positions at Septon on the L'Ourthe River. The 1st Battalion, 290th Infantry Regiment, was attached to the 3rd Armored Division on December 23 and during that night marched to an assembly area east of Erezée.

Early on the morning of December 24, Company A was picked up by 3rd Armored Division half-tracks and taken east to Manhay, which was being shelled (Christmas fireworks?) and then back west to Grandmenil and then south to Oster. We mounted an attack to clear the high ground east and south of Oster and encountered small groups of panzergrenadiers from the 2nd SS Panzer Division who managed to disorganize our attack so that about two platoons were left with the company commander, who ordered us to dig-in over the objections of the two platoon sergeants. The captain then wanted two men to return to Oster, and I was volunteered—my one true "Christmas gift"—although I was not too happy at the time. After we left, the Germans surprised the group and killed three men, including one digging in the hole I had started, since it was deeper than his.

At this point, the CO pulled the company off the hill, and we started to march out, when the battalion commander (or exec) ordered us to return to the hill. Then the captain had to be evacuated, and 1st Lt. Giles Jenerette, the company exec, took command. We returned to Oster, where we spent the night in houses and barns, taking turns on watch and seeing fires burn to the north where the 2nd SS Panzers were taking Manhay and Grandmenil.

Christmas Day dawned bright and clear, and we saw the contrails of bombers flying east. P-47s were attacking south of us, and one came back over the ridge trailing smoke. When the pilot parachuted south of us, he came toward Oster with his .45 automatic pistol drawn and was quite relieved to find that we were Americans.

We moved up to the tree line and dug in, where we enjoyed our Christmas dinner, consisting of some stale bread and a C-ration shared with two other men. How I berated my stupidity in leaving a fruitcake my mother had sent me in my duffel bag in Hoeselt for some rear-echelon commando to enjoy.

In late afternoon, Lieutenant Jenerette led a large patrol around the edge of the woods to a crossroads. There we observed the Germans walking up and down the road in their long overcoats which I always envied, since they seemed so much more practical than our short ones.

About dark, the lieutenant sent some of the patrol back and continued on with the rest of us and eventually attacked Odeigne, where more men were killed, wounded, or captured. Lieutenant Jenerette was among the wounded, suffering a severe chest wound. For this action he received several decorations, including a Distinguished Service Cross.

When the patrol returned to Oster, we found that the rest of the company had come down off the hill. Late on the 26th, we were issued our first rations—our squad got a ten-in-one box—but before we could eat it, we were ordered to move out. We moved by foot until after dark, when we were picked up by trucks and taken to Blier.

The next day, the 27th, we had our "Christmas Dinner"— turkey, dressing, and all the trimmings. Our enjoyment of the meal and our relief of being out were colored by the realization that the company had over thirty casualties— killed, wounded, missing, and sick. The next day was my twenty-second birthday.

—*The* Bulge Bugle, *November 1993*

George Karembelas
A Company, 333rd Infantry Regiment, 84th Infantry Division

George Karembelas describes the miserable conditions endured by some American soldiers fighting in the Ardennes on Christmas Day and the heartbreak of leaving your wounded buddies behind in battle.

THE BLINDING FLASH AND THE DEAFENING EXPLOSION were followed by screams. The medic, who a minute before was kneeling over me to give first aid, groaned and slumped on me.

"I'll help you," I said, but he was already dead.

And this is the way it is when riflemen are sent to fight tanks.

It was Christmas night, December 25, 1944, and the Allied armies in Europe were locked in a desperate and costly struggle, since known as the Battle of the Bulge. Snow that Christmas was not one of nature's beautiful decorations but an enemy just as deadly as the German machine guns and tanks.

Some of the events that took place on the night of the 25th are only hazy recollections; others are still very vivid and will never be forgotten. Some of these events are responsible for saving my life, while others may be viewed as premonitions of the impending tragedy. Every year at this time I find myself reflecting on these events, and I wonder!

Christmas was uneventful except for the bright sun and clear sky, which permitted our air force to become operative after a prolonged period of inactivity due to bad weather. The elation I felt at seeing thousands of planes on their way to bomb the German panzers was short-lived because I knew that there was still a long, long road to travel before sanity would return to the world.

"All right, you guys, pack up; we're going for a nice little walk," barked the platoon sergeant. We crawled out of our foxholes, a few miles from Marche, and after marching, waiting, and freezing for what seemed an eon, we stopped at last in the courtyard of a large farmhouse. Orders, we were told, had not come through as expected, and we would have to sit. A nearby barn, filled with hay, provided a perfect haven, and as I crawled into the hay to warm my freezing feet, I thought how wonderful it would be if orders were delayed until morning and I could spend a whole night in luxurious comfort. The heavy guns roaring in the distance seemed very far away, and the whole war seemed to detach itself from my little world. At the moment, the only thing that mattered was that I was under shelter and among my friends.

John Shaw, a close friend who always took meticulous care of his overshoes, said to me, "What kind of situation do you think we're in, anyway?"

"I don't know."

"Hazard a guess."

"I can't even do that. I've got a sense of foreboding, that's all."

With the customary abruptness, orders were passed around to assemble in the courtyard. There were moans and groans from everyone; our little haven was about to crumble. In the courtyard, I remember thinking that this would probably be just another "hurry up and wait" affair because we were totally unfamiliar with the terrain, and it would be suicidal to send troops on a night mission without adequate briefing. I was sure that a night mission was out of the question, and worse, we would maneuver for position the rest of the night. We were told briefly that German paratroopers (about one company) had occupied a strategic hill, but since we would attack with an entire battalion, it would simply be a matter of policing-up, just like we did in camp. (In camp, soldiers were formed into a rank and went along picking up trash; this was known as policing an area or simply police-up.) I said to John Shaw, "If anybody has the notion of ordering us to attack now, he's crazy."

No answer.

"John, didn't you hear me?"

"I heard you."

"Then why the hell don't you say something—?"

"I will, when I get my overshoes stashed away in a good, safe place." We had been ordered to remove our packs, overcoats and overshoes.

Soon, we started marching toward a hill silhouetted against the sky. I wasn't particularly frightened, but I kept wondering if we would find only a company of German paratroopers. I remember seeing a truck pulling an antitank gun up the hill, skidding, and going into a ditch. The sight of the antitank gun didn't register at that moment, but I have thought since about it a great deal and wonder if someone knew that antitank guns, and plenty of them, were the main thing needed for that mission.

During the march to the top of the hill, I kept stumbling for no apparent reason; I even dropped my rifle and was afraid that the bore might be plugged up. Shortly thereafter, I dropped one of my grenades, and going through a few strands of barbed wire, I feel sure that they were warnings. I had never before dropped my rifle. At the time, however, I was more concerned with cleaning it and catching up with my platoon.

Someone was firing tracers behind us. "Shaw! Do you see those Roman candles?"

"I see them."

"And you aren't nervous in the service, buddy?"

"It's only grazing fire, don't worry."

▲ GIs guard a portable bridge with a machine gun. The U.S. Army's leadership in Europe decided in late 1944 that the very rural Ardennes would be a great place to rest battle-worn divisions and introduce newly arrived divisions to combat. *National Archives*

▼ A GI is armed with a Colt .45 automatic pistol. Many historians suspect that Hitler's plans for the Ardennes Offensive of December 1944 (then known to Americans as Operation von Rundstedt and later as the Battle of the Bulge) were first conceived in July 1944. *National Archives*

◀ American soldiers stand watch behind a 57mm antitank gun. Hitler informed his generals of his planned Ardennes Offensive in September 1944, although he had given priority in delivery of new tanks and artillery to those units to be used in the Ardennes Offensive starting in August 1944. *National Archives*

▲ GIs are preparing to go out on patrol. Hitler was well aware of just how thinly stretched were the U.S. Army units stationed in the Ardennes. He believed his forces could break through the forest and then drive on to the main Allied supply port of Antwerp, Belgium. *National Archives*

◀ Spearheading Hitler's Ardennes Offensive n December 1944 were his panzer (tank) divisions. The most formidable German tank in service at the time was the seventy-ton Tiger B tank, seen here. It was armed with an 88mm main gun. *National Archives*

▲ During the Battle of the Bulge, a squad of German paratroopers on the rear deck of a Tiger B heavy tank shares a cigarette with a Waffen SS soldier on a motorcycle. By this time of the war, few German paratroopers had ever had jump training. *National Archives*

▲ A Waffen SS panzergrenadier (motorized infantryman) is motioning his fellow soldiers forward in this Battle of the Bulge–period photograph. The Waffen SS was the armed element of the Nazi Party and was generally better equipped than the German army. *National Archives*

▲ Typical of the type of turret-less tank destroyer employed by the German military during the Battle of the Bulge is this restored Jagdpanzer IV owned by a private collector in England. Such vehicles were cheaper and quicker to build than turreted tanks. *Bob Fleming*

◀ Two Waffen SS panzergrenadiers take a smoke break during the Battle of the Bulge. It was the Waffen SS that pioneered the wearing of camouflaged uniforms and helmet covers, as seen on the soldiers pictured. The German army adopted camouflaged uniforms late in the war. *National Archives*

▲ A German half-track on the right side of the picture is covered with branches to hide it from any American aircraft on the prowl. On the left is a captured U.S. Army half-track. German soldiers often pressed captured vehicles into service. *National Archives*

◀ Two Waffen SS officers in a Schwimmwagen are checking a map to make sure they are heading in the right direction. The Schwimmwagen was the amphibious version of the Volkswagen Kübelwagen, the German equivalent of the American Jeep. *National Archives*

◀ German soldiers are stripping the footwear off of dead American soldiers during the Battle of the Bulge. The German offensive began to slow toward the end of the first week due to the terrain, supply difficulties, and growing American resistance. *National Archives*

▶ The mainstay of the U.S. Army tank inventory during the Battle of the Bulge was the M4 Sherman medium tank series, pictured here in a whitewash camouflage scheme. Crewed by five men, the original version of the tank was armed with a 75mm main gun. *National Archives*

▲ The U.S. Army M36 tank destroyer was based on the lightened chassis of an M4 Sherman tank. Armed with a powerful 90mm main gun in an open-topped turret, the M36 had the firepower to take on German tanks like the Tiger and Panther. *National Archives*

▲ GIs are using bed sheets as camouflage for themselves and their water-cooled .30-caliber machine gun. While Hitler belittled the fighting abilities of the American soldier, the German soldier soon found how tough they could be during the Battle of the Bulge. *National Archives*

◀ The M3 105mm howitzer was a cut-down and lightened version of the U.S. Army's standard M2 105mm howitzer mounted on a modified 75mm towed-gun chassis. The M3 was issued to the army's airborne divisions by 1944. *National Archives*

◀ A GI stands guard behind a 57mm towed antitank gun designated the M1 by the U.S. Army. The M1 was a license-built copy of a British-designed weapon with a longer barrel. However, its poor penetration abilities made it unpopular with Allied troops. *National Archives*

▲ Awaiting an enemy attack is this U.S. Army M10 tank destroyer armed with a 3-inch (76.2mm) main gun, which proved to have poor armor-penetration abilities. The British Army mounted a far superior 76.2mm gun referred to as the 17-pounder in their M10s. *National Archives*

▲ GIs stand guard against German aerial attack with an automatic cannon designated the 40mm gun M1 in the U.S. Army inventory. The weapon was a license-built version of a Swedish-designed gun known as the Bofors and could fire up to 120 rounds per minute. *National Archives*

▲ Abandoned and snow-covered, a German Tiger B heavy tank is being inspected by a passing GI who, no doubt, is impressed with the vehicle's massive size when compared to American tanks. Allied soldiers also referred to the vehicle as the King Tiger or Royal Tiger. *National Archives*

◀ Painted in a winter camouflage scheme is an open-topped U.S. Army M3 half-track configured as an armored personnel carrier (APC). It is armed with a ring-mounted .50-caliber machine gun at the front of the vehicle. *National Archives*

◀ A GI looks over a captured German six-round rocket launcher designated the 15cm Nebelwerfer 41 in the German military. American soldiers who had to face this weapon in battle nicknamed it the "screaming meemie" due to the sound the rockets made in flight. *National Archives*

◀ The savagery of combat can be seen in this picture of a GI posed over the body of a German soldier he killed with his M1 Garand rifle. The Garand was a gas-operated, eight-round, semiautomatic rifle. *National Archives*

▲ Off to the front is an open-topped U.S. Army M18 tank destroyer armed with a 76.2mm main gun. The M18 was lightly armored and powered by an air-cooled radial engine that provided the vehicle a top speed of fifty-five miles per hour. *National Archives*

▲ A major premise for Hitler's Ardennes Offensive was that the poor weather conditions that prevailed at that time of the year would ground Allied air support and allow his forces to operate unhindered by ground-attack aircraft like the Republic P-47 Thunderbolt. *National Archives*

◀ Surrounded paratroopers of the 101st Airborne Division in Bastogne drag off an air-dropped package containing much-needed medical supplies. It was the airlift that made it possible for the Americans to keep the Germans from taking Bastogne. *National Archives*

▶ Brigadier General Anthony C. McAuliffe became the acting commander of the 101st Airborne Division when it was surrounded at Bastogne by German forces. It was he who told the Germans "Nuts!" when they asked for his troops' surrender. *National Archives*

▲ On December 26, 1944, Gen. George Patton's 4th Armored Division broke through encircling German forces to link up with the Americans trapped within Bastogne. Leading the attack were up-armored Sherman "Jumbo" tanks, like the one pictured. *National Archives*

▲ Paratroopers of the 101st Airborne Division march out of one of the roads leading into Bastogne to do battle with the German forces surrounding the town. The enemy would occupy the area around Bastogne until mid-January 1945. *National Archives*

◀ This winter-camouflaged vehicle was the U.S. Army M29 cargo carrier, nicknamed the "Weasel." The open-topped, unarmored vehicle had excellent off-road mobility, could be made amphibious, and could carry up to four people or 1,200 pounds of payload. *National Archives*

◀ American soldiers are riding on and marching alongside an M4 Sherman tank. As late as January 4, 1945, the Germans were making plans to capture Bastogne. However, on January 3, the American armies in the Ardennes launched their own counteroffensives and disrupted the German plans. *National Archives*

◀ The frigid and heavily wooded terrain of the Ardennes was an infantryman's nightmare during the Battle of the Bulge. Thousands of GIs would be pulled from combat due to trench foot and frostbite. *National Archives*

▶ A captured German soldier rides into captivity on the hood of an American Jeep. Waffen SS soldiers seldom made it into the POW stockade during the Battle of the Bulge due to the massacre of American troops at Baugnez (Malmédy), Belgium, on December 17 by Waffen SS troops. *National Archives*

◀ A GI stands on the hull of an abandoned German antiaircraft tank armed with four 20mm automatic cannons in an armored, open-topped turret. This type of specialized vehicle was aimed at redressing Allied air superiority. *National Archives*

▲ American GIs in snowsuits have taken a small group of German soldiers as prisoners. By the beginning of January 1945, the German generals knew that they stood no chance of success. However, Hitler resisted their pleas to withdraw from the Ardennes. *National Archives*

◀ GIs are lined up for a chow break. American troops did not get proper cold-weather gear until the tail end of the Battle of the Bulge. The generals had placed transportation priority on ammunition and fuel rather than on cold-weather gear. *National Archives*

◀ A couple of GIs examine a small, abandoned German armored half-track. It is unclear if the Germans put white stars on the vehicle to confuse American soldiers, or GIs did it to indicate to all concerned that it had been captured and was not to be destroyed. *National Archives*

▲ Hundreds upon hundreds of destroyed or abandoned German vehicles could be found littering the Ardennes upon the conclusion of the Battle of the Bulge. Americans captured this abandoned, unarmored German half-track prime mover and used it to tow a 105mm howitzer. *National Archives*

▶ One of the most impressive German tank destroyers of World War II was the Jagdpanther (Hunting Panther), seen here being examined by curious GIs. On January 8, 1945, Hitler finally gave permission to his generals to begin a partial withdrawal from the Ardennes. *Patton Museum of Cavalry and Armor*

◀ A U.S. Army Signal Corps cameraman is seen taking a picture with a destroyed German Tiger Ausf. E heavy tank behind him. By the time the Battle of the Bulge was over on January 28, 1945, it was estimated that the Germans had suffered one hundred thousand casualties. *National Archives*

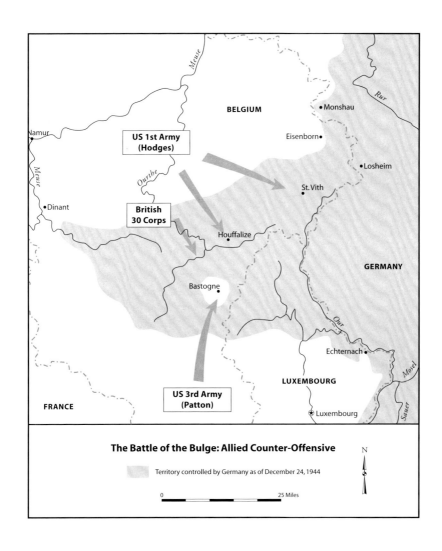

Meuse

BELGIUM

Monshau

Rur

Eisenborn

US 1st Army
(Hodges)

Namur

Losheim

Meuse

Ourthe

St. Vith

Dinant

British
30 Corps

Houffalize

GERMANY

Bastogne

Our

Echternach

LUXEMBOURG

Mosel

US 3rd Army
(Patton)

FRANCE

Luxembourg

Sauer

The Battle of the Bulge: Allied Counter-Offensive

N

Territory controlled by Germany as of December 24, 1944

0   25 Miles

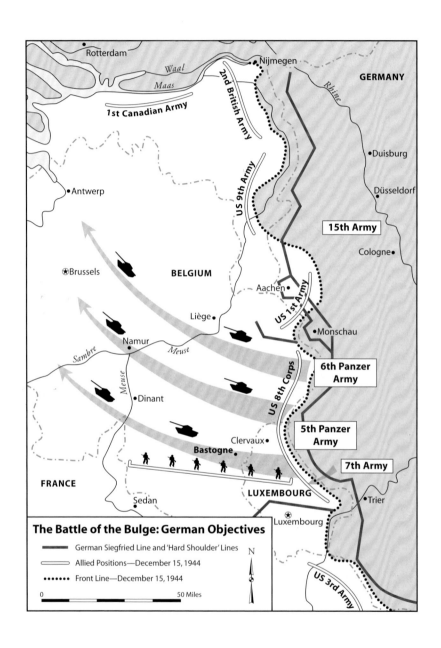

Rotterdam

GERMANY

Waal

Maas

Nijmegen

1st Canadian Army

2nd British Army

Rhine

•Duisburg

US 9th Army

•Antwerp

•Düsseldorf

15th Army

❁Brussels

BELGIUM

Cologne•

Aachen•

Liège•

US 1st Army

•Monschau

Namur•

Meuse

Sambre

6th Panzer Army

Meuse

US 8th Corps

•Dinant

Clervaux•

5th Panzer Army

Bastogne•

FRANCE

LUXEMBOURG

7th Army

Sedan•

•Trier

Luxembourg

The Battle of the Bulge: German Objectives

━━━ German Siegfried Line and 'Hard Shoulder' Lines

▭ Allied Positions—December 15, 1944

••••••• Front Line—December 15, 1944

N

0   50 Miles

US 3rd Army

The hill was very quiet, and I remembered the scout in the Indian movies saying, "Yeah, it's too quiet." One platoon attacked the Chateau of Verdenne on the hill, but very little firing ensued, and we were told that the castle was taken and not to worry about it anymore. We were then lined up and told to proceed through a designated section of the woods, firing and screaming in order to demoralize the Germans. The woods consisted of a few large trees and many smaller ones fairly close together. There was a wide path or road on our left flank, and we were told to stay away from it but to guide on it. I was about ten yards from the road, blazing away from the hip and screaming like mad. Someone was firing from my left and a little to my rear but too close for my comfort. "Hey, burrhead," I yelled, "do me a favor and point that peashooter at the krauts instead of me."

"Sorry, George, I'll get up on the line with you."

It was my platoon leader.

All of a sudden the Germans began to return our fire; their machine guns appeared to span the entire width of the woods. I didn't feel particularly concerned about the machine gun fire, and I don't think anyone else did. After all, we had always dealt with German small-arms fire before; it was their artillery we feared. I don't think anyone in my immediate area was wounded, but we began to crawl and continued to fire; the screaming was far less enthusiastic, and soon no one screamed. I reached a small clearing in the woods near the road. The lieutenant came up and asked me if I could see anything. I said no, but I thought I had spotted a machine gun nest and would try to hit it with a rifle grenade.

As I edged toward the road, the machine gun opened up again for a few seconds, and the lieutenant cautioned me not to get too close to the road. In order to fire at the position I had picked out, I had to get on one knee to clear some trees. I fired

187

the grenade, saw it hit, and felt certain that I had knocked out the German machine gun. As I turned to crawl back, I felt something crash into my left thigh. It felt as though someone had struck me with a baseball bat. The blow knocked me backwards, but I managed to crawl away from the road without much difficulty. I felt only surprise and amazement that I had been hit; after the initial pain, I felt only a mild burning sensation.

The lieutenant came up and asked me where I was hit.

"In my thigh."

"Medic!" he called.

The medic crawled up and said to me, "I'll check it to make sure an artery hasn't been severed."

I was flat on my back with my feet toward the Germans, and this position saved my life. The medic kneeled beside me, examined the wound, and said it wasn't bad, no broken bones. He told me to take my sulfa tablets, while he applied a dressing.

The medic had come to our company just a few days before, and I didn't even know his name.

As he started to leave, I felt an explosion which seemed to be right at my feet and felt a sharp pain on my right foot. I heard the medic groan, and he fell over me. I tried to help him, but he was already dead. The shrapnel from the German tank almost cut him in half. Then I heard screams from all around. Several of the men were hit, and some were calling for a medic, while others were just crying. I remember two in particular, one who spoke English with an accent kept saying, "I die, I die," and the other was screaming about a wound in his back, and he couldn't move. I started to crawl toward the voices when another explosion, practically at the same place as the first one, knocked me unconscious.

I don't know how long I was out, but when I came to, I thought I was dead. What had been pitch dark before was now fairly bright, with fires burning in some places and flares going off. My first thought was that I was in hell. Slowly, I regained my senses, but when I started to move, I knew that my legs had been shattered. I tried to sit up just as another shell came in, and I fell flat again. This time I was very frightened because a small fragment hit me above the eye, and the blood impaired my vision; I thought I was blind. When I wiped the blood away, I could see and turned to examine my legs. My right foot felt as though it was held on hot coals.

I reached down to feel it—I suppose to make sure that at least it was there—when I heard a voice to my right ear saying, "George really got it that time; I think he's dead."

I turned my head and said, "Hell, I'm not dead; where is everybody?"

"Orders have come through to withdraw. Somebody must have admitted that we can't fight tanks with rifles."

Time had lost all meaning, and I had no idea how long this whole thing had taken. I tried to get up, hoping against hope that somehow I could walk, but soon resigned myself to the fact that I would not get out of the woods under my own power. I crawled over to the other men; there were at least five whom I had known very well.

I asked, "How badly are all of you guys hurt?" They seemed to have their legs shattered so completely that the slightest movement was impossible.

Then I asked the question that combatants have been asking since the first two tribes of primitive men clashed: "Why hasn't help been sent to take out the wounded?"

Someone answered, "That's what I'm up here for, but now I'm hit and can't even help myself."

He was sure that no one would venture into the woods. Earlier, most of the wounded had been taken out, but now nobody would return.

"We can't stay here," I said, "the Germans might come through at any minute and finish us off. Nobody is returning their fire." All agreed, but there didn't seem to be much point to try to do anything. I searched around with my hands, hoping to find a rifle. All the weapons had suddenly disappeared; the only thing I had was a grenade in my pocket.

After trying to think of something to do or something to say, I also joined the mood of the little group, which seemed to be if help doesn't come, we're lost, because there's nothing we can do by ourselves. From the German lines, machine guns sprayed the area periodically but not even close to us.

Finally, one soldier spoke up and said, "If anyone thinks he can crawl, he'd better start because the krauts will be here in no time."

"I can crawl," I said, "but I don't know how far, and I don't want to become separated from the rest of you. I haven't any idea how far back the others have withdrawn. I'll try it with somebody else."

Compared to the others, I was in fairly good shape, and I would have to try to get back and send help. The next few minutes were the most heart-rending moments I have ever known. I am sure that all the wounded doubted that I would ever get back and knew that even if I did, help for them would not arrive in time. They gave me messages for their wives, sweethearts, and families (two of the men had babies that they had never seen) and last farewells to their loved ones, which made me break down. (I may add that all of the wounded died, but I did not contact any of their families.) After reassuring them that I would have help back in no time, I started crawling away from them. It soon became apparent to me that I would never get through the woods but would have to risk the road. I crawled to the edge of the road, was unable to see any sign of a human being, no gunfire of any sort, and decided to crawl as fast as I could.

The next period of time is very hazy. I am almost sure that I got up and walked a few steps, but I can't be positive. In the meantime, the Germans had started firing again, and I remember watching their tracers overhead. Nothing seemed to matter, however, except finding friendly troops because I knew that before too long I would pass out and freeze to death. At last I arrived at the point where we entered the woods some hours before. I was very tired by this time and crawled to the ditch to rest for a little while. I don't remember how long I was there, but when I tried to crawl again, I knew that I had reached the end. I heard someone walking toward me on the road and became very frightened because I was certain they were Germans and that they would see me and finish me off.

I took the grenade from my pocket, pulled the pin, and called out, "What company are you guys from?"

"A Company, 3rd Platoon," one of them said in a surprised voice.

I replaced the pin. "Help me get to the first aid station, and then get word to headquarters that there are still wounded in the woods, and tell them to be quick about it."

But self-preservation comes to the fore at such times, and the soldiers probably felt I would be too much of a burden to them. They suggested I be carried to a nearby shack, and they would hurry back to get help. I pleaded, threatened, cursed, and did everything I could think of to persuade them to take me with them. At last they made a seat with a jacket and their rifles and carried me to the aid station. I remember passing out several times on the way, and I knew what a burden I was to those two soldiers. Needless to say, they saved my life, and I am very grateful. The aid station was set up near some trenches in which stretchers had been placed. I was lowered into one of them, covered with a blanket, asked where I was hit, and given first aid, which consisted mainly of applying a dressing over any spot that was wounded. It was impossible to cut away clothing and boots for proper care.

Daylight came and with it a Jeep. I remember being lifted out of the trench and placed on the hood of the Jeep. A very kind voice asked if I was cold and gave me another blanket. In fifteen minutes or so I was in a building, placed on a table, and attended to by an army medical officer. I don't remember what he told me, but I felt very reassured. He gave me a tin of hot coffee and a tube to drink through, and then I saw what remained of my company. They asked about friends, and I asked if help had been sent for the others, but nothing really made any sense.

Shortly thereafter I was placed in an ambulance with some of my friends, and was told that we were going to a hospital. Before long I began having terrific pains and asked the attendant to please give me something. He did, and I remember falling asleep with two of my friends looking at me. I woke up in a hospital ward and looked for my friends, but they had been taken elsewhere. Soon I was transported to Paris and began the long route through hospitals to my eventual discharge from the army. To this date, I have seen only two of the men in my company, but wherever they are and whatever they are doing, may God bless them all; they were the greatest.

—*The* Bulge Bugle, *November 1990*

Harold Lindstrom
F Company, 289th Infantry Regiment, 75th Infantry Division

Harold Lindstrom describes what he went through on Christmas Eve during the Battle of the Bulge, when he and his unit encountered a German tank.

ABOUT 10 P.M., CHRISTMAS EVE, we were marching across a long, gentle, treeless hill in front of Grandmenil. I will call it a slope. I was the 60mm mortar assistant gunner in the 4th Platoon. I think it was the entire F Company—marching single file on a narrow road. We knew we were getting close to combat, as during the day we had met Jeeps with wounded and had passed an area where another company of the 289th Infantry Regiment had met a column of German tanks. By the looks of things, many must have been killed or wounded. There were Jeeps on the road that had been crushed to a flat metal scrap pile from being run over by the tanks; burning trucks in a clump of trees alongside the road; and much equipment lying around, such as helmets, rifles, canteens, and whatnot.

Until now, we had not been fired upon—I didn't think we would be this time. The night was beautiful. A bright moon glistened off the white, clean snow. I was very tired so just kind of shuffled along behind the guy ahead of me. Surprisingly, I wasn't frightened by what I saw. There were many burning buildings in the small village of Grandmenil about a half mile ahead and down the slope. What's more, there was fighting going on down there! I heard the rapid fire of German machine guns in the village. Their tracer streaks went out toward an area on our side of the village but farther down the slope. Slower-firing American machine guns were firing back. Their tracer streaks went into the village. The whole thing fascinated me. I seemed to be a ringside spectator. I learned later the Americans were K Company, 269th Infantry Regiment, who had taken the village and then were driven out by a German counterattack.

Suddenly, my unrealistic thinking that I was a spectator was shattered. A machine gun of a German tank fired at us! I heard the sharp crack of the gun being fired directly at me, and tracers streaked across the road just ahead of me. Instantly, I awoke from my dull dream world and looked for cover. There was no ditch or protection by the road. I spotted a slight terrace-like surface to my right and up the slope—slightly ahead of me. There was a fence next to the road, but I went through it as though it didn't exist. I hit the ground on top of the terrace just as the Germans fired again. They swept the area from right to left with a long burst. They seemed to know approximately where we were, but I do not think they could make out individuals. I was very much afraid. I had never been so frightened before or have ever been since. I was sure they could see me—dressed in dark clothes, lying on the gleaming white snow. The German bullets plowed into the ground ahead of me, spattering pieces of frozen dirt onto me. Some were very close. I found a bullet hole in my shovel carrier flap the next day! One of the bursts hit the 60mm mortar base plate in front of Ralph Logan's head (the mortar gunner). When they hit the base plate, the bullets made a ringing sound, made orange and red sparks, whistled, and made tracer streaks as they flew over him. Someone squirmed and moaned to my left, indicating he had been hit. I froze in fright—didn't move a muscle. I decided to move though. I was lying on top of my ammunition pack, which positioned me above ground surface. If I had my say, I would be lying under the ground! We lay there some time. I began feeling cold as the snow under me began to melt and come through.

Finally, our platoon sergeant, Laverne Ives, said, "Men, we can't lie here all night and wait to get hit. Immediately after a burst sweeps by you, start crawling up the slope toward that clump of trees." Boy! That was comforting to receive some directions. Up to now, I just lay there not knowing what to do. I waited for that next machine gun sweep. They hadn't fired for a while. I heard the tank engine start, run a little, and then stop. Someone yelled something in German and laughed. I don't understand German. I hoped they wouldn't decide to drive up the slope and crush us. I decided to start crawling up the slope. I was afraid to make a broadside target as I turned around to crawl up to the trees, so I crawled backward. It was pretty difficult. My belt and equipment would catch on the ground under me. My coat wanted to slide over my head. When far enough up the slope, I turned around and crawled faster, head first. Farther up the slope, I got up and ran the rest of the way. When near the trees, I was stopped by one of us. He asked for the password. I was so frightened I couldn't remember it at first but finally did when I heard him cock his rifle.

He told me the guys were in the woods. I was surprised to see so many. I thought I was the only one out. Only two men in our platoon had been hit. Many of us were to be hit later.

I have thought of that night during every Christmas Eve since.

—*The* Bulge Bugle, *November 1993*

James Herrington
327th Parachute Infantry Regiment, 101st Airborne Division

James Herrington recalls how under the worst conditions, his thoughts still turned to the home fires and family on Christmas.

IN BASTOGNE OUR SITUATION WAS CRITICAL. In addition to being surrounded and outnumbered, there were eighteen thousand mouths to be fed. Carbine and M1 ammo was in short supply, as were bazookas and artillery shells. The harsh weather was yet another enemy, against which we had little defense, and frostbitten feet were not altogether uncommon.

On the morning of December 23, all lookouts were ordered to watch for the first aircraft. The weather, which had been hazy, was finally clearing. At 0935 hours an MP rushed into 101st Airborne Headquarters to tell Colonel Kohls that several

Allied aircraft were circling the sector. By 1150 hours, sixteen more aircraft appeared and dropped desperately needed supplies by parachute northwest of Bastogne at Sans-Souci Lane and the Marche Road. We felt a renewed sense of hope that enabled us to continue our fight.

By afternoon of the 23, the sky filled with 241 Dakotas and P-47s. The air support offered by these was a significant factor in turning the battle in our favor during the next few days. They were dropping 75-pound bombs in an effort to reduce our enemy's numbers. However, battle lines were still very ill-defined, and German and American troops were in close proximity on the ground below. Consequently, our own troops had to hit the ground when we heard the roar of the plane and the distinctive whistling sound of the bombs, even though it was "friendly fire."

The fighting continued December 24 and 25 and throughout the remaining days of December. There was no opportunity for communication with the outside world. No letters were coming in or going out—we were lucky to have received supplies of food and ammunition. That didn't stop us, though, from being aware that back home it was Christmas. I wondered about my family and whether they were concerned about me. This was my third Christmas away from home, and I hoped I would be alive to be there for the next one.

—*The* Bulge Bugle, *November 1993*

Harold Herrer
75th Infantry Division

Harold Herrer recalls the hunger he experienced during Christmas Eve during the Battle of the Bulge when he and his small patrol became lost.

ON DECEMBER 24, A SMALL GROUP OF US was picked to go on reconnaissance. Our mission was to seek out the enemy, discover his strength, and bring the information back to the company. It sounded easy, and we were to be back in a short time.

Again, plans didn't go as intended. We got lost in the forest and came front-to-front with the Germans at the edge of a small Belgian town that was dug in and had a Tiger tank to protect it. It was already night, and they sprayed us with rifle and machine gun fire. Luckily, only one of our men was hit and not seriously. We withdrew deeper into the forest, always trying to find a way out and get back to our company. This continued during the night and the next day, with other encounters with the Germans.

We had our weapons, ammunition belts, two bandoliers, bayonet, canteen, hand grenades, gas mask, shovel and whatever else a dog face might need. The one thing we lacked was food, as we were to be back early.

As I was walking up and down the hills in the snow with all this weight, and I knew it was Christmas Day, I could only think of the folks back home, who might be eating goodies and doing the things they like. I was getting hungrier by the minute and could only think, "Boy, what a Christmas."

We found our way back to the American lines Christmas night. Being without food for thirty hours is certainly no record. But to me it was a new world, and each Christmas I think back to those days. I've had many wonderful Christmases since those days and am very thankful.

—*The* Bulge Bugle, *November 1993*

Howard Peterson
Combat Command A, 4th Armored Division

The 4th Armored Division of Patton's Third Army learned on December 21 that it was to advance north and break through to Bastogne. Howard Peterson describes the fighting that went with that task up through Christmas Eve.

197

On December 16, 1944, I was in Rheims, France, as a member of the 325th Glider Infantry Regiment, 82nd Airborne Division. On December 20, 1944, I was in Arlon, Belgium, as a rifleman replacement as part of CCA (Combat Command A) of the 4th Armored Division. "Old Blood and Guts" Patton had ordered Hugh Gaffey, commander of the 4th Armored Division, to "haul ass" up the Arlon-Bastogne road to break the encirclement of the 101st Airborne Division in Bastogne.

After a hellish ride from Rheims to Arlon in a "deuce-and-a-half" (truck), we loaded in some half-tracks and about 1600 hours started north out of Arlon on the Arlon-Bastogne road. Progress was slow, and we did not close on the blown bridge over the Sure River at Martelange until about 1300 hours on December 22. By now we had covered about twenty of the twenty-eight miles from Arlon to Bastogne. While we waited for the engineers to finish the bridge over the Sure, we had a feast when one of the guys pilfered a ten-in-one ration off one of the tanks.

I drew guard duty about 0400 hours, and because it was a bright, moonlit night, I thought I would be less of a target if I stood in the shadow of a tree. While leaning up against a small tree I could feel this lump on my back. When I moved to see what the lump was, I found out it was about ten pounds of TNT wired to the tree with primer cord so that in case of retreat the engineers could blow the trees as a form of a road-block. I chose some other place to stand to finish out my tour of guard duty.

As we were closing on Martelange in the half-tracks, we rounded a curve and climbed a slight rise. As we emerged from a cut in the road, it seemed like there were a hundred 105s (artillery pieces) on both sides of the road, and they all opened up at the same time. The sky suddenly became bright as day, and the noise was deafening. I think it was at this time that I had the first of my laundry problems. To the uninitiated, that means that I was "scared shitless."

About 0800 hours we got across the Bailey bridge over the Sure and fanned out. CCA was given the main Arlon-Bastogne road. CCB was on the left flank, using the secondary roads as its route to Bastogne. CCB was flanked on its left by the green, newly arrived 75th Infantry Division. CCA was flanked on its right by the "Blue Ridge Mountain Boys" of the 80th Infantry Division. We rode along on the backs of the Shermans. I had on my GI long johns, olive drab pants and shirt, two pairs of socks, jump boots, four-buckle overshoes, knit sweater, banana cap, helmet, tanker overalls, and extra pair of socks under each armpit, my K-bar knife, and my GI gloves. I had thrown away my gas mask. I had an ample supply of toilet paper inside my helmet, and my pickers were stuffed with K-rations, candle stubs, cigarettes, grenades, and 2 1/2-pound blocks of TNT complete with fuse to blow myself a hole in the frozen ground, if necessary. I had my good old M1 with the regulation belt load of eight clips ball and two clips armor piercing, four and one on each side; bayonet; canteen; first-aid pouch; two extra bandoliers of ammo; and three bazooka rounds.

By now it had snowed, and just about everything was hidden by this white blanket, and the temperature was at least twenty degrees below zero. As we rode on the backs of the Shermans, we stood on one foot and hung on with one hand for as long as we could stand the cold, and then we switched hand and foot and tried to get some circulation going in the hand and foot we had just used. This was made more difficult because the tank turret was being constantly traversed from right to left and left to right. The tank I was riding on and three others fanned out in the fields to the left of the main road. Suddenly the tank I was on, the lead tank, stopped, and the sergeant "volunteered" another GI and me to investigate what appeared to be a squad of German soldiers moving along in extended order. "They" turned out to be a row of fence posts, but to this day, I was sure at first that I had seen my first krauts—another laundry problem. One of the other tanks broke through a barbed wire fence, and a strand of barbed wire slapped a GI across the face, turning his face into raw hamburger. A GI wearing an unbuttoned overcoat jumped off his tank, and when the coat tails billowed out behind him, they caught in the tracks and sucked his legs into the bogie wheels of the tank.

Suddenly, the tank I was riding on stopped, and one of the other tanks fired a whole belt (over two hundred rounds) of tracer ammunition at a haystack alongside a barn about two hundred yards in front of us. No sooner did the tracers bounce off the haystack when the other two tanks opened fire and destroyed a German tank that had been trying to hide in the haystack. I guess that the tankers had learned from experience that tracers don't bounce off haystacks.

We moved forward about another twenty yards and the tank I was riding on got mired down in a small stream that had become hidden due to the heavy blanket of snow. I must have managed about fifty yards when fire from a German Nebelwerfer began falling around the stuck tank.

They assembled us foot troops back on the road (there were twenty-six of us in this one bunch), and we started north again toward Warnach, a wide spot in the road about two miles farther ahead. We walked strung out in a line in the ditch on the right-hand side of the road so we wouldn't be such good targets for those damned 88s. A little way up ahead was an American two-and-a-half-ton truck nose-down in the ditch, and it had a big, red Nazi flag with a black swastika on it across the front of the radiator. We had to climb the road embankment to get around the rear of the truck, and as I passed by the cab of the truck, I could see another good kraut sitting behind the wheel with the top of his head blown off.

About another five hundred yards up the road, we came upon three tanks surrounding a farmhouse where they had a sniper trapped. The sniper had already hit three GIs, and they said the sniper was a woman, and by the way she fired she must have an M1 with plenty of ammo. The three tanks proceeded to blow the farmhouse to a pile of rubble. I don't know if they ever got the sniper or if the sniper was a woman. Our orders were to "Get the Hell to Bastogne" so we took a break in the pig pen to get out of the cold. There were a half-dozen pigs and some sheep in this pen that measured about twenty feet square. There was also a dead pig and two dead sheep in the pen. We all smelled the same, so nobody complained or paid any attention: I mean the GIs or the pigs.

The town of Warnach was where the Germans had set up their command center. If you were passing Warnach in a car and sneezed, you would probably miss it altogether. To enter Warnach, you make a right turn off the main Arlon-Bastogne road. I was walking along behind a tank, taking full advantage of the warm air from its radiator, when suddenly I had this funny sensation in my ears and the sky turned red (it was about 0400). Then the same thing happened again. A hidden German self-propelled gun in an orchard ahead had hit the tank twice and set it on fire. I saw two GIs jump into a ditch alongside the tank and start to get one of those new folding bazookas ready to fire. They didn't have much luck, and one of them yelled, "Let's get out of here," and they jumped up and ran. I was young, but my mommy didn't raise no dummy, so I proceeded to "haul freight" too. In the process, my feet became entangled in some old chicken wire in the ditch, and when I started to run, I fell forward on my face. To this day, I don't know how I did it, but my guess is that I broke that wire with my hands.

201

As I ran back toward the Arlon-Bastogne road along a brush-filled ditch to my left, I heard somebody yell, "Hey, infantry." I hope that that tanker realizes how lucky he was that I didn't shoot him, but he told me he had a fellow tanker man whose right hand had been almost severed and was only hanging by some skin. I put the wounded tanker's left arm over my shoulder and his buddy did the same with the mangled one. We would walk three, four steps, and the wounded tanker would pass out, and we would drag him three, four steps, and he would come to and take three, four steps and pass out again. We managed to get him to a medic.

I got back to my squad, who had assembled alongside a barn, and when I got there, I saw about a dozen German prisoners standing with their hands against the side of the building. All but one of the prisoners were Wehrmacht soldiers, but the one on the right end was an SS Panzer soldier dressed in black coveralls. He was a handsome S.O.B. with a head wound and blood running down the left side of his face. None of the Wehrmacht soldiers had guts enough to turn around and ask for some gloves to cover their hands, but not the SS Panzer soldier. He turned around and in perfect English demanded gloves for his hands. A small American GI standing close by said, "I'll give you some gloves, you kraut son-of-a-bitch," and pole-axed the SS trooper. They all turned around and put their hands back on the wall. The GI with the Thompson offered to return the prisoners to a POW camp to the rear, but they wouldn't let him go because he had just gotten word that his brother had been killed in the South Pacific. Later we watched about twelve to fifteen P-47s doing their job on some German columns. They were too far away to hear, but we could sure see them plainly enough.

We were told we were going to spend the night here, and by the time I got the message, the only place I could find to lie down was at the top of the stairs. All I took off were my four-buckle overshoes, and I used my helmet for a pillow. It seemed like only a couple of minutes but was really several hours when a sergeant came running in yelling that a bunch of German paratroopers had landed to our rear. Everybody engaged in organized confusion.

It was about 0400 hours, so I sat up on the top step and started to put my overshoes on when I got the damnedest cramp in the calf of my leg that I have ever had. But being smart, I figured that by the time I got the other overshoe on, the cramp would have gone away. When I started to put the other overshoe on, I'll be damned if I didn't get a cramp in the calf of that leg. I beat on them with my fist to no avail, and they finally went away.

We were told that we were going to attack Warnach again. By the time we got started it was daylight, and this ninety-day-wonder looie lieutenant wanted someone to use the .50-caliber on top of the tank to rake the roadside and "scare the hell" out of the Germans. I was getting smarter by the minute, and I remembered the old army adage, "don't never volunteer for nothing." After about a hundred rounds, the .50 jammed, and the GI bailed down off the tank. As we turned the corner to the right, there in the middle of the road sat one of those German motorcycles with the tracks at the back (an SdKfz 2 Kleines Kettenkraftrad) as a sort of roadblock. The ninety-day "shavetail"—lieutenant—told the sergeant that he would back off a bit and then blast the motorcycle out of the way, just in case it was booby-trapped. No sooner did the tank fire than a hidden German self-propelled gun fired and set the tank on fire, but this time they were ready, and two other tanks blew the German SP gun to perdition. Suddenly, somebody yelled, and two krauts broke out of a copse of trees about two hundred yards farther down the road, where it took a sharp turn to the left. One of the German soldiers took a half-dozen steps and then retreated to the safety of the trees. The other one ran along the fence for about two hundred feet, calmly climbed over the fence just as you or I might do it today, and started to run up the road. Another twenty or twenty-five feet and he would have been safe, but all of the sudden he went about ten feet in the air, came down face first, and never moved. When the two German soldiers had broken out of the trees, we all started to fire at them—M1s, Thompsons, BARs, carbines, grease guns, and maybe a couple of .45s too.

An officer came running over and ordered two other GIs and me to search this farmhouse. As it turned out, I was the only one with any grenades left, and I had bent the pins over to make sure one of them did not come out while the grenade was in my pocket. Because of my cold hands, I couldn't get the pin out, so I tossed the grenade to one of the other GIs. He got the pin out, but as close as he was to the door, he should have lobbed it underhand, but instead he threw it overhand and missed the doorway. The grenade hit the edge of the door and bounced back into the yard. The GI yelled, "I missed the door," and took off. I knew what to do, too, so I hauled ass behind a pile of rubbish in the corner of the yard. It seemed like forever and the grenade hadn't gone off. I stuck my head up to see what was going on just as the grenade went off. I guess I was just plain lucky. I had an M1, one of the other GIs had an M1, and the third guy had a Thompson sub (machine gun). I was second through the door and emptied a full eight-round clip through the door in front of me. The other (GI with the) M1 emptied his through the door to his left, and the Thompson gunner emptied his clip up the stairway to his right, and there we three stood just like the Three Stooges.

As we stepped back out into the yard, a Sherman started to rake the side of the building with .30-caliber, starting at the eaves and working his way across the building and then down and across again. I am almost certain that I managed to hide my whole body under my helmet while the tanker was hosing down the wall of the house. Suddenly, out of nowhere a cow came around a corner of a nearby burning building, followed by an old woman who looked to be in her nineties and carrying a switch with which she was chasing the cow. The cow and then the old woman in pursuit disappeared around the other corner of the building and were gone. Where she came from I don't know, and where she went I don't know.

I got mine (i.e., wound) on Christmas Eve; had to wait over four hours to be evacuated. I was supposed to be air evacuated back to England, but the friggin' fog had come back in, so I wound up in a field hospital in Commercy, France, on Christmas Day, naked as the day I was born, with a small Red Cross package sitting on my chest.

The records show that the taking of Warnach cost America five Sherman tanks and sixty-eight GIs killed or wounded. The Germans lost 135 dead on the streets and in the houses, with a like number either wounded or taken as POWs.

—*The* Bulge Bugle, *February 1993*

Harold Horowitz
K Company, 119th Infantry Regiment, 30th Infantry Division

War can be series of close calls, as Harold Horowitz attests in his recollections of an incident during the Battle of the Bulge.

I WAS ORDERED TO THE 119TH INFANTRY DIVISION as a replacement. Curly, the BAR man, said, "Kid, stay close to me, you'll be alright."

On Christmas Eve, our company was poised to attack at dawn. My squad was out in front, moving in single file at daybreak. Two badly wounded soldiers were dragged by medics. They were outpost men, shot in the semi-darkness. As the sun came up, German artillery pounded our positions as machine gun fire raked our squad. We were pinned down behind hedge rows and dug foxholes in the hard ground. A heavy concentration of 88s, tree bursts, mortar, and cannon laid a pattern of bombs saturating the entire area miles behind the rear echelon. Sweating, I discarded my frozen overcoat in this below-freezing weather because it became too heavy and troublesome. Curly and I talked during lulls in the incoming barrage. Fifteen feet away from me, he asked to change foxholes. "I have a better field of fire from yours," he said.

"I dug this. I'd rather not!"

Hours later Curly received a direct hit by a mortar shell and was blown to unrecognizable pieces.

At night we advanced to a farm house; it was pitch black inside, and I stumbled over a dead cow. Searching the basement, we took prisoner the two Germans who had fired the machine guns. Moving ahead, the next few days we passed many German frozen corpses, left where they fell.

Eventually I was evacuated with frozen feet.

Americans can be proud of the combat soldier. He put aside his fears and courageously faced his worst nightmare.

—*The* Bulge Bugle, *February 1993*

George Sperl
F Company, 290th Infantry Regiment, 75th Infantry Division

Christmas Day would be the first day of combat for George Sperl of the 75th Infantry Division during the Battle of the Bulge, and much to his surprise, he survived it.

WE SPENT ABOUT A WEEK IN THE COUNTRY just outside of Rouen, France, when suddenly we were told to stack our duffle bags and take only our bedrolls and light packs as we boarded 6x6 trucks to go to a railroad station.

No one knew where we were going, but we figured it was somewhere toward the front. I remember on the forty and eights (French railroad boxcars) looking out at night and seeing a buzz bomb going off overhead. Along the way, French or Belgian civilians would give us bottles of wine, and we gave them chocolate and cigarettes from our D-rations. When we reached our destination (probably somewhere in Belgium), we again got on 6x6s and took off in the middle of the night. Those drivers went like a bat out of hell through small villages, et cetera. About dawn we got off the trucks in what must have been an artillery emplacement. We still didn't know about the Bulge or where we were. That night, I was one to four guys picked up by our sergeant (I believe his name was Olds) to go out on patrol. Needless to say, we were all scared as hell, but we returned without incident.

Later, we were told to get ready to move out. We hiked along roads for quite some distance and came to some farm buildings. We were told to go up in the barn and get some sleep on the hay. Near daybreak, the kitchen crew caught up with us and gave us a warm breakfast. We moved out along a road at sunrise on what turned out to be a clear, sunny Christmas Day. We still didn't know our mission but later found out we were to retake some high ground that another company in our division had taken the day before but got overrun that night by a German counterattack.

After going about a mile, spread out on either side of the road, we saw our first dead German soldier. He was lying in the road at an intersection holding a machine gun in firing position. Behind him was a small antitank gun. At that instant I believe we all realized we must be very near the front, and it could very easily be one of us instead of that enemy lying there. We moved slowly most of the day until afternoon, when we left the road and moved across a pasture with a few trees on it. Suddenly, we heard 88s coming overhead and exploding behind us. I crouched next to a large log as something hit my backpack, but it was only a piece of wood from a tree. I recited what little I could remember of the Twenty-third Psalm.

We moved up to a road where there was a 6x6 parked on the road with a single bullet hole in the middle of the driver-side door. We crouched in the ditch next to the road with a plowed field ahead of us on a gradual upslope toward a woods at the top. Our sergeant spread the word down the line that when the captain blew his whistle, we were all supposed to rush up the hill, firing like hell. This seemed more like a Civil War tactic, but we did it with bullets snapping past our heads. I believe none of us ever thought any of us would get to the woods. After covering about a quarter of the way, I saw one of our guys fall. Later, I found out he got hit in the elbow. (I believe his last name was Black, and he always talked about wanting to be a boxer.) About halfway to the woods, I saw some movement, and as I got closer it turned out to be one of the GIs from the previous day's assault who was wounded and lay there all night. I assured him the medics would be there soon, as we had to press on. Incredibly, when we got to the woods, the firing ceased, and we all looked at each other in disbelief at how we got up the slope. Only one other guy was hit—a flesh wound in the calf of his leg. One of the guys in our company was showing off a Luger that he took off a German officer after he shot him.

I have often puzzled about why a few German soldiers with automatic weapons could not have mowed us all down as we advanced up the hill. The only explanation I can figure is that by Christmas Day their drive had stalled, and perhaps their defense was getting stretched, not to mention that they were experiencing supply problems and were rationing ammo, although that didn't seem to be the case when we were charging up the hill.

So that was our baptism of fire, and we were all quite relieved that we had accomplished our mission in good shape.

—*The* Bulge Bugle, *May 1999*

4 | CLOSING THE BULGE

Al A. Alvarez
C Company, 16th Infantry Regiment, 1st Infantry Division

The Allied commanders had from the very first agreed that once the German Ardennes Offensive had run its course, they wanted to seize the initiative, erase the enemy salient, and set an offensive in motion to cross the Rhine River. Al Alvarez talks about his unit's response to the German attack.

"RECON, YOU FIND 'EM; ENGINEERS, YOU FIX 'EM; tanks, you fight 'em; and tank destroyers, you finish 'em!" With these emphatic but crystal-clear adjurations, Lt. Col. Henry L. Davisson set the tempo for his task force subordinate commanders. It was December 16, 1944, and the yet-to-be-named Ardennes Offensive had exploded. The krauts' massive tank penetration now was creating the northern shoulder of what was to acquire the sobriquet the Battle of the Bulge.

In response, hastily thrown-together units from the vaunted 1st Infantry Division, "The Big Red One," would acquire their title from the aggressive commander of the 634th Tank Destroyer Battalion Lt. Col. Henry L. Davisson. Task Force Davisson (TFD) was thus quickly formed as a lightly armored, tank-killing reaction force. Major Olson, the TFD S3 (operations officer), designated the line of march and handed out strip maps for a southward reconnaissance.

Our armored convoy consisted of the 1st Recon Troop heading out with puny 37mm-armed M8 Greyhound armored cars. Intermingled came the 1st Combat Engineer Battalion's A Company, riding its soft-skinned vehicles. Now came D Company of the 745th Tank Battalion with its measly light tanks, armed also with 37mm guns, but backed up by its 75mm assault gun platoon. Spread out and looking for targets, C Company of the 634th Tank Destroyer Battalion came with their 90mm guns, claiming the ability to compete with German armor. All were ably supported by "the King of the Battlefield," our four-man forward observer Charlie artillery observation party (with the commo [radio communications] capability to call down division artillery and corps artillery barrages, or "serenades").

Our battery veterans of the "Lucky 7th" Artillery Battalion, who had fought German armor in Tunisia, Algeria, the beach at Sicily, and in the fields of Normandy, spoke out in warning to our little observer party: "Be ready. This TF Davisson is outgunned by the huge Panthers and King Tiger monsters reported coming your way. Remember, your tank-destroying force needs to equal or outgun those battle-tested German behemoths and also mount sufficient armor to protect themselves from the superior German antitank weapons. In other words, you better be killer tanks rather than tank killers. If not, you will have to stop 'em with indirect 105mm or 155mm artillery concentrations."

Despite these knowledgeable words, we heard only the spurrings of Colonel Davisson. Quickly, the TFD saddled up and cautiously commenced traveling south through snowy Belgium. The lengthy convoy slid out of Sourbrodt and Robertville and clanked into Walk and Waimes, small villages recently vacated by U.S. Army medical units.

The weather was frigid cold and damp, but the fog was dissipating, and for once, artillery would have wonderfully clear observation! Here we were, the Lucky 7th's forward observation party, on high ground, salivating at the abundance of lucrative targets! Spotting from our town's church steeple with our twenty-power scopes, we saw German convoys, to include tanks, traveling west across our front from (artillery coordinates) 863-020 to 863-024—an artilleryman's dream. Compounding our good fortune, our battalion had recently been supplied with the previously secretive ammo employing the proximity fuse constructed around its nose plug, which activated when the emitted radio beam encountered an object within fifteen yards. We were going to have the proverbial field day . . . and we deserved it!

Our parent organization, the "Fighting First" Infantry Division, was still recuperating from its horrific bloodletting in "the Hurtin' Forest" this past November, where the krauts had grounded us into the Hürtgen Forest and past. Surely now was to be payback time, but the war gods frowned and said no, not yet.

The American artillery ammunition supplies across the entire First Army front were dangerously low, contriving to place quotas on all "shoots." Our radio pleas to the fire-direction center for fire missions received a "wait out." Our frantic telephone messages informed us their priority was to our east. There, our sister regiment, the 26th Infantry Regiment "Blue Spaders," were in continuous battle with German armored thrust at Büllingen and Bütgenbach. There, Lt. Col. Derrill M. Daniel and his 2nd Battalion would successfully blunt the German Colonel Peiper's rampaging westward drive and dream. That portion of the northern shoulder would remain firm.

So now it was to be our turn. The German 1st SS Panzers Division, frantically searching for a route on the *rollbahnen* (highways) to the west, then side-slipped and proceeded to smash at us. Task Force Davisson now intermixed with 3rd Battalion, 16th Infantry Regiment, at Weimes. Our front erupted with tank fire and reported infantry advancing, plus intensified artillery fire in our immediate front. Our first indication was a flying buzz bomb smashing into the battery area and wounding three gunners: Cpl. Homer A. Jerome, Technician 5th Class Raymond A. Fink, and Pfc. Erlo Baton. We were further alerted by a commotion reported on our eastern outpost, which luckily forewarned everyone in town. Speeding down the only street in Weimes came two GI Jeeps overly loaded with krauts. Firing madly and careening widely to escape our firing-gallery response, they crashed off the road on the west side of the village.

Colonel Davisson then ordered, "Recon, send a squad to investigate and recover bodies and/or the vehicles!" Lieutenant Cangelosi, our forward observer, took over the viewing scopes from our lofty OP as the submachine-armed Recon Squad gingerly approached the overturned vehicles. They sprayed the area, righted a Jeep, and returned with a WIA (wounded in action) spread-eagled on the hood. Another German captive was shoved into the copilot's seat, hands on his head. Arriving at the town square, now crowded with a rubbernecking GI throng, the Jerry prisoners held center stage. Looking like a "Right out of Hollywood" with his peaked hat and black leather topcoat and gloves, in excellent English, a captured German officer demanded medical attention for his men. In response, someone in the crowd belted him with a rifle butt. He was saved further harm by the NCOs, who held back the provoked soldiers. It appeared that in breaking through our outpost, the Germans had hailed in English then fired and killed and wounded the surprised guards. These angry crowd members were old-time buddies of the soldier killed by this *ruse de guerre*.

Later, with his head now bandaged, the German officer was carted off to the 16th Infantry Regiment's S2 (intelligence officer). Subsequent interrogation divulged he was an officer-courier transporting the photographic proof of this explosive and successful German penetration through the American lines. The following day, angered regimental staff members descended and oversaw a search of the snowy Jeep-accident area and found this valuable film. These important photos, immediately developed at the rear headquarters, received prominent world attention as the classic "Bulge" combat film, showing smiling German paratroopers as "successful warriors in action."

With our shooting priority reestablished and our observation still A-OK, our artillery observer party initiated fire missions with visibly outstanding results. Lieutenant Anthony Cangelosi, our latest FO, who would break the bad-luck cycle of officer casualties and proceed to make it to the war's end in Czechoslovakia, took targets under fire. First, we fired on enemy troops forming for attack, then followed a mission on enemy vehicles. Finally, we observed for a divisional artillery TOT (time on target) on an enemy assembly area. With the horizon ablaze, we continued with harassing fires throughout the night. Corporal Maurice Vacher was our instrument corporal, who would be promoted and get the Purple Heart the following week. He would return, bandaged, with three new stripes and stories of great chow in the medical rear. I, now a Tech 5 (corporal's pay without the authority) and my cohort, Tech 5 René Coté, our dependable driver, rounded out our crew. At first light, all of us, now professionals after six months on the combat scene, poured destruction on the advancing white-painted enemy armor and accompanying white-clad infantry. After four missions and 275 rounds expended, we reported "enemy activity ceased and one tank burning."

Later, during a slow afternoon, Capt. Fred F. Chirigotis, from the 745th Tank Battalion, asked us to observe for indirect fire so they could "use up" their 75mm ammo. With a total expenditure, their tanks would be able to acquire new 76mm tubes. Jumping at the chance, I got some invaluable and exhilarating shooting experience and contributed some damage, too!

During another quiet period, on Coté's watch, he asked, "What the hell are those guys doing?" An engineering squad seemed to be laying a hasty minefield in the road leading south into the town of Faymonville. Apparently these engineers must have been short of mines because the engineering sergeant had his squad scrounge up dinner plates from the nearby Belgian homes. His squad, laden with this ample supply of dishes, was pacing off the distances and placing plates face down on the road and adjoining fields. This sight piqued our interest. "Look at him now. He's putting some real mines amongst those kitchen plates!" Finally, the squad members covered these actual metallic mines with large, porcelain dinner platters "Very clever, these Americans! Those porcelain covers will inhibit the mine metallic detectors." Later that afternoon, as it snowed, our forward area was dimpled with the ingenious defensive preparation.

German counterfire reintensified and seemed to be directed at our high ground and steeple, so we moved into town to the second floor of the town hall or barroom. Kaboom! The biggest tank you ever saw blew our Jeep to kingdom come. No one was hurt, but we sure were happy we had gone to church the previous Sunday! We countered with "purple smoke," our air-strike marking rounds, as FDC insisted that there were "no aircraft available." A couple of more rounds that landed first, then whistled after, and whew, he backed out of view somewhere back into Faymonville. The troops were understandably quiet as we hurriedly plastered the town with high-explosive shells and white phosphorus and set numerous fires, everyone privately hoping he was through with us good guys.

Our chief of detail and my boss Staff Sgt. Joseph Desforge and Motor Sgt. "Shorty" Hofer came up during darkness with a replacement Jeep. Besides replacing our food and bringing extra radio batteries, they told us we were stopping an enemy armored attack on the northern shoulder of something called "the Battle of the Bulge." After that illuminating information, we settled back in but encountered some new problems. Our "posit" rounds were exploding at their maximum ordinate as premature bursts over our heads. Apparently, the sensitive fuses were set off by clouds! As if that was not enough, Sergeant Ringer's howitzer, back in the firing battery area, had a muzzle burst, and the gun was destroyed, but luckily with no gunner casualties. Probably the intense cold on the metal tube and the sudden heat of the morning firing caused it. My remembrance of this December is the bitter cold, with all the troops occupied with ways of keeping warm. The approved method was putting on layers of any clothing. Many brainy GIs wrapped blanket strips over straw around their boots and created an incredibly large footprint in the snow— anything for insulation to stave off trench foot while occupying their foxholes.

During our lengthy and boring time on watch, someone mentioned, "Today's Christmas! This'll make our third Christmas overseas for our 'Lucky 7th' Artillery Battalion." Coté reminisced about Christmas 1942 in Africa and on the moors in England on Christmas of 1943. Lieutenant Cangelosi celebrated by knocking out a machine gun position at 864-013 with two direct hits. The doughs cheered and waved their arms and weapons, stamping their cold feet, too, in their exposed foxholes. Afterward, when I sneaked down to the chow line in an adjoining cellar, the cooks told us "Boomers" (artillery observers), "You're doing a bang-up job." But more importantly, they slipped me an extra helping of meat and potatoes.

From Christmas to New Year's, it was just continuous fire at enemy troops in the open and enemy tanks. Our records show we averaged over 1,800 rounds per day during the last days of December 1944. This wall of steel both harassed and hampered the enemy's efforts to exploit and enlarge his armored thrust. Our uninterrupted night defensive fires, requested by our supported 16th Infantry Regiment, commenced with the coming of darkness and carried over until daybreak. Even so, another strong tank counterattack was repulsed in the vicinity of 053-013 (railroad tracks near Steinback, Belgium) by the direct fire of the 634th Tank Destroyer Battalion and 74th Tank Battalion. The blackened hulks of destroyed German tanks stood out against the snow. The bodies of German infantry were not as easily discerned.

New Year's Day opened with hordes of German aircraft strafing our positions. As usual, the poor, bloody infantry suffered the casualties, and as always, it was the new replacements. We boomers hid in our cellar as the bomb explosions rattled around us, watching the lieutenant celebrate by drinking his liquor ration as we underaged peons looked on.

Rumors were now flying that we would attack Faymonville the first week of January 1945. So we took under fire all possible enemy positions in the town. Methodically, we increased the destruction by dropping HE rounds through the roofs, then followed up with WP to burn the houses. Most of them, however, were constructed of stone and resisted all our bombardments. Still, slowly, Faymonville was now systematically pulverized.

During that first week of January, we carefully, in conjunction with the mortars, fired in support of a patrol attempting to retrieve the body of Lieutenant McLaughlin of L Company, killed in action days previously.

Lieutenant Cangelosi "had the word" (ordering another attack) and got us ready by checking our equipment, clothing, and footwear. "I want constant commo while on the attack," he said, adding, "The infantry is going to get us on high ground every chance they can and protect us, too." That's good, but for me, first I must get and be warm. Layering of clothing was the answer. So it was long underwear, shirts, jackets, many trousers, ponchos, wrapped blanket strips over straw, and joining the "monster footprint brigade." With a French foreign legion "kepi" look, I covered my helmet with a white pillow slip with a flap covering my neck. Then I enclosed myself in a white bed sheet, a snow cape, and emerged through the slit for my head. Finally, I connected up the radio and set it on a German wooden sled with a fifty-foot on/off switch for the lieutenant's use. We were "ready for Freddy." I threw some cardboard ammo cartons filled with coffee, sugar, and cans of cream on the sled and loaded my pockets with goodies.

Now, as the last preparation, I ate everything I could of rations: crackers, cheese, meat and beans, cocoa, sugar, candy—anything for energy. "Now bring on those krauts. I'm warm, full, and have dry feet. I can shoot, scoot, and communicate!"

On January 14, 1945, with heavy snow falling, the 16th Infantry Regiment's 3rd Battalion, commanded by Lt. Col. Charles T. Homer, commingled with portions of TF Davisson's tanks, assaulted Faymonville. We (with me pulling the radio sled) accompanied I Company and then later L Company. As we slowly trudged into the northeast portion of Faymonville, mines in the snow took out some of the A Company, 745th, tanks, but the doughs continued despite incoming mortars. The first reports were twelve KIA and fifteen MIA (missing in action) for our 3rd Battalion. We stopped at nightfall and ran a line to the nearest company to hear reports of seventy casualties for the 3rd Battalion. We fired harassing missions and kept everyone awake.

The next morning dawned crisp and sunny, and Lieutenant Cangelosi returned from battalion briefing. We are going to take Schoppen, the next town to the southeast. "Let's move it!" Trudging again through the snow, we encountered some woods where MG fire erupted. Lieutenant Cangelosi quieted it with an HE concentration. We held up in these woods with no fires, no hot chow, and tried stomping our feet all night to stay warm. Only good thing was a can of sliced peaches (kept warm in my armpit) for breakfast from my food stash.

The following day, January 15, we accompanied the 3rd Battalion's L Company, which seemed to be in reserve, since we stepped in the footprints of the lead company. The snow was knee deep, and it was snowing fiercely, with drifts piling up. Someone passed the word down the line, "We are in a blizzard!" Observation was impossible—we could not see anything, but better still, the Germans could not see us. My day consisted of struggling through the snow, laying a line back on the road, finally meeting our artillery liaison wire crew, and then splicing the line with frozen fingers and hearing the two parties conversing. We tried bumming rides on the only vehicles moving, Weasels, some type of a lightweight, covered, tracked vehicle. They seemed to be ambulances, carrying WIA and flying their Red Cross flags. Everyone on the road now piled on a tank dozer for a slippery, dangerous ride back, and I followed my line back into a house. Thank God, the troops had fired up a stove, and it was crowded and cozy. While Lieutenant Cangelosi and Sergeant Vacher observed upstairs, I dried up and tried heating my radio batteries on the stove to restore their strength: "Eureka, I think it works!"

The artillery liaison bunch gave me the bad news that "Jonsey," A Battery radioman, was KIAed when we hit Faymonville. The word was he was hit by a sniper. We were losing a lot of doughs, but they were strangers to me. Jonsey was an artillery buddy. I had just returned a quarter-mile reel of commo wire I'd borrowed from him.

We continued through the snow at the proverbial snail's pace, the doughs plodding through snowdrifts, the tanks sliding and slipping off the roads. I noticed some troops had wrapped barbed wire around their boots for traction; they claimed it worked. My salvation was my sled and wrapped boots. The lieutenant was pleased with his constant commo as I dragged the sled. The troops were pleased with his instantaneous fire mission at any obstacle, seen or unseen. I was pleased with my available food on the sled!

We entered Moderscheid and fired normal missions on enemy troops, and then, strangely, we gave them four missions of propaganda shells! We continued with 13 missions on enemy troops at command posts and observation posts with approximately seventy hits on houses containing troops, with resulting fires. Then we continued with harassing fires throughout the night—nobody sleeps!

The next morning—don't know the date—we commenced preparation fires prior to forward displacement, meaning "move out and drag the sled!" It seemed to be getting lighter in weight—probably from my eating the rations and throwing away the used batteries.

Great news! The 16th Infantry was squeezed out of the advance by the 18th Infantry Regiment, so for us, immediate support became general support, and another team took over. We were lucky—the food just about ran out! Sergeant Vacher quartered us in a large barn, while Lieutenant Cangelosi checked with 3rd Battalion for "hot scoop." We cleaned up the equipment, gassed up the Jeep, set up a stove, and cooked some liberated food!

We were in heaven: no observation duties, in a warm barn, bellies full, just radio watch and waiting for the lieutenant to take us home . . . kaboom! A round came through an opening in the front wall and out the back wall—with a startling, crackling explosion that showered us with debris. Straw flew everywhere, and we were covered with shards of wood, powdered stone, and animal droppings! No one was physically hurt, but someone had to change his laundry. We moved next door to another barn, smaller, but with stone walls.

It was January 31, and we were pulling radio watch only while putting in land lines to artillery liaison. Listening on the artillery net, we heard a rare command given to the guns: "Battery C continuous fire to the right at five-second intervals with a converged sheath," for an expenditure of forty-five rounds at the same target. Contact by telephone to my old buddies at artillery battalion tactical operations center disclosed that a subsequent 18th Infantry Regiment patrol reported a German battery of six 150mm guns abandoned their positions and guns at the coordinates of that strange concentration!

It was the beginning of February. The sun came out, and it seemed that Task Force Davisson, having halted, then chased the Germans out of Belgium, simply faded away with the spring thaw!

Bob Hagel
L Company, 320th Infantry Regiment, 35th Division

The top Allied commanders decided on December 25 that the German advance in the Ardennes had lost its momentum and that it was now time to lash back at the attackers. Bob Hagel recalls his small role in pushing the Germans out of the Ardennes.

THE 35TH DIVISION WAS PART OF Patton's Third Army and was en route to Luxembourg to fight in what was known as "the Bulge."

We departed Metz early in the morning of December 26 by truck and traveled all day in the rain and cold until sometime after dark, when we were finally able to bed down in an old barn. We were awakened in the early morning by an artillery barrage (our own), and after a hasty breakfast we departed for the front line, passing through several badly shelled towns, one of which was Bigonville, Luxembourg. That was the last time we had a warm meal or slept in anything other than a foxhole for the next ten days. The weather turned colder, and it started to snow. L Company was held in reserve the first day but then moved up into the line. The 35th Division's job was to keep the road from Arlon to Bastogne open so the Third Army and supplies could continue to flow north. We found out later that we were facing the infamous 1st SS Panzer Division, and their orders were to cut the supply road no matter what the cost.

We probably didn't move more than a mile or so in the next ten days. Every day was almost the same. Around 2 p.m. we would attack the enemy position, push them out with small-arms and mortar fire, dig in, fight off counterattacks, care for and ferry back our wounded, and bring up supplies. We were fighting in heavy pine forests and mountainous terrain with no roads. Everything had to be moved either by carrying it or pulling it on sleds that we had found in towns along the way.

At night the temperature would drop to near or below zero degrees. The only food we had was K-rations that we tried to warm by burning cardboard boxes during the day. We wore every piece of clothing we could find. Many men had their feet frozen because of the shortage of galoshes or winter boots. Our blankets froze and looked like plywood. When you would climb out of your foxhole in the mornings, you would find two to six inches of snow.

To make matters worse, there was a lot of confusion. At times we would lose contact with our sister companies on our flanks. Several times we were told we were surrounded, which made it tough trying to get our wounded back and our supplies up to us. Another thing that had to add to the confusion was the number of new replacements in L Company. I believe the figure had to be about 30 percent when we moved into the lines. I'm sure the veterans worried about us as much as the enemy. Needless to say, it wasn't easy. I was told later, after the war ended, that L Company lost over one hundred men, either killed or wounded, from December 27, 1944, until they were pulled out of the line on January 8, 1945.

Because of the forest and terrain, we were fortunate that we had very little contact with enemy tanks and not much in the way of heavy artillery. We had very little support from our own artillery, probably because of the confusion I mentioned earlier and the fact that we were within fifty yards of the enemy most of the time. We could hear them talk and dig their holes when it got quiet at night and could even hear their wounded moaning.

Even though I had never fired a bazooka in basic training because of a bad right eye, I was told to carry one after the former bazooka man was killed. . . . I then became attached to the light machine gun section, where my duties were, as mentioned before, helping carry the wounded back and going for supplies. My rifleman buddies accused me of being "rear echelon."

The busiest people at this time were the medics. There was not a lot of heavy fighting, but it was constant, and there were casualties every day. You can imagine that if we lost over one hundred men in two weeks, the medics had to be overworked. That, plus not being able to get a vehicle within a mile of the front line, didn't help. Granted, there were some wounded with minor injuries and able to walk back themselves, but when a man was seriously wounded, a medic had to help get him back to the aid station and then return to help another.

On January 6, I had been talking to the machine gun crew and then returned to my foxhole about twenty feet in the rear. Five minutes later a shot was fired, hitting the gunner in the head, killing him. We immediately got back in our holes and started digging them deeper. A few minutes later, I was shot through the shoulder and chest by the same sniper, was knocked down, and passed out. When I regained consciousness a while later, I was told by those in the hole with me that they were unable to get me out because one of the two medics that had come up to get me was shot through the red cross on his helmet and killed. Another man had been shot through the neck. He eventually recovered.

It was an hour later before the company commander came up with the second medic and some help to get me out of the hole, onto the stretcher, and carried back to safety. I was taken by sled, Jeep, and ambulance to the aid station and field hospital, where I was operated on. Eventually I ended up in England for treatment and rehabilitation.

I was the lucky one. I had the million-dollar wound, which got me out of the fighting but didn't cripple or disable me. I'll never forget the medics or the machine gunner, even though I never knew their names. I also felt sorry for the ones that never got touched but had to fight on for months, not knowing if and when it would happen. They were the heroes.

—*The* Bulge Bugle, *February 1992*

Luis R. Rodriguez
C Battery, 240th Field Artillery Battalion

Throughout the Battle of the Bulge, American artillery played a pivotal role in defeating the German Ardennes Offensive. Luis Rodriguez recalls the conditions in which the artillerymen in the battle served under.

I SERVED IN C BATTERY, 240TH FIELD ARTILLERY BATTALION, as a cannoneer with 155mm guns, oftentimes referred to as "Long Toms." We were in the area of Stolburg, Germany, and preparing to move to Düren, Germany, when we got word of the German offensive. On the night of December 23, we made our move to assist in the Battle of the Bulge, arriving in the early hours of December 24 in the town of Stavelot, Belgium. We set up our guns and fired 4,051 rounds of ammo in the first ten days in support of the 82nd Airborne Division, attached to the XVIII Airborne Corps.

Our guns had fired many rounds of ammo, having gone into combat on August 18 in the Falaise Gap in France, so a rush was executed to supply us with new gun barrels or tubes. It was a one-day operation, so by evening we were back into action again. I will have to say that as artillerymen, we did not have the discomforts that our frontline troops experienced, but the cold was equal. We had poor winter clothing, especially sleeping bags. I made a sleeping bag out of two GI blankets plus two civilian blankets wrapped with a piece of tent material. This worked out quite well.

The extreme cold weather raised problems with our guns. It would freeze the hydraulic oil in the rams that assisted in the raising and lowering of the barrel plus also the recoil mechanism. One time we had only one gun operable, so twenty-four rounds of ammo were fired with the one gun, all in rapid fire. I will mention that we painted our guns with powdered milk to blend in with the snow. After all this firing, the barrel was brown in color from overheating. A short time later this same gun blew up, scattering pieces for one-half mile.

—*The* Bulge Bugle, *February 1992*

George Nicklin
K Company, 47th Infantry Regiment, 9th Infantry Division

One of the special operations conducted by the Germans during the Battle of the Bulge involved dropping paratroopers behind the American front lines on December 16 to seize some ground to help the Sixth Panzer Army advance. George Nicklin was a medic during the Battle of the Bulge.

I WAS A COMBAT MEDIC DURING World War II. I had just started my pre-med studies at the time of my drafting and had completed a single term. I was "asked," after two months of regular infantry combat, to accept transfer to combat medic status. Medics were in constant short supply, as they have the highest infantry casualty rate of any frontline soldier. Needless to say, I was not particularly happy with this request, as I had been surviving quite well as a 60mm mortar gunner. I had even achieved a degree of fame for my accuracy, which was the reason behind my company commander's obstruction of my transfer. On December 16, the beginning of the Battle of the Bulge, he could no longer do this. So, after months as a regular infantryman on the front lines, fighting near Aachen, Germany, I was transferred to the 9th Infantry Division, 47th Regimental Surgeon's Unit, commanded by Maj. Donald Roberts, for a three-day first aid course.

As the Battle of the Bulge was beginning, the regimental aid station was quartered in the Ardennes Forest, in a commandeered house. We were transported in trucks to the area, which had been overrun by the Germans. The 9th Infantry Division had been rushed into the northern corner of the Bulge with instructions to hold the corner and not permit any further falling back. The positions we entered were "empty" 99th Infantry Division positions, which had been "emptied" by either casualty or surrender when the Germans initially overran the area.

I soon learned that we would be very busy in the aid station treating German paratroopers who had inadvertently been shot or wounded either during the drop or after capture. Wounded prisoners were then brought to the regimental aid station for treatment. Usually they had been shot in fighting prior to capture; occasionally, one would be shot accidentally after capture. Thus, in the beginning of my medical career, all my patients were Germans!

I discovered that U.S. military intelligence was ecstatic about the paratroop drop, as the first two prisoners they captured were the German colonel in charge and his aide-de-camp. They carried with them several shoe boxes of index cards that listed the names of all the men in the drop. This made it possible for us to check off prisoners as we killed, wounded, or captured them, thereby giving us an excellent idea of what percentage were still at large. In a few days, most of the German drop was eliminated as effective soldiers.

Because of the activity in the aid station, my three-day first aid course was extended until two days past Christmas. During this extended time, I saw an interesting set of American casualties: they had come to the Aid Station complaining of blindness. The story eventually unfolded that we captured German V1 "buzz bomb" launching platforms. With them were large drums of a clear liquid labeled "Alcohol." Unfortunately, this was *wood* alcohol, not grain alcohol. Wood alcohol breaks down into formaldehyde when it enters the body, attacking the optic nerve initially and then the brain itself. The troops who drank the wood alcohol—usually with cans of grapefruit juice—would find themselves initially afflicted with blindness. They would then often die from the attack of the formaldehyde on the brain structures.

So, to my amazement, I did not see many Americans wounded, but I did see a fair number of American casualties. At the end of ten or eleven days, during which I had an extremely pleasant Christmas (with turkey!), I was transferred back to K Company, 2nd Platoon. We were located in the lovely town of Kalterherberg.

In late December the front line of the Bulge had been stabilized, and the Germans were being pushed back. Kalterherberg was a beautiful, tiny town of pastel-colored houses with three-feet-thick concrete walls. They were ideal for maintenance of our defense. All of the villagers had been evacuated from the town—by either the Germans or the Allies—and we were using the houses in the town as our defense points. We had also stationed units in the fields to the east, our outpost should another German attack occur. I especially remember the beautiful Catholic church, which had been left with all its doors standing open. It seemed to be in excellent condition despite the snow that had drifted in onto the floor. There was an amazing spiritual stillness as I walked into the church, and I sensed that even under these terrible conditions, there was a presence of the Divine Spirit on this, the front line.

I remember two prominent characteristics about Kalterherberg: One of them was the unlimited supply of beef. We had steak almost every day when we were living in the houses because of the cattle that had been killed in the fields surrounding the town. They had of course been frozen due to the cold weather. The other prominent characteristic was the highly beneficial fighting. We would send combat teams, usually of platoon size, to attack German outposts. I was a participant in one such team—I was the medic. We had about eighteen or twenty men in the unit and succeeded in killing or wounding about twenty Germans and capturing another twenty, with only one minor casualty. This was a source of great jubilation. The general came down from division headquarters and immediately presented Lt. Donald Ingram and the platoon sergeant, Steven Milotich (who had led the attack), with Bronze Stars. I also noticed about two or three weeks later that we were mentioned in *Stars and Stripes* under "Attack Activity"!

—*The* Bulge Bugle, *February 1991*

John E. McAuliffe
M Company, 347th Infantry Regiment, 87th Infantry Division

The 87th Infantry Division arrived in Western Europe in early December and was briefly employed as part of the Third Army before being transferred to the First Army. John McAuliffe describes his time in the fighting.

I ARRIVED IN FRANCE AS A REPLACEMENT without an overcoat (stolen), blanket (misplaced), or helmet. I was an ill-equipped soldier expected to fill in the gap in the battle line. Fortunately, I was refitted at the replacement depot and ready to join my new outfit, M Company, 347th Infantry.

After the commanding officer, Capt. Green "Big Jake" Keltner, briefed us in a barn, the platoon sergeant took four of us out into the snow-filled woods and told Sgt. Joe Kelly of the first mortar section to select two men. He said, "I'll take Manley and McAuliffe," and then pointed to the ground and said, "Okay, there's your hole." Luckily, we were spared the task of digging that one, as the ground was brick hard. My first night of standing guard was a cold one and lonely, as I stood under the snow-laden firs and was told to be on the alert for German patrols with dogs. We were along the Sauer River.

A couple of nights later we moved up into a log hut with a makeshift stove, probably built by the Germans earlier. This was better than sleeping on the ground. It didn't last, though, as the division soon made a mass move to the Saint-Vith area by truck convoy to relieve the 17th Airborne Division beyond Watternal, Belgium. The names of these towns and units were unknown to me at the time, and it was only years later upon reading the division history that I was able to put the pieces together. Being in the 81mm mortars, we did not always see the enemy, and upon asking what we were shooting at on one occasion, the sergeant growled, "Never mind that, Mac, just attend to your job." Likewise, I envied our platoon leader, Lt. Ray Erickson, because he carried maps of the immediate area, and I was always curious as to our position and that of the enemy, and just what our location was. But like so many things in the army, we weren't supposed to know everything but just take care of our job at hand.

As we boarded the trucks for the trip to the Saint-Vith area, I purposely sat on the rear, hoping to catch a good look at the countryside. I didn't realize the others were vying for seats behind the cab to be more out of the cold and perhaps for protection. A slightly built, fair-skinned lad placed his kit containing his razor and some personal belongings under my seat by my feet and entrusted them to my care. Did I look that confident and secure?

The convoy moved out, and we stopped for nothing. Being on the tailgate, I was the one who emptied the urine from the steel helmets that were passed down. Along the way I saw many wrecked vehicles, disabled tanks, and strewn equipment: the ravages of the initial German breakthrough.

Houses were bombed out and gutted, and the countryside was a very bleak sight and covered by deep snow. We passed through a little town and two hours later I saw the same scene again. The driver lost the convoy, and we were riding in circles. After eighteen hours of cold trucking, we got to our destination only to find the kitchen closed, and we had no supper. Tired from the long trip, I completely forgot about the kit, and that kid gave me hell for not minding it. Why he didn't choose to hold onto it himself, I'll never know. It was like he lost his only possession. I never saw him after that.

As we walked along the road among some displaced villagers, I tried my high school French on them. It was bad and didn't work anyway: they were Belgians.

That night our platoon slept in a small country Catholic church. The pews had all been removed, and the men spread out on the floor with their gear. I was a religious person, and having attended strict Catholic schools, my first impression was that we were desecrating the sanctity of the church. But those notions were quickly dispelled by the graveness of our situation, and my mind turned to prayer. I remember ascending the three steps to the altar where the relics are kept, on which the sacred chalice and host are placed during mass. I put my hand over the spot and prayed for our protection and then found a place to lie down on the floor.

The next day was typically cold and bleak, and we were out on the road again. We came to a bend in the road where five GIs lay dead off to the side, one body propped against a wall. It was then the shells started to come in, bursting all around us. Black soot settled on us, and the acrid smoke filled our nostrils. It was like that spot was a chosen target for the German 88s. I was scared; the invoking of God's name came easily. We pressed onward and again were hit up the road a bit. I slipped and fell three times on the icy roads under my heavy equipment. No one helped me up; all were hustling toward the protection of a group of houses up ahead in the evening darkness. We took comfort in the seclusion afforded by that small compound of houses. In looking for our platoon OP, I ran smack into the muzzle end of an M1 pointed from a darkened doorway. I was challenged; I was lost, and I returned to my squad room. Those guys in the OP never did get their evening rations.

Up near Manderfeld we came to the edge of the forest, and a lieutenant was sending the men out across a clearing at spaced intervals. As I came up to him, he looked me over and said, "That's too much!" meaning too much to be carrying. Besides my regular gear, I was carrying forty-two pounds of HE-light mortar bombs. I said nothing, and he said, "OK. Go now." About one hundred yards out, several rounds of 88mm shells burst near me, and I fell face down in knee-deep snow. The shelling was scary enough, but my next concern was getting myself up from under the weight I was carrying and from the deep snow. I weighed only 154 pounds, and all the gear and ammo must have come close to 80 pounds.

On the other side of the clearing in the forest, shelling started pouring in again. This time it was the devastating tree bursts, and the shrapnel was scattering every which way. A fellow named Huber from Baltimore and I took cover under a fallen fir tree. When we came out, there was a guy sitting on the log holding his blown-up knee. I looked around for help and hollered, "Where is everyone?" Someone yelled, "They're down in the bunker." I asked, "What bunker?" Behind a camouflaged mount, I found the stairs leading down inside. This was in the West Wall, near Ormont.

The squad slept in the bunker that night. It had been evacuated by the Germans. It was a relief to remove my boots and galoshes for the first time in weeks. When morning came I was asked to go on detail to guard an ammo stockpile. Sergeant Kelly yelled, "Alright, Mac, what's holding you up?" I was taking forever to put my boots and galoshes back on over my aching and numbed feet. They really never thawed out until the beginning of March, when we had our first hot shower in two months. That winter I wore long woolen underwear, two sets of olive drabs, and a sweater and field jacket, with a scarf and overcoat, and with two pairs of woolen socks under my combat boots and galoshes. I had no feeling in my toes for two months, but the two guys who wore the shoe-packs were evacuated with frostbitten feet. We never saw them after that.

—*The* Bulge Bugle, *February 1993*

Henry Hooseker
87th Infantry Division

The VIII Corps of the First Army would begin a major counteroffensive against the Germans in the Ardennes on December 30. The 11th Armored Division and the 87th Infantry Division would lead the main brunt of the attack. Henry Hooseker, belonging to the 87th, shares a funny reminiscence about a few hours during that advance.

ON THE CELEBRATED FORCED MARCH of Patton's Third Army from the Saar to the Battle of the Bulge (our destination was Libramont), we alternately traveled on foot and on trucks. On our foot marches we slogged through wind, snow, sleet, and rain. At the end of one of the truck interludes, we were unceremoniously dumped someplace in Kreis Echternach in Luxembourg. (I was sure this was Kreis Echternach unless the Germans had changed the road signs.) At least the body heat in the truck had provided some warmth, and usually we had rested on the truck rides. We were told to get some rest! The area was deserted except for some ruined buildings that had had it from shell fire. These remnants lay in two parallel lines along what may have been a street. The whole area and remnants were covered with a good ten inches of snow. It was very quiet and cold. My thoughts were that it was a miserable place to spend the night. During all of this, our hunger went unabated, and the measly K-Rations we received hardly satisfied our wish for something hot and more solid.

We looked at this forlorn spot that was covered with snow and started to pick our lodgings among the ramshackle, mostly ruined buildings that were probably barns and cattle pens. Although they provided some cover, it certainly wasn't a place you'd write home about.

It didn't take long for the company to spread out in the buildings along each side of the lane or street. The place was desolate, and a dead silence reigned except for the occasional rattle of gear and good old GI bitching.

As we settled, nestled down, and got as warm as possible, an unbelievable sight appeared. Right in front of us, a very large pig started wandering down the center of the street. You couldn't say Jack Robinson before you heard the simultaneous sound of three or four shots from M1s. It was obvious that this casualty was a non-combatant—but what a welcome target. The pig was dead.

It didn't take long before the former farmers in our company butchered and dressed the pig. Some pork chops were fried in mess kits. I still remember the fine smell.

What mystified me for fifty-three years was how the rest of the pig was prepared—it was a big pig. We did eat heartily.

—*The* Bulge Bugle, *November 1999*

George Schumacher
D Company, 345th Infantry Regiment, 87th
Infantry Division

The general mission of the 87th Infantry Division, along with the 11th Armored Division, was to swing around Bastogne, capture the heights south of Houffalize, and secure the Ourthe River line. George Schumacher recalls a small combat action during the fighting.

MY VIVID REMEMBRANCE LEADING to the Battle of the Bulge was the sub-zero biting cold and the freezing trip in open trucks from the Saar Basin campaign to Belgium. Our first battle assignment in Belgium was to take the town of Moircy; the date was a few days after Christmas.

As we crossed the frozen fields, our initial attack was met with enemy artillery and mortar fire that swept the fields leading into the town. Another GI (name unknown) and I were able to capture several prisoners who came out of the woods to surrender. One was a young, beardless Jerry, about my age (I also hadn't begun to shave). In trying to move these prisoners back to the rear, we were hit by an enemy mortar barrage. Several of our prisoners were wounded by their own shells, and one was killed. Finally, there was a short pause in the shelling. We then left the dead man, double-timed across the open field, and quickly moved the prisoners to the rear. After turning over the prisoners, I rejoined my unit.

We then set up a machine gun in a barn at the far end of town. The right wall of this barn was constructed of corrugated metal. Our water-cooled .30-caliber was positioned just inside an open doorway, at the rear of the barn. This gave us an excellent field of fire that covered the rear fields and hedgerows. A building to our right was on fire, and as darkness fell, this fire afforded some illumination of the snow-covered terrain. The two of us, Jay

Morgan, in position as gunner, and I, acting as his second gunner, protected the rear of the town. We talked in hushed tones about the possibility of a counterattack—and we waited.

Later during the night, we could hear the faint sound of voices carrying over the cold air; they were not speaking English. Unexpectedly, from a dark hedgerow to our right front, we heard sounds—then movement. The outline of one soldier came out, followed by a full squad of men. It was the enemy in their long, dark overcoats and coal scuttle–like helmets.

As I watched, Morgan tracked the machine gun to fire. We had a quick, whispered discussion and decided not to fire until the squad was at the center of the field, between each hedgerow. When the squad reached center field, Morgan opened fire. Taken by surprise, they never had the opportunity to return our fire. Several men who were not hit by our machine gun fire tried to make a run for it to the next hedgerows. With my carbine, at a rear window, I picked off the runners. There was no movement on the field—their counterattack was nowhere.

Suddenly, there were popping noises all around us. Farm equipment, harnesses, tools, et cetera, hanging on the wall to our left began falling to the ground. A heavy piece of timber—it seemed like a huge wooden door or a workbench in the darkness—fell and pinned me to the floor. Struggling to free myself from under the timber, I managed to lift it off my back. Morgan called to me that he was hit. Dazed and blood running down the right side of his face, he continued to fire. Looking around in the dark, I saw the metal wall to our right was now full of bullet holes. Fire light from the adjacent burning building was shining through the holes, making the wall look like a sieve.

I now realized there was an enemy machine gun in the right front hedgerow, covering their infantry's advance, and was now firing directly at our position. Morgan continued returning fire until our ammunition ran out. Now, mortar shells were bursting directly in front of the open doorway. Fortunately, neither Morgan nor I were hit with shrapnel; however, from the bullet that hit his helmet, Morgan was now semiconscious and going into shock from loss of blood.

Half carrying and half pulling him, I crawled to the front door. Some GI in his "infinite wisdom" had parked a two-and-a-half-ton truck parallel to and against the front door, blocking our egress. What to do? We had only one choice. Crawling underneath the vehicle, I dragged Morgan with me into the open road. Fortunately, I recognized the red cross arm band of a medic down the street, and his quick examination revealed that a bullet had struck Morgan's helmet and grazed his skull, causing much bleeding. The medic said, "You're a lucky SOB: an inch to the left and you would be dead!"

Morgan's luck ran out several months later—he died in action. By any standard, Sgt. Jay Morgan was a true hero. May he rest in peace.

> Now night her course began, and over heaven
> Inducing darkness, grateful truce, impos'd
> Her silence on the odious din of war;
> Under her cloudy covert hath retired
> Victor and vanquish'd.
>
> —John Milton

—*The* Bulge Bugle, *May 1999*

Wendell C. Obermeier
899th Field Artillery Battalion, 75th
Infantry Division

The small number of German special operations commandos who operated behind American lines during the Battle of the Bulge caused a great deal of concern for all GIs. Wendell

Obermeier remembers how his physical appearance caused him some problems during the Battle of the Bulge.

DECEMBER 16, 1944, HITLER STARTED his all-out offensive to drive a wedge through the Allied forces. We know that operation as the Battle of the Bulge.

The 75th Infantry Division arrived in France on the same day this great battle started. My unit, the 899th Field Artillery Battalion, was part of division artillery. We fired our howitzers at the enemy on December 29. We were now in the battle.

When the German attack started, they attempted to disrupt the Allied defense by parachuting English-speaking, highly trained German soldiers, dressed in American uniforms, carrying U.S. weapons, and wearing dog tags. These spies attempted to cause chaos by changing road signs, misleading troops, and many acts of sabotage. These Nazi spies were dropped behind American lines and caused real problems in some areas.

To counteract this, Allied forces set up roadblocks and checked all soldiers. At the checkpoints they would ask everyone questions referring to American slang—baseball talk, such as line drive, Texas leaguer, et cetera: things that only true Americans would know.

On January 2, 1945, my survey crew and I were making a reconnaissance for new battery positions in case we had to displace to support our unit. We were stopped at one of these checkpoints. Evidently, my answers to the questioning were not conclusive that I was not a spy. I was disarmed and separated from my crew, who were also under interrogation. From the checkpoint, I was taken, at gunpoint to MP headquarters and questioned further. Probably part of the problem were my characteristics. I am of German descent, six feet tall, blond, fair-skinned, blue eyes, butch haircut, and name on my dog tag: Obermeier. No wonder they were hard to convince! I finally persuaded them to contact my division through corps headquarters. A couple of radio calls and I was released and my weapons returned. I rejoined my survey crew. We continued on, finished our mission, and returned to our unit.

When anyone asks me, "Were you a prisoner of war?" I have to say yes and then explain I was a prisoner of war of our own forces for a short time. This was my most unusual incident in my two years overseas.

—*The* Bulge Bugle, *August 1999*

Carl Ferguson
Headquarters, 75th Infantry Division

The slightest slip in combat can cause losses, as is attested to by Carl Ferguson.

In Abrefontaine, our artillery command post occupied the nearly destroyed building that the 82nd Airborne Division's artillery had used as their advance command post about a week before, during the battle to take that city. GI blankets covered the windows to keep out the blasts of cold air and to maintain good blackout discipline at night. However, the walls and roof of our building were intact. Most buildings in town had suffered considerable damage by friendly artillery and machine gun fire in the fight to drive out the Germans.

As I had been up all night the previous night, as soon as the CP was established, I took my bedroll and climbed the narrow, winding staircase in the musty, cobweb-lined attic and unrolled my "sack" on a mound of threshed wheat. The very loud crack and crash of a battalion of friendly 155 howitzers in position only a block or less behind our CP, although deafening, did not keep me awake. During succeeding nights, the loud, bursting crack of incoming artillery shells became rather common.

Each night, usually before midnight, a single enemy plane, known as "bed-check Charley," circled overhead, trying to pinpoint vulnerable American positions. On moonlit nights— and we had several at this location—the town of Abrefontaine could be seen quite easily from the air. Obviously, his mission was one of reconnaissance and intelligence, with possibly the secondary motive of dropping a bomb or two on any target of opportunity that we might have carelessly exposed to the aerial observer, by failure to observe strict blackout precautions.

Division headquarters had been noticeably lax in blackout discipline in previous positions, and they paid dearly for their negligence here. During their first night in Abrefontaine, a small enemy plane dropped an antipersonnel bomb through the roof of their headquarters mess, killing a lieutenant colonel, the division signal officer, and two enlisted men. Several large holes in the roof of their shelter had leaked through light to reveal their position to the enemy pilot. Major Broyles, 75th Division artillery medical officer, had established his aid station across the street and was first on the scene.

—*The* Bulge Bugle, *November 1999*

Michael V. Altamura
750th Tank Battalion, attached to the 75th Infantry Division

Church can sometimes be a haven from the death and destruction that is so much a part of any war, as recalled by Michael Altamura.

WE WERE IN A PICTURESQUE, SNOW-COVERED valley in Belgium during the Battle of the Bulge in December 1944. It was Sunday morning. A small Catholic church stood on a slight slope overlooking the snow-covered fir trees. At the other end of the valley was a coal-fueled electric power plant. Every once in a while a German buzz bomb came over, attempting to knock out the power plant. A group of tankers and infantrymen decided to attend church that Sunday morning. We stood in the back of the church with our guns slung over our shoulders as the priest gave the mass in Latin. The congregation was kneeling in prayer.

We heard the "put-put" of a buzz bomb overhead, and then the sound cut off. When the sound ceased, we knew the rocket engine had stopped propelling the airborne buzz bomb, and it would fall, exploding when it hit the ground. The congregation looked upwards as if to accept their fate. The priest's intonations stopped. The bomb hit pretty close to the church. The ground shook; a few of the stained glass windows cracked. No one moved or said a word. The priest resumed his mass in Latin. I thank God for sparing us that Sunday morning in a small Belgian church during the Ardennes battle.

—*The* Bulge Bugle, *February 2001*

Charles R. Miller
A Company, 290th Infantry Regiment, 75th Infantry Division

The biggest issue for the Allied generals in late December was how to deal with the German salient in the Ardennes. Should it be pushed back to its starting point or cut off close to the shoulders? Charles Miller describes the fighting through January 1945 to pinch off the German salient.

On December 19, 1944, we left Yvetot by railroad, riding in the infamous forty and eights (French railroad boxcars). We were told that our planned destination was Wiljre, Netherlands, but apparently this was changed en route along with our assignment to the U.S. First Army. We arrived at Tongres, Belgium, at 2200 hours, December 20, and marched approximately eight kilometers to Hoeselt (Belgium), arriving at 0120, December 21, and were billeted in houses and barns. At 0045 on December 22, we left Hoeselt and traveled, preparing a defensive position along L'Ourthe River. It was very cold, and the open 6x6 trucks provided little shelter. I remember trying to open the meat can from a K-ration and having to hold the opening key between my teeth because my fingers were too cold to grasp it. It was warmer when we arrived at our position, and the physical labor of digging holes was welcome. While we had no direct contact with the enemy, during the night there was continuous heavy gunfire somewhere south of our position. As I was to learn later, a battle was being fought in the vicinity of Soy and Hotton, where the enemy was trying to break through, and it was the uncertainty of the outcome of that action that had caused us to be put in our position to help defend along L'Ourthe River.

On December 23 the 1st Battalion, 290th Infantry Regiment, was attached to the 3rd Armored Division, while the rest of the regiment moved to a position along the Soy-Hotton road. During the night of December 23, the 1st Battalion, including Company A, marched to the vicinity of Erezée. We were burdened by heavy packs, and it was difficult to keep up the pace set by the battalion commander; many men fell out, and many more straggled. When junior officers and NCOs mentioned to the battalion commander about the pace, he told them that he was ten years older than most of the men and that he had orders to be at our destination by midnight. The NCOs pointed out that he was carrying only a musette bag and carbine, and, besides that, his orders were to have his battalion with him. I remember marching through small communities and discussing with my comrades the reason that most of the vehicles parked next to the houses had their engines running. We decided that the vehicle operators had run wiring into the buildings for lights and were operating the engines to keep the vehicle batteries charged. If we had known that there had been a big enemy breakthrough, we would have realized the engines were running so that the operations could "bug out" if necessary and not be delayed by difficulty in starting a cold engine. But we knew nothing about the enemy attack until much later. When we arrived at our destination, we were told to dig slit trenches for protection and get some sleep. This proved almost impossible because we were in the midst of numerous artillery positions (probably 105s), which fired almost continuously.

Early in the morning of December 24, we were picked up by 3rd AD half-tracks, which carried us to Manhay. That name stuck in my memory because it seemed to me a peculiar name for a community in Belgium. Manhay was being shelled by the Germans—the first time we were under enemy fire—and we stayed there only a short time before retracing our route to the west as far as Grandmenil and then turning south to Oster, where we arrived about 1000. Dismounting from the half-tracks, we formed up to attack the high ground to the southeast of Oster, advancing in an open formation with two light trucks moving on trail roads on either flank. As we moved across the open fields, approaching a dense stand of planted evergreens, we were fired on by a small number of the enemy armed with Schmeisser machine pistols—the infamous "burp gun," which made a sound that you never forget once you have heard it. Several men were hit immediately, including our platoon leader, who took a burst on the left side. I remember him sitting on the ground with blood streaming from his left arm and shoulder but waving us on with his right arm and saying, "Go get 'em, boys!" A number of us moved into the edge of the woods and took dubious cover behind rather small trees. The company commander was fifteen or twenty feet to my left, lying behind a small tree and yelling at the men to move forward, but I followed his example and stayed put. Then, one of the platoon leaders came forward and, standing beside me, told me to shoot and start moving. I told him, "Lieutenant, I don't see anything to shoot at." He said that it didn't matter, but just to shoot and move. He managed to get the company on its feet and moving again. Thus, we learned about "marching fire," which the experienced units were using but which we had not been taught.

As we continued up the hill, encountering no more Germans, the company drifted to the left, and we lost contact with the tanks on the right, which promptly turned around and returned to Oster. As we neared the top of the ridge, the CO decided we were too far left and ordered the skirmish line to move right in single file, which frightened me, since we didn't know if there were more enemy in the woods. We moved some distance to the right, losing contact with the tanks on the left, and came to the top of the ridge overlooking a valley. There we saw an enemy tank down below. A check revealed no bazookas among us, and, in fact, we only had the first and second platoons and no officers except the captain. We withdrew a short distance, and the captain placed outposts and ordered us to dig in. I leaned on my rifle against a tree, took off my overcoat, and started digging. I had one of the new-style entrenching tools that could be used as a shovel or a hoe and quickly got my hole down knee deep.

The two platoon sergeants tried to convince the captain that we should return to Oster and reassemble the company, which had become scattered as we maneuvered through the woods. The captain said that he wanted to hold what he had gained, to which the two sergeants replied that he hadn't gained anything. As you might expect, the captain prevailed and told the sergeants to select two men to return to Oster and advise the executive officer to send up the Jeeps and trailers with the bed rolls and ammunition. I was selected by my platoon sergeant, who then took me and the man from the other platoon aside and told us to tell the executive officer what the situation was and ask him to come up with the Jeeps and convince the captain to withdraw. As I was putting on my overcoat and other gear, one of the men in my squad asked if he could move over into the hole I was digging, since it was much deeper than his. I told him, "OK," and started down the hill with the other man. We were cursing the captain and two sergeants all the way, since we were convinced that we had bypassed many Germans as the company advanced up the ridge. Fortunately, all we met were several groups of men from the company who were wandering around trying to flush out any of the enemy they could find. We reached Oster and were telling the company executive officer what both the captain and the platoon sergeants had told us, when we heard small-arms fire up on the ridge. Shortly thereafter, we saw the men we had left on the ridge streaming down the hill led by the captain. As I learned later, the Germans had surprised them and killed four men, including the men on the outpost and the man digging in the hole I had left. As soon as the captain reached us, he told the executive officer to get the company on the road and ready to move out.

It was getting dark as we marched out to Oster, and we had gone about one kilometer north when we met the battalion commander, who asked the captain where he was going. When the captain told him that we were "pulling out," the battalion commander told him that he couldn't pull out because C Company had taken their objective, and if A Company pulled out, it would leave C's flank exposed. This was not true, as I was to learn much later. And, in fact, most of the 2nd SS Panzer Division was between A Company and C Company, moving up the road in the valley the other side of the ridge we had attacked earlier, on their way to assault Manhay, which they captured later that night. It also explained the audacity of the handful of the enemy who had stood their ground in the face of a reinforced rifle company supported by tanks: we had been skirmishing that day with SS panzergrenadiers from one of the most notorious of the SS panzer divisions.

When the battalion commander told the captain that he must take the company back on the ridge that night, the captain fainted and was placed on the battalion commander's Jeep. The company executive officer was ordered to take command and move the company back to Oster and up on the ridge. We marched back to Oster, but, rather than going back on the ridge that night, the new company commander positioned outposts and occupied some houses and barns on the north end of Oster. The next morning, Christmas Day, we did move back on the ridge and dug a line of foxholes on the slope overlooking Oster. We had not been re-supplied, and ammunition and food was in short supply. I remember sharing a C-ration with two other men. We also had a little bread, which had been found in an abandoned house in Oster.

Later that day, the company commander was ordered by the commander of the 3rd Armored Division task force to which we were assigned (TF Kane—Lt. Col. Matthew Kane) to have a patrol work the woods southeast of Oster to search for tanks. The company commander elected to lead the patrol himself, and I was assigned to it, in part at least because I was armed with a rifle grenade launcher. We worked around the edge of the woods and in the afternoon were lying on a hillside overlooking a small group of buildings gathered around an intersection where a road crossing a small stream turned west from a north-south road which we were following. We watched as a number of Germans walked up and down the main road in their long overcoats, which I always envied because they appeared much warmer than our short ones.

At one point, there was an attempt to contact someone on our company back-pack radio, and shortly thereafter a number of artillery rounds fell on the crossroads, so a decision was made not to use the radio again, since some felt that the guns had ranged on the radio. It's more likely that it was just interdictory fire on map coordinates. At this time, most of the remainder of the Task Force Kane was in Freineux and Lamormenil, so the Germans were on a direct route between A Company and the rest, but it was possible to communicate through La Fosse.

About dark, part of the patrol returned to the company position, while the rest of us turned east toward Odeigne, leaving the woods and walking along the road. After we had gone a short distance, a machine gun to our left fired on us. I wanted to use a rifle grenade but was told not to do so. I heard explosions, as someone had worked up to the machine gun and used grenades. The patrol proceeded on to Odeigne, where a very chaotic action took place, and two men were killed and another captured. As the patrol broke up, we heard that the company commander had been killed, and, with another man, I made my way back to Oster. We went to the house of M. Achille Lerusse, who invited us in and told us that there were other Americans there. He directed me to a room on the left side of the hall, and on opening the door, I saw about six weapons aimed at me from a number of armored division soldiers who were sleeping there without any guard posted. Although we knew it was a foolish thing to do, my friend and I were very tired, so we joined them and slept through the reminder of the night.

The next morning, December 26, we found that the remainder of the company had come off the hill and also learned that the company commander had not been killed but was badly wounded—shot through the chest. He survived and rejoined the company in Germany toward the end of the war.

The rest of the 26th was uneventful; the weather was clear and sunny, and the ones who had been on the patrol the night before were excused from any duties. Toward dark we were issued a ten-in-one ration—the first food we had been provided since December 23, but before we could finish eating, we were ordered to move out, since the task force was withdrawing to the line established by Field Marshal Montgomery on December 24. This line ran from Trois-Ponts southwest through Manhay, Grandmenil, and Amonines. We followed the rest of the task force along a trail road west to Sadzot and on to Blier, where we spent the rest of the night in a barn. In three days the company had over thirty casualties—killed, wounded, captured, missing, or sick.

I had taken off my boots for the first time in five days, and when I woke on the morning of December 27, my feet were so swollen that I could not get my boots back on. I put on the overshoes and managed all right until after lunch, when I was able to get my shoes on again. The cooks prepared our Christmas dinner, which we had missed on the 25th, and we gorged ourselves. Later in the day, we moved into defensive positions in Amonines. My platoon occupied the last house on the road that leads west out of Amonines past the church. It was the first time I had seen a barn as part of a house.

Our time in Amonines was mostly uneventful—some patrols and night road blocks but not a lot of active enemy action. Our platoon sergeant and his assistant (the platoon guide) were both wounded by mortar fire as they crossed a small stream behind a church—a spot where the platoon sergeant had warned us to be careful because numerous fins from mortar shells indicated that the area was under observation.

While we were in Amonines, I spent two days in the battalion aid station with a bad throat and laryngitis. For most of that time, the platoon sergeant from the second platoon was there also, then he was evacuated for further treatment, and I returned to duty. The aid station was in a large house on the main road with a wall around it, so the medical Jeeps could stop on the road and carry their litters through the gate. As we would watch, the medics would bring some in the house for treatment and take the dead soldiers around the side where they were stacked like cordwood. It was rather disturbing, since we had to go around that side of the house to relieve ourselves.

On January 4, we were ordered to prepare to move out, so we put on all of our gear and were sitting around in the house. With our coats on, it was very warm, and most of us were half asleep when the quiet was shattered by a rifle shot. One of the men had shot himself in the leg (probably accidentally). The medics came and took him away, and as things were quieting down, again there was a sudden explosion in the kitchen—all of the lids blew off of the wood stove, and the stove pipe flew all over the kitchen. Our first thought was that a mortar shell had hit the kitchen, since the Germans had been directing mortar fire at us for several minutes. It turned out that some idiot had dropped a can of meat and beans in the stove, and when the liquid boiled and turned into steam, the can exploded.

We soon moved out, following the advance, and when C Company had taken Magoster, we dug in at the edge of the woods on the east side. Sometime after dark, the kitchen truck came up, and our canteen cups were collected and returned to us full of food. This provided a rather unique dining experience, since in the dark I was not sure of some of what I was eating, although I knew it was familiar. I am sure that there was a canned peach half for "dessert," since it was thoughtfully placed on the top of the mélange. Interest was added by the German artillery, which was shelling the woods behind us, and shell fragments were buzzing through the trees like angry bees. Without helmets on and the collars of our overcoats turned up to cover our necks, it was more annoying than dangerous.

On January 5, the battalion moved through Beffe and A Company took up defensive positions to the south, while B Company extended the line from Beffe west to L'Ourthe River. My platoon was in a house on the high ground overlooking the river valley, and my position was a hole near the edge of the bluff with a hedge between it and the house. I didn't like this position because the hedge limited contact with the others, and the man with me did not hear well. The second night we were there, I heard something moving behind the hedge, apparently trying to work through it. When I received no reply to several low-voiced challenges, I took a grenade and was ready to pull the pin when the hedge parted and a dark shape came through it—a cow.

On January 7, the battalion launched an attack to the south, with B Company on the right and A Company on the left. As our platoon left our holes, we received automatic weapons fire from our right flank, and several men were wounded. This was apparently fire from friendly troops who took us to be the enemy. As we moved into the wooded area, I was one of the scouts for our platoon (going ahead of the rest of my squad). The other scout for the platoon was one of the nineteen replacements the company had received on January 1, 1945, while in Amonines. Most of these men came from service troops—quartermaster, ordnance, signal corps, and the like—and had little or no infantry training and little experience with the M1 rifle. This proved to be the case with the other scout.

We had moved only a short distance into the woods when he fired a shot. Everyone stopped and looked around and, when nothing more happened, I asked him what he had fired at. He replied, "Nothing, I caught the trigger on a button on my overcoat." I told him to lock his weapon until he saw something to shoot. This was standard procedure to prevent accidents.

We moved two or three hundred meters into the woods when I saw a soldier about thirty meters in front of me. We both stopped and looked at each other because, with camouflage nets on them, American and German helmets looked very similar at a distance. I finally decided that he was a German and fired at him, possibly wounding him slightly, because he cried out and ran off to my right and took cover in a foxhole. He then began firing from the hole, which was protected by logs on the sides as well as overhead. All I could see was his rifle sticking out when he fired, and my shots going into the side of his bunker were not having any effect. The German was almost directly in front of the other scout, but, when I called for him to shoot at the German, he replied, "I can't; my rifle won't work." Apparently he forgot to unlock it. At this point, my platoon leader called to me, "Quit firing! You are shooting at B Company," to which I replied, "B Company— Hell, the woods are full of Germans in here!" The Germans opened up with a machine gun, raking the woods, but fortunately firing slightly over us as we lay on the ground. After watching the bullets striking twigs just above me, I called on my squad leader to come up to my position as he was supposed to do. When he didn't respond after two or three calls, I told the platoon leader, "Lieutenant, either someone comes up here with me, or I am coming back there with you!" The lieutenant then ordered my squad leader to do something, so the sergeant ordered the BAR man to advance. The BAR man responded by running up and kneeling beside me, asking, "Where are they,

Miller?" I replied, "Right in front of us." He then fired a full clip of twenty rounds from his BAR at the same time one of the company officers to our left was calling for a machine gun to be brought up. Apparently, the Germans realized that we were more than just a small patrol, so several surrendered, and the rest retreated.

We advanced through the German position but had to hold up to wait for B Company to catch up and, as a result, were ordered to dig in for the night. As usual, I dug a deep hole and put some branches over it, and I was happy that I had done so when it snowed during the night. The next morning as we were preparing to resume the advance, the artillery forward observer advised us to get back into our holes as he called for a barrage to clear out the woods ahead. Again, I was glad for a good, deep hole when several rounds fell short. We resumed the advance without encountering any enemy except one dead German in a wheelbarrow which apparently one of his comrades had used in an effort to help him. Around the middle of the day, we reached Marcourt, where we stayed in defensive positions until January 9. Nothing eventful occurred at Marcourt except that we found the Belgians upset because the Germans had slain a number of civilians.

We left Marcourt by truck at 1515 on January 9 and at 1823 reached Basse-Bodeux and ate supper. We left Basse-Bodeux on foot at 2230 and arrived at Mont at 0036 hours, January 10. We had little rest, and I remember being so tired that I went to sleep walking and woke up when I walked into the man in front of me.

On January 11, we left Mont and hiked about five kilometers to Goronne. I was selected as one of two scouts to lead the battalion since A Company was at the head of the column. We were told that the I&R (Information & Reconnaissance) Platoon had been over the route the night before, but it had

253

not snowed, and we noticed that there were no tracks in the road, so we decided to be especially cautious. However, nothing eventful happened, except that at one point we were challenged by some troops from the 291st Infantry Regiment (also part of the 75th Infantry Division) and told we were in front of their lines along the Salm River. Our route turned more to the southwest, and we reached Goronne and went into division reserve.

On January 12, we left Goronne at 1800 and hiked about four kilometers to Rencheux. There we took up defensive positions. A Company was in a Belgian military installation on high ground north of Rencheux, and I was with three other men in a cellar that had a window that overlooked the Salm River, Vielsalm, and some distance to the east. It was a quiet time other than occasional artillery fire from the German side—usually a single gun that would be answered by a number of American guns. There were several patrols, but I did not participate in any of them.

On January 15, the 75th Infantry Division began an attack across the Salm River—the 291th Infantry Regiment north of Vielsalm and the 289th Infantry Regiment south of Vielsalm as part of a classical maneuver known as a double envelopment. The 1st Battalion, 290th Infantry Regiment, including A Company, was supposed to attack Vielsalm, but patrols into the town in the early hours of January 17 found it deserted. So at 1145 hours we crossed the Salm on a railroad bridge at the north side of Vielsalm.

Since the enemy showed no signs of withdrawing, the commanding general of the XVIII Airborne Corps ordered the commanding general of the 75th Infantry Division to press on, so the 1st Battalion, 290th Infantry Regiment, moved through Vielsalm and on to the east through Ville du Bois and Petit Thier. As we proceeded east from Ville du Bois, we observed isolated groups of the enemy to the south, and an effort was made to put out flank protection, but we were not able to keep up with the column because the snow on the fields made for slow going. At one time when a number of Germans were seen some distance south of the road, an order was given to fire on them with a heavy machine gun, but the gun and tripod were separated because the men carrying them had not been able to keep up with the column. We were the second company in the line of march, and, as I observed, a number of men carrying very heavy packs were falling back. I recalled our march of December 23. These men were probably replacements because we soon learned to dispose of all but the essentials. We had been joined by two armored vehicles—possibly at Petit Thier, although I didn't actually see them until much later. I thought they were tanks, but it turned out that they were tank destroyers.

It was getting dark as we marched through Petit Thier, where we were greeted by enthusiastic Belgians offering us calvados and other liquid refreshments. It was dark by the time we reached the crossroad at Poteau, and as the leading company attempted to enter, they were fired on by automatic weapons and stopped. The battalion commander came back and discussed with our CO the possibility of A Company flanking the crossroads through the fields on either side. After considering the problems the snow had caused earlier, the battalion commander asked the tank destroyers to move up and fire on the Germans in the crossroads. The tank destroyers' leader asked if the road could be swept for mines and learned for the first time that we had no mine detectors with us. His companion told him to move to the side as he took his firing position so he could move up to support him. His reply was, "No use both of us getting knocked out," which didn't indicate an optimistic state of mind, but actually the tank destroyers had only to fire its machine guns, and the Germans withdrew and permitted us to move in. As we took cover in foxholes dug by U.S. Army's 7th Armored Division troops as part of the defense of Saint-Vith from December 16 to December 23, the Germans shelled the crossroads, killing at least one man.

The next morning, January 18, as we prepared to resume the offensive to the south, a German gun fired on the crossroads. After observing from inside one of the ruined buildings, the commander of one of the tank destroyers trained his gun up the hill, moved his vehicle from behind the cover of the building, and fired two quick rounds up the hill. He then returned the tank destroyer to its hiding place behind the building. He reported that he had destroyed a German SP (self-propelled) gun, but no one really believed him until the SP was found two days later with two holes in it. A little later, we spread along the road to the west of the crossroads and prepared to attack south across an open field and into the woods. Enemy small-arms fire was intense, and the attack never really got started. The artillery FO (forward observer) said that our move the day before had carried us out of the range of the 105mm guns because their impact area was so large that shells might fall on us.

We spent the night in a house west of the crossroads and resumed the offensive the next morning with more success since the enemy had withdrawn from the immediate vicinity of the crossroads, retreating to prepared positions farther south. As we moved deeper into the woods, we encountered increased opposition, and an intense action developed as we attempted to cross a firebreak or trail road. When we left Rencheux for Vielsalm, I had been armed with a submachine gun commonly called a "grease gun" because it superficially resembled an automotive maintenance tool. I would have much preferred to have kept my M1 rifle with which I was proficient but was not given the choice. When we encountered the strong enemy position, my weapon would not fire because of the intense cold and neither would the BARs. Since I had been trained on the BAR, the platoon sergeant instructed me to see if I could get them to operate. I advised the men carrying them to remove the cartridge clips from the weapons, stuff toilet paper into the receiver, and set it on fire. I did likewise with my submachine gun, and thus we succeeded in warming them enough so that they started working. The cold affected the M1 rifle as well, but the bolt on the rifle could be closed manually and the weapon fired single shot to warm it. The automatic weapons depended on the speed of the bolt closing to fire them, so it was necessary to warm them. After crossing the firebreak, we continued the advance through the woods, but encountered much less resistance. Over a hundred prisoners were taken, but most of them surrendered to the support company following behind us after letting us walk over them in their well-concealed foxholes.

That night A Company occupied a large house or tavern a few hundred meters south of the Poteau crossroads, although it was much farther by the route we had taken through the woods. It was a bitter cold night and, while it was comfortable enough in the building, standing guard outside was a chilling experience, especially for the feet, since we had only garrison-issue clothing, including regular combat boots and overshoes rather than the much warmer shoe pacs that were issued later.

The next day, January 20, we advanced some distance with little contact with the enemy. We came to a place where the larger trees had been cut and the snow was waist deep in the open areas around the younger trees, and we had to travel on the road. I went with a patrol that was sent forward to reconnoiter before the company advanced further. We went some distance, finding conditions much the same and no sign of the enemy until we heard a tank moving somewhere ahead of us. We then returned and reported to the company commander. When he found that we had no bazooka ammunition, he decided to withdraw a short distance and dig in the woods near the road. In a little while, a large number of vehicles proceeded south along the road past our position: tanks, trucks, Jeeps. We found that they were from the 30th Infantry Division. Seeing that we had been bypassed and were no longer in contact with the enemy, I advised my platoon sergeant that I was going to the battalion aid station to have my feet checked since they were bothering me. I got back as far as the large house where we had spent the night before and found it occupied by C Company of our battalion. After spending the night there, I caught a ride on a 30th Infantry Division truck the next morning. They took me to Recht and left me at a building occupied by an artillery unit. After giving me my first hot meal in almost a week, they transported me to Petit Thier and our battalion aid station. After my feet were examined, I was evacuated to the division clearing station in Rencheux and from there to a hospital clearing company in Spa. During the course of the five-day action, the company had fifty casualties: a large number of them, especially toward the last, were due to weather rather than enemy action.

—*The* Bulge Bugle, *February 2001*

James A. Steinhaufel
C Company, 134th Infantry Regiment, 35th Infantry Division

It was General Patton who insisted that the German Ardennes salient should be cut off and the German armies caught within be engulfed by a vise closing from north and south against the shoulder of the Bulge. James Steinhaufel describes his unit's encounter with the much-feared German Tiger tank.

THIS STORY OCCURRED IN JANUARY 1945, perhaps the middle of the month, during the Battle of the Bulge. The Allies were recovering the lost ground and were beginning to push into Germany. We were in Belgium near the Luxembourg border. After being wounded in the leg by grenade fragments at Habkirchen on December 13, I had recently returned to Company C. At this time the 35th Infantry Division was part of General Patton's Third Army. I was with Company C of the 134th Infantry Regiment.

I looked up into the morning sky. We had been struggling through the snow for a few days. It was very cold. We sought shelter whenever it was available. We had been sleeping in the snow at night. It was a long way from the bridge at Habkirchen and the hospital. My leg still felt tender as I pushed through the snow. About twenty-five of us from Company C were in the area. I was in a squad of six or seven soldiers. Our patrol was moving near a battle area. In this region of Belgium and Luxembourg, there was no front line. We were trying to clear a small area of the Bulge.

As we trudged through the snow, we came upon two burning American tanks. The acrid smell of smoke and burned flesh hung in the air. It had not been long since the two Shermans had been knocked out. The two American tanks had come out of the woods together, side by side, and were knocked out by a German tank patrolling the area. The American tankers had tried to get out. Some men were dead, and one was hanging out of a hatch. We lowered our heads as we walked on. Shuffling through the snow, some following in the footsteps of those ahead, a few making their own new trails on the flanks, everyone was alert, looking with twisting eyes.

As we patrolled along a road, we heard and then spotted a large German tank with a patrol walking with it. The soldiers were the outside eyes. The tank was probably a hunter providing the infantry intimate close support. I recall that the tank could have been a Panzer VI Model E Tiger I heavy tank or a Panzer VI Model B, King Tiger heavy tank. Both were equipped with an 88mm, twenty-two-foot-long barrel, if I remember correctly. The Tiger I was probably the most famous and most feared tank of World War II. The Tiger I weighed fifty-five tons and had 2.4 to 3.2 inches of side armor behind the tracks, while the King Tiger weighed sixty-eight tons and had 3.2 inches of side armor.

When our Company C Commander, Capt. Wallace Chappell, saw the German Tiger, he ordered us into a very narrow ravine. The gully sloped down away from the road into the dark Ardennes Forest. The woods were of intermixed birch and pines that provided some cover in the narrow confines of this slash in the earth. Nevertheless, the patrol and German tank saw us take cover in the gully.

We were watching him and the German squad. The tank was above us. The tanker could look down into the ravine. It was about 150 yards from the tank to the gully. We crouched and pressed into the small recesses. I knew we had been spotted. We couldn't run.

Through the cold air, I could hear the distant sound of hatch covers clanking shut. The tankers had been riding with the hatches open. As we crowded into the gully, I listened to the grinding of the turret as it twisted toward us. I pushed lower into the small recesses. Hiding was impossible.

Once, I looked up. It was possible to see the menacing, dark, growling bulk silhouetted against the dark, cloudy sky. The tank was above us. The barrel lowered, searching, and pointed. We were dark, stationary lumps in the snow. I buried my face deeper into the frosty granules. I didn't notice the biting cold as the snow pressed into my check. My hand held the steel pot tightly to my head as I tried to edge further under it. The vision of death had come to us many times before. I thought how this would be a carnival shoot for the tanker. Our squad was directly below the steel-grinding hulk. The sound of the engine, protesting the movement of the turret, rolled over our heads. The engine seemed quieter than the pounding, racing beats in my chest. My senses were on high alert and were working very well.

Another patrol was farther into the ravine. They were probably from another company of the 134th Infantry Regiment. They had taken cover in the bends and twists, behind a stump, at the base of a tree, or a hump of dirt, just below us. The snow mixed with our rifles and gear as we pressed into sides of the ravine. I know that Pvt. James Graff was somewhere nearby.

I felt the first blast of cold air directly above my helmet. As much as the German tanker would try, he couldn't lower the barrel far enough to shoot directly at us. You could hear the barrel being adjusted and then the engine's protesting as the barrel came to a stop in its lowest position. It was terrifying. He hit a guy farther down in the gully, but the tank was not able to lower his muzzle further to get to me. So the 88mm rounds were going over my head.

After the first shells swooshed over our heads and crashed into the gully below us, we understood that the tanker was hitting the troops below us. You could hear shouts, then calls for help. We heard moaning and a call in the crisp, cold air for a medic. The shells were so close I decided to take my pack off. It was good the German tank couldn't depress his turret further. I could hear a swish, then the boom from the barrel, as the shells were traveling faster than the explosive sound traveled. The sounds were very close together, but the swish seemed first.

The patrol below us was taking all of the tanker's fire. I didn't know then which company, but they were from the

134th Infantry Regiment. More shells slashed overhead and crashed below us. A tree was thrown upward. We knew that all of the pieces arching in the air and bouncing off the trees was not all rocks or wood. My hand gripped tighter to the steel helmet. We were trying to push deeper into the snow. Then the shooting stopped.

I could make out the grinding sound of the tank moving away from us. The crunching of protesting snow reached our position as the German tank moved. The turret searched and pointed, looking for targets. I do not know why the tanker stopped shelling us. Perhaps he sensed vulnerability in his position. Or the German patrol had sighted one of Patton's armored division Sherman tanks. He may also have known we were just wasps in a nest below him, I guessed. He had tried to take out a few of us, perhaps to push us back or gain some time, while the German patrol accompanying him moved for protection.

The German tanker's real adversary was not the wasp nest in the ravine. It was our tanks in the area. The German tanker must have known he was in a battle with Patton's scattered Sherman tanks.

In a battle like this, there seems to always be a tear-jerker. The battle in the gully was like many battle scenes. Two brothers were serving in the area together. Here in the gully one of the brothers was killed. As the lumbering sound of the creaking-clanking tank moved away from us, A GI came into the gully and shouted a name, his brother's name. He rushed from group to group, calling his brother's name. Someone in our patrol replied that we didn't know his brother. It could have been Graff or one of the replacements. I remember glancing at his boots and wondering if his feet were cold like mine.

The tension of the shelling drifted away. We brushed the snow from our pants and coats as we rose to stand. I wondered how any of us would get our feet warm again. We often didn't.

One person in our patrol shouted to the snow-covered GI that there were other troops below us. He should check there. He could now hear the guys below us moving. Calls for help had stopped drifting up to us. The searching GI's face tightened as he looked down the gully and realized we had motioned to the area where the tank shells had been exploding. As his face tightened and his eyebrow lowered, he stepped around us and slogged down the ravine. We learned later that his brother was one of those killed in the crashing, exploding shells.

The night before the gully incident, two of us had been on guard duty at an outpost when several GIs came and took our .30-caliber machine gun from us. The reason for our manning the outpost must have been over. We went back to Company C. In the morning we moved off on the patrol. We didn't have the heavy .30-caliber machine gun, if we had needed it. We had been lucky.

Captain Chappell sent a sergeant down into the gully to tell his troops to move out. Shortly the sergeant came to our patrol, and we were told to leave the gully, and go to the cabin. We were happy to leave the terror. The sergeant didn't have to tell us twice. We moved back into the trees away from where the tank had been. At this time the American Sherman tanks came up, from around the bend, and into a good position. They took out the German tank that had been shelling the ravine. I don't recall that the German patrol accompanying the tank had fired at us. When the Sherman hit the tank, the German patrol ran away and into nearby trees.

The company was moving out. There was no front line. I recall now that it seemed the 35th Infantry Division, of which the 134th Infantry Regiment was a part, was up on the front line more than any other unit. We had to walk up a hill to the rundown shack-like cabin. It was about ten feet by ten feet in size. An American Sherman was parked alongside the cabin, maybe twenty to twenty-five feet away.

After we were inside and beginning to get warm again, the Sherman started shooting from its hidden position. After we realized the American tanker was using the shed as cover, it didn't take us long to understand that we needed to move and move fast. We bailed out of the cabin and took cover away from the Sherman. As a group we watched the shoot-out. The cabin allowed the Sherman to shoot from a concealed position. It had to be hidden for protection. Close in, the American tank could take the turret off the German Tiger. But a German tank's 88mm shells could rip through the Sherman easily if it were caught in the open.

The American hit the German two or three times with no effect. The two tanks were five hundred yards apart. You could hear the swoosh-thump of the shells from our hidden position. The shootout lasted only a few minutes. Ten to fifteen shells were exchanged. I had left the shack during the shooting. The Sherman would move forward from behind the cabin. He would shoot a shell and then draw back. You could hear the tank engine surge as the driver kept the rev up to quickly move. In a few minutes the tank would move forward again. The American kept repeating this maneuver. The guy in the Sherman was missing all the time. The Tiger was by himself. We couldn't see any sign of a patrol. The cabin and the American Sherman tank were about five hundred to a thousand yards apart. Other American troops were closer to the Tiger, but we didn't see them during the shelling.

One of the American tanker's shells hit in the narrow two-to-four-inch space just over the track of the German tank. The tankers considered this a soft spot on the German tanks, especially the Tiger. The armor was only two to two and one-half inches thick behind the treads. On a Tiger tank I had inspected earlier in January, my hand would barely fit in the space above the track, and I could just barely touch the thick armor behind the track. Thus, the Sherman made quite a shot, given the distance. A lucky hit! When the Tiger exploded, a German tanker came out of the lower hatch and ran away. We could hear more explosions from inside the bucking hulk. It became quiet except for the sound of burning mixed with an occasional exploding shell.

We had been standing in the trees watching the battle. The sound of our boots stomping and crunching the snow mixed with the sounds that drifted from the burning tank. We were well hidden. No small-arms fire came from the German patrol. We had not fired toward them. After the ravine, we didn't want to attract more attention.

It was possible that this was the German Tiger that knocked out the two Sherman tanks that we had seen smoldering, two hours earlier, before we got into the gully. After the German tank was hit and a few minutes after the German tanker was running up the hill, our patrol walked back to the cabin. We were standing outside the cabin talking, swinging our arms and stomping our feet to get warm. Someone shouted that a Kraut patrol was coming toward us.

The German patrol would have had to come down through the same gully we had been hiding in. They held their arms high above their heads. Most of them had thrown their helmets to the ground. They began to shout, "Comrade, Comrade." They had also dropped their weapons, packs, and ammo belts before coming up the hill toward the cabin where we were standing. They had winter hats stuffed inside their coats.

It was not normal for surrendering German troops to shout "Comrade" as they came toward us. These same krauts did this as they walked toward us: Comrade, Comrade. So, we moved down toward them. We stopped and waited for the ten

265

German soldiers to come up the hill the remaining distance to us. They were through with this war and they knew it. We surrounded them and put our rifles on them. At this they bunched up. They were all standing at attention.

They had a hauptmann, equal to a captain in the American army. If this rank is correct, he was probably with the Waffen SS. It was strange to see a German officer with such a small detachment as his patrol. He was not a tanker, so he could have been Waffen SS or from the regular German army known as the Heer, part of the German Wehrmacht. The officer and these men could have been part of the Wehrmacht Waffen SS.

As the German patrol trudged toward us, I wanted the medals on them, so I walked in close with my M1 pointed into the group. I walked up to the officer, pointed the M1 close to his chest, and said, "Nicht schiessen," German words we used with prisoners that were supposed to mean "no shoot." The officer still had his helmet on. I indicated for him to take it off. His long coat opened as he raised his hands again over his head. As the coat opened, it was possible to see a small leather pistol holster on his right hip. It could have been a backup weapon. I motioned to the holster with my rifle muzzle.

I again told the German "Nicht schiessen." He recognized my meaning, and his glare turned, looking now toward the pistol on his hip. He loosened his belt and slid off the holster. His eyes rose from the holster. He looked directly into my eyes as he handed it to me. It was a burning glare. He didn't want to surrender to a common soldier. He was stiff and unbending. I could feel some of the tensions subside, as he knew his war was over and we would not schiessen.

Seeing the officer was unusual. You didn't capture many German officers in the heat of battle. It was obvious that this officer was not pleased to have had to surrender. Especially now! He must have felt it was very degrading and without traditional ceremony. I'm sure he would have preferred to surrender to an officer. He was not happy.

I took the small holster and pistol from the German officer's hand. I opened the holster and could see the butt of the pistol. The German officer's Walther pistol was a smaller automatic pistol than the normal Luger worn by most officers. The small pistol was made to be worn concealed. Before the war, the German secret police often used this model. I quickly put the pistol in my backpack so an American officer would not take it away (as they seemed to think they had the right to do).

We didn't talk with the prisoners. The mystery surrounding why this officer was carrying a small Walther 7mm pistol will probably never be known. Nor his name! We will never know why he was with this patrol. I don't recall what happened to the German patrol, but it was normal for one or two GIs to take them to the rear after we had made sure they had no weapons. The GIs would turn them over to the first American unit they came upon and then return to our unit. Someone else took the officer to the rear.

I have often wondered why the German officer and patrol surrendered to us. They must have been tired of the war and recognized that it was going bad for them. Sometimes surrendering German troops would hug you and smile. Other times they could be quite nervous and serious. Often, you could understand that some of them were quite relieved, especially when it was clear to them that we would treat them kindly.

This was a typical day in the life of a GI. I had been scared to death, and then I had captured a German officer, all in a matter of moments.

—*The* Bulge Bugle, *November 2000*

James V. Christy
B Company, 109th Infantry Regiment, 28th
Infantry Division

The British Army also played a part in the Battle of the Bulge,
as is recalled by James Christy.

LIKE ANY OTHER SURVIVOR OF THE BULGE, I have war stories to
make your hair stand on end, but here is one that probably
few people have heard.

The 109th Infantry Regiment, commanded by Lt. Col.
James E. Rudder (formerly of the 2nd Ranger Battalion
and Pointe-du-Hoc fame on D-day), served in Belgium and
Luxembourg in December 1944. We bent with the onslaught,
but we did not break, and though our losses were fearful,
Colonel Rudder somehow managed to hold the regiment
together until elements of the 80th Infantry Division relieved
us just before Christmas in the vicinity of Colmar-Berg,
Luxembourg, and continued on toward Ettelbruck. I was at
that time a first lieutenant and executive officer of B Company.
We thought we were through and due for a break, but soon
found ourselves attacking on Christmas Eve the little village
of Gilsdorf as part of Task Force Rudder with tanks of the
10th Armored Division. We took Gilsdorf, but that is really
another story.

Shortly after Christmas, we (the 109th) were trucked
to the rear around Neufchâteau and to an area of the north
flank of the German salient near Saint-Hubert. There we were
backing elements of the 87th Infantry Division and doing a
lot of rear-area patrolling, mostly motorized. On New Year's
Eve at 2400 hours I was in a Jeep tooling down a back road
in freezing weather. I simply could not resist welcoming the
New Year by letting off half a belt from the pedestal-mounted
LMG (light machine gun). A day or so later I got the mission

to contact British troops who were supposedly coming down to help us. I was assigned twenty men, to include two bazooka teams and two LMGs, with one one-and-a-halfton truck and two Jeeps. We took off in the direction of La Roche.

At one point along the way, we spotted tracked vehicles on the same road coming in our direction. We all bailed out, and I got the bazookas and LMGs in position to do some damage. They were Bren gun carriers from a British recon unit. Those things were not much bigger than the Weasels we had used too much in the Hürtgen Forest. After an exchange of pleasantries, we both continued on our way, the Brits south, us north. Shortly we found ourselves approaching a town in which a hot fire was in progress. This could have been La Roche or some smaller village nearby.

I halted my little group at the edge of town and started to deploy for a fight. About a hundred yards ahead at a crossroads I spotted a character with a black beret and a swagger stick who seemed to be directing the action. I told my second in command to go over and find out the situation. In short order he was back and stated as follows: "That guy would not talk to me. He asked me my rank right off, and when I said staff sergeant, he asked if there was an officer with us. He would talk to the officer only."

You better believe that got me a bit warm under the collar! In the past two weeks I had seen soldiers fight, bleed, and die almost every day without regard to rank or position. I myself wore no visible insignia for reasons I need not explain to combat-experienced people. And by the way, I am a West Pointer.

To come to the point of the story, I marched up to this jerk, and if I remember correctly, addressed him in these exact words: "Just what the Hell is your problem, Mac?" He immediately asked for my rank. I told him first lieutenant, United States Army, and demanded his. He said he was a major in the British Army, but actually a French national. I refrained from commenting on how French and British screw-ups were the reason we Americans were in Europe, but I was sorely tempted.

It turned out that the British soldiers had the situation well in hand, and our help was not needed. The Germans in the village were only stragglers. I reported the contact and situation to my battalion CO, and that was the end of that.

—*The* Bulge Bugle, *February 1991*

Harry Scheff
B Company, 22nd Tank Battalion, 11th Armored Division

The 11th Armored Division was in training in England when the German Ardennes Offensive began. General Eisenhower ordered the division into the Ardennes as part of the First Army on December 17. Harry Scheff recounts his introduction to the Battle of the Bulge.

MY FIRST ENCOUNTER IN THE BULGE was on December 27, 1944. Company B, 22nd Tank Battalion, had moved up on the line between Houffalize and Bastogne. James Salisbury, the Jeep driver, 1st Sgt. Daniel Boone, and I were told to stay with the 55th Infantry Regiment kitchen until the commanding officer, Captain Bell, called us to join the company. While walking two days, we were attacked by enemy planes in the morning and evening of December 28 and 29. On December 30, we tried to contact our company by radio, to no avail. At that point we took off for the front, asking men we met on the way if they knew where Company B, 22nd Tank Battalion, was. When we pulled in to the company area, we saw First Lieutenant Sowden walking toward Headquarters Company. We called to him and saw an amazed and then happy look on his face.

When we told him where we were, he said, "No officer was informed." Captain Bell was seriously wounded in the leg. First Lieutenant Sowden was in command and on his way to report the three of us missing in action. When we were told that, I said, "If we had known that, we would have gone back to Paris," and, as a result, all our tensions were relaxed and we all had a good laugh!

—*The* Bulge Bugle, *May 1993*

Wilfred "Mac" McCarty
B Company, 21st Armored Infantry Battalion, 11th Armored Division

Eisenhower decided on December 28 to allow the green 11th Armored Division to be used to counterattack the German positions in the Ardennes. Wilfred McCarty recounts how little time he spent in battle before being wounded.

ON DECEMBER 30, 1944, MY COMPANY made contact with the enemy near Jodenville, Belgium, and forced them to withdraw to the high ground southwest of Chenogne. During our battle outside Jodenville, a German 88 shell and I tried to share the same space (the Germans thought that I was a tank). The shell landed next to me, and while most of the shrapnel fell over me, I was knocked silly and sprayed with shrapnel. It was like fifteen people had kicked me in sensitive parts of my body with heavy GI shoes. I thought that I was going to die, and I did not know for sure what country I was in—Belgium or Luxembourg (it was Belgium).

I was suddenly surprised to see a GI that I did not know standing near me. He had been hit in the face with shrapnel— probably from the same 88 shell that hit me. He seemed to be in shock, and for some strange reason, I thought that his gloves were bloodier than mine. So as not to cause him any more anxiety, I suggested that we exchange gloves—which we did without a word. I then remembered that we were supposed to take eight tablets with water if we were hit. I counted out the tablets one by one and gave them to the other GI, but I forgot to take any tablets myself. I did, however, give myself a shot of morphine.

Someone in the tank that the Germans had missed then threw me a blanket and moved on. I was now a foot soldier lying in the snow with what felt like frozen legs. Then a Jeep came out with bullets still firing, and I was taken to a tent hospital to be treated. They eventually moved him out of my line of vision.

After my operation, I saw the soldier who had been hit in the face with shrapnel. He was not badly wounded, but the blood on his face had made the injury look worse. We laughed when we saw each other. (We had been two scared GIs.)

I was then sent back to England for further operations. When I was better, I was sent back to the front a second time via boxcars that were used in World War I. The sign on the boxcar read, *"Hommes 40, Chevaux 8* (40 men or 8 horses)."

—*The* Bulge Bugle, *February 2001*

Hal O'Neill
83rd Infantry Division

The 83rd Infantry Division was located on the southern shoulder of the German salient in the Ardennes and was caught by surprise, as was everybody else, by the enemy advance into the Ardennes. Hal O'Neil was a military postman and kept the mail going throughout the Battle of the Bulge.

THE 83RD DIVISION WAS PULLED OUT OF GERMANY and sent southwest across Holland into northern Belgium. Bumper-to-bumper military vehicles stretched for miles on a road on top of a dike surrounded by flooded fields. Air cover patrolled overhead, and when a vehicle broke down, it was pushed off into the ditch or field. I was transferred to a messenger Jeep that now required three men instead of two. The MPs stopped us repeatedly to ask about the winner of the World Series or Betty Grable's leading man in some movie. This was to detect English-speaking Germans in our rear areas.

The Jeep had chains on all four wheels, and the windshield lay on the hood to stop reflections. We put up a ten-inch board for a windshield and drove with a bobbing motion, peeking over it to see the road. Welded to the front bumper was a six-foot-tall angle iron with a notch to catch and break cables strung across the road at night. We carried K-rations and sometimes ten-in-one rations that we heated on the engine block. You had to remember to punch a hole in the can or it would explode, and the Jeep smelled of burnt eggs or Spam. Jeeps had no winch, so larger vehicles had to pull or push us out of drifts or ditches.

We wore long johns, wool shirt and pants, and mackinaws instead of overcoats. Finger gloves were useless, so we traded with German prisoners for their fur-lined mittens and a rabbit fur vest. The cost was only a few cigarettes. I wore three pairs of socks with size twelve boots instead of my normal size nine. Towels with eye holes protected our faces. Wet feet meant trench foot, and frostbite was a problem. We usually had a pair of socks drying from armpit warmth, and growing a beard helped.

The messenger Jeeps ran between the divisional HQ and the three infantry regiments' HQs. With units on the move, the info was often out of date, and we spent two or three days on the road before returning to divisional HQ. Thirty-five-year-old Pop did most of the driving, and I did the navigation. Teenage Elmer did a lot of sleeping. We rotated sitting in the back seat, since it was the coldest.

The army issued single-blanket sleeping bags, so we stopped at an aid station to pick up blankets with the least blood stains. Outdoors or in a building, we put six or seven blankets underneath and as many above. Only our boots were removed for sleeping.

One bitter night we parked between two blazing buildings for extra warmth, and another time we slept on the second floor of a windmill. Heavy Elmer collapsed the staircase, so Pop and I used our tow rope to get down. We threatened to put him on a diet.

Near the end of the Battle of the Bulge, we picked up an illegal trailer that had no lights or brakes. It carried a small pot-bellied stove, stovepipe, briquets of coal dust and molasses or something, a 220-volt radio, allo-volt radio, souvenirs, wine for Pop, rations, and a tarp for a ground sheet. Also, there were army overcoats or mackinaws, depending on how close we were to returning to divisional HQ, and extra cigarettes or coffee when we passed a farm with people still living there.

None of us even caught a cold, and we were happy when told to head to a coal mine for delousing and showers. The lice came from sleeping in barns and were known as mechanized dandruff.

Message center is the post office for military mail. The messenger Jeeps made regular runs from division to higher HQ and to lower HQ: regiment and some attached units. Normally, there were no overnight runs, but the Bulge was very different. Before a run, I would check the division's wall map for our destination, gas points, and unrepaired bridges. The HQ assigned often had moved, and it took all day to find them. We did not drive at night, even with blackout headlights, because all the other traffic was bigger than our vehicle.

There was a lot of "Help your buddy." If you saw someone in trouble, you stopped to help or they stopped to help you.

Truck drivers told us of road and bridge conditions, a farm house that had chickens, wine, a place to sleep, et cetera.

Signal got free cartons of cigarettes, and since I did not smoke, they came in handy to swap with German prisoners for mittens or swastika-decorated daggers or other items. We had few flat tires, but used to get them fixed for a few cigarettes before the Bulge. During the Bulge we drove on the rim until we found a wrecked Jeep and removed a wheel.

Some Jeeps never returned. Mostly this was caused by road accidents. Drivers using the throttle because their feet were too cold to use the gas pedal were slow to react to a curve or blocked road. The brain told them to hit the brakes—and then added, push in the throttle. If you turned over in a Jeep, you were dead if not thrown clear. We lost one vehicle to enemy action. A shell exploded near the Jeep, and the driver went off the road.

On one run in bitter weather, we had only one item in the mail sack. It was a clerk's afterthought to an earlier message: division-rear officers' showers will open at 0930 hours instead of 0900 hours. We turned back to an undamaged farmhouse and went to sleep. Routine paperwork went on, covering late morning reports, maintenance records on truck trailers, et cetera.

We believed that if the army ever lost all the typewriters, it would grind to a halt. We wondered, if the U.S. Army was so confused and stupid and yet was winning the war, what was it like in the German army?

The weather cleared and the sky was full of our planes, which we could hear bombing and strafing in the distance. A thaw set in and the roads were a mess.

Before being pulled out of the Bulge, we made a special run to, and got arrested by, the rear-echelon-area MPs. Charges were: unshaven, filthy uniforms, filthy vehicle, unauthorized modifications to vehicle, no driver's licenses, and no shot records. We happily pleaded guilty and looked forward to a warm cell. A disgusted MP captain ordered us to get out of town and back to our unit. I bet he had the office deloused after we left.

We detoured by a dock full of new Jeep trailers, and one followed us, so we adopted it. It towed well, had brakes and tail lights. We painted new numbers on it and our unit designation.

Once the Battle of the Bulge was over, the 83rd was pulled out to rest and train replacements. Some of us were filthy lousy, had trench foot, a little frostbite, and only the clothing we stood in. A delousing center was set up at the shower house of a Belgian coal mine. You put your valuables in a sealed envelope, stripped, and entered the very large mine shower room. Over a hundred men were showering under pipes set in the ceiling. There were no stalls or partitions, and some men lay on the floor in six inches of warm, dirty water, while others wandered about seeking the ideal temperature. The pipes nearest the boilers gave very hot water, and those farthest away gave icy cold. Every twenty minutes, a sergeant ordered us out to make room for others. Some stayed anyway, and others were asleep on the floor. After we dried off, a medic checked for trench foot, half-healed injuries, and skin diseases. Then, we were issued brand-new uniforms, underwear, and boots. My buddies and I ran back to our Jeep, removed the new outfit, and put on another set of dirty clothing. We then got back in line, and I ended up with three new outfits plus boots.

Outside of Hamouir, Belgium, nine of us enlisted men lived in a greenhouse with a glass roof and two potbellied stoves that heated anything within four feet of us. We had cots, many blankets, and lots of housekeeping items. At dawn I awoke and without getting completely out of bed, started a fire in the stove next to me using wood and pressed coal bricks kept under my bed. As the stove warmed up, I put a large (unwashed) frying pan on the top. Someone else got the other stove going and put on a big, unwashed (to preserve flavor?) coffee pot. I put a huge chunk of butter in the frying pan to melt for frying slices of bread. As it was eaten, I put in Spam and fresh eggs. Civilian plates from our large supply from wrecked houses were passed from cot to cot followed by mugs of coffee. Used only once, unwashed dishes and mugs joined a pile in the back garden after each meal.

Since we all rode messenger Jeeps, we were able to live quite well. My notes show that on one day we brought in a ten-pound chunk of frozen chop-meat, a large can of British marmalade, dried apples, French bread, and four kinds of wine. All day coffee and hot soup simmered for those coming in from a run half-frozen. If desperate, we could eat at the company mess. The CO often put troublemakers into the Mess Section. I remember watching a partly sober cook with two large pots— one to mix pancake batter and one for regurgitation. I suspect he sometimes got the pots mixed.

As Sherman said, "War could be Hell, if you let it!"

Eduardo Alberto Peniche
C Battery, 81st Antitank-Antiaircraft Airborne Battalion, 502nd Parachute Infantry Regiment, 101st Airborne Division

Some of the strongest attacks on Bastogne, held by the 101st Airborne Division, occurred after the Third Army had broken through to the town. Edurado Peniche remembers one violent battle that kept the Germans out of Bastogne.

THE NEW YEAR OF 1945 WAS WELCOMED with a big bang in our sector; it seemed that our division's artillery and mortars had joined every gun on the Third Army front in a midnight barrage, all of them pouring high explosives toward the German lines. By this date, the entire Bastogne area was deep in snow that had been coming down in intervals during the seven days of the siege.

We had left Camp Mourmelon in France at 1500 hours Monday, December 18, 1944. In our deployment toward Bastogne, Belgium, our AT Squad (C Battery AT, 81st AT/ AA Airborne Battalion) was assigned to Company D, 2nd Battalion, 502nd Parachute Infantry Regiment. By dawn on Tuesday, December 19, we took defensive positions in the outskirts of the village of Longchamps. We emplaced our 57mm AT gun (it was a British gun, a six-pounder) on the knoll overlooking a valley. We were covering one of the main roads leading into Bastogne. Our main mission was to protect the roadblock on that road. We had piled all the plows and other farm implements that we could find in the area to set the roadblock, and we felt that we could defend and hold the position against any German attack. We had dug the gun in until the barrel was just barely above the snow. Down in front of us was no man's land.

On January 3, 1945, the 502nd Parachute Infantry Regiment was attacked in force and its main line of resistance was overrun by enemy armor. The action began around 1330 hours. The enemy armor came down the road which runs southward from Compogne to Longchamps. In a well-planned maneuver the German tanks, about fifteen or seventeen of them, fanned out for the attack. They were being followed by infantrymen and panzergrenadiers. It was a fierce and determined attack against our front. As the German tanks and infantry began to advance against our position and toward the road block, our squad leader, Sgt. Joe O'Toole (Vincennes, Indiana) gave us orders to engage the enemy—the enemy fire was effectively raking our positions. The entire Longchamps-Monaville front was under attack!

I am sure that at that moment everyone else was scared as I was. . . . Private First Class Lafred Steen (Bronx, New York) was ready to load the piece again as PFC Darrell Garner (Florence, South Carolina), our gunner, was finding the range. I quickly moved two more antitank shells to the gun position, making sure they had armor-piercing fuse, a new type of high-velocity shell.

Several air bursts exploded between us and the roadblock; our machine gunners to our right were keeping the grenadiers from reaching the road block. As a Mark VI Tiger tank approached that point in the road, we hit it twice; the second shot took its turret off, and as the crew was leaving the burning tank, they were riddled with machine gun fire—our AP ammunition was proving to be very effective AT ordnance. Behind our position one or two armor vehicles (either TDs or captured German half-tracks or SP guns, not too clear which) sporadically came up the ridge to lob a shell or two against the attacking force. The German 88s were proving to be accurate and devastating—shells and bullets were spraying our emplacement. In reality, once an AT gun is committed to battle, its position is easily spotted, and the situation becomes one of do-or-die. There are no avenues of retreat nor room for maneuverability.

I crawled back to our ammo dump to bring more AT shells and assisted in loading the gun. As we destroyed a second tank, all hell broke loose around us. We were determined to offer a heavy resistance, but the German gunners zeroed in on our emplacement; we were being hit with everything that the enemy could fire. It was the hour of the mad minute. It was that terrifying moment when all the weapons on the line seemed to explode violently all at once. The incoming shells were so numerous that the ground shook. One gun took a direct hit and was destroyed. All three of us, O'Toole, Garner, and I, were hit by shrapnel. The battle raged on all around us, and the TDs and our mortars were hitting the advancing German infantry. The German tanks were not advancing but were continuing their murderous fire. The mad minute indeed was upon us at Longchamps, and yet, our other AT squads were joining the firefight.

By this time, I crawled to assist O'Toole, who had been severely wounded in the hip and leg. He was bleeding profusely and looked like he was going into shock. To mitigate the pain, he had given himself a shot of morphine. Darrell was hit in the face and shoulder. My left leg was numb above the knee, but my knee was hurting a lot. I looked down and saw the blood on my muddy trousers. Voices and moans of some other men could be heard. I remember praying both in English and Spanish. As I crawled on the snow toward the ridge, I heard the bullets and the shrapnel cutting the air above me, but I needed to reach our CP just behind the knoll. We needed medical attention. The entire mad episode could not have lasted more than fifteen or twenty minutes.

I finally reached the CP and reported what had happened and was happening. While the medic was tending my wound (foreign body, left knee), I heard our artillery rounds heading toward the advancing Germans. It was then I realized how close I had been to being killed in action. It was then that I realized once again that we were heavily engaged with the enemy. Casualties on both sides proved to be numerous.

The attack lasted three hours. Several of our division artillery guns were ordered to assume antitank positions in anticipation of a possible breakthrough. More TDs were being thrown into battle, and thus our line held. The crisis at Longchamps was over for the moment. Our wounded were being evacuated to field hospitals. My ambulance was on its way to Arlon. The trooper on the stretcher below me mumbled something, and I agreed—for us the Battle of the Bulge was over.

In summary, we had been exposed to terrible moments of adversity before a determined attacking force, but we had given a good account of ourselves. Of our five 75mm guns attached to the 2nd Battalion, 502nd Parachute Infantry Regiment, four were knocked out during that afternoon, but in the meantime we performed splendidly. The antitank gunners of Battery C, 81st AT/AA Airborne Battalion, were credited with knocking out ten Mark IV tanks, but in effect two of those tanks were Tiger tanks, Mark VI, destroyed by our squad.

As for me, although I received the Purple Heart and the Bronze Star with "V" for bravery, my greatest award at Longchamps was, and has been, that Almighty God allowed me to rub shoulders with such gallant comrades-in-arms as I did that afternoon of long ago, where I experienced the mad minute in battle.

—*The* Bulge Bugle, *December 1992*

George Nicklin
K Company, 47th Infantry Regiment, 9th Infantry Division

One of the most respected men in any infantry unit was the medic. They would do almost anything to help a wounded man and therefore suffered very high losses in battle. Medic George Nicklin recalls how the death of one man has affected him so much.

NO ONE HAS HAUNTED ME MORE DURING my lifetime than my friend Lone Prophet. He is indeed a man with a bizarre name. When you hear this name, you would assume in our financially burdened world that the spelling should be "Loan Profit." Lone

281

Prophet is, however, decidedly the real name of a real man, who lived in the United States and Europe during the 1940s.

How did I become to be so haunted by him? Where has this led me? It has led me into the unexpectedness of life with which all of us must struggle. I met Lone Prophet just before New Year's Day in 1944. It was a very cold late December. We were in beautiful, picturesque Kalterherberg, a village of about two hundred to three hundred pastel-painted houses in the German Ardennes Forest. The houses were amazing in that they had three-feet-thick concrete walls. In the middle of the town was a beautiful Catholic church, whose doors stood wide open with the snow streaming in and forming drifts on the floor of the sanctuary. A hallowedness pervaded me as alone I explored the empty church.

I was coming back to a group of men with whom I had entered combat on October 22, 1944, in the intense fighting centered on Aachen. I had been with them until December 18, a week earlier, when I had left for an intense course in emergency first aid treatment. Previously in the U.S., I had had a term of pre-med education. I had discovered from experience on the front lines that medics were at a high premium. They had an amazingly short life expectancy. When the army notified me that they wanted to use my medical expertise as a medical corpsman, I was horrified, or—perhaps more accurately—mortified. I realized that the risks were considerably higher than my previous job of being a regular infantryman.

I had the good luck to be assigned as a medic to my former company—K Company, 2nd Platoon. The company had four platoons but only three medics—weapons platoon did not have a medic. Members of that platoon were taken care of by the three other platoons' medics.

Shortly after my return to K Company, I ran into Lone Prophet. When he told me his name, I was astonished. I asked him about the origins of his name. Prophet said that his mother liked the name Lone Prophet. He replied that he viewed the name as indicative of the family he came from. Prophet revealed that he came from a small village in the hills of Kentucky, near the Tennessee border. Time has dimmed my memory as to the name of that village. His family and their neighbors were characterized as hillbillies. He was very reticent about addressing this, but there was a hint of the hillbilly evident in his accent. The accent was a throwback to spoken English of the sixteenth or seventeenth century.

As the days and weeks wore on during the winter of 1944–45 in that snow in Kalterherberg, I saw Lone Prophet at least every two or three days. He was a medic for the 3rd Platoon, and I for the 2nd Platoon. I do not recall the name of the medic for the 1st Platoon, though perhaps the shortened life expectancy of medics had left the 1st without one. When we met, we were always very pleased to see one another. After reassuring each other as to our respective healths, we would discuss the state of our platoons' medical supplies. Usually one, if not both, of us had been to the battalion aid station the previous day to stock up on medical supplies. We would exchange bandages, adhesive tape, syrettes of morphine, et cetera, so that our medical kits would be adequately supplied. Prophet and I developed a strong sense of affection for one another. We were both very pleased with our continued mutual well being.

We were on the northern hinge of the Bulge. How many wounded did we have to treat? It did not seem that we had many wounded. The fighting was very desultory, though there were spurts of extreme fighting followed by quiet accentuated by the snow. The snow was very deep. Our foxholes, previously occupied by the Germans, were very comfortable. We emerged from the foxholes several times a day to assess the situation. Occasionally, we would have combat sorties into German lines, where we would capture prisoners and kill some Germans. As we got farther beyond January 1, the German ability to attack diminished. By the end of January we had advanced several miles within the Hürtgen forest, part of the Ardennes.

Toward the end of January my supplies were low, and I thought it might be easier to secure them from Prophet, who was in a neighboring dugout. I arrived at the dugout within a few minutes. Prophet's dugout had the advantage of being in a well-forested area. The dugout's undesirable characteristic was that the German-built dugout's entrance was open to the German lines. The entrance was capacious, two door widths wide, as was the interior, which included several stoves for heat. The dugout was reasonably well lit with candles.

As I moved through this dugout's entrance, Prophet and I discussed our need for medical supplies. After separating our pooled bandages and morphine, we exchanged different widths of gauze. We had iodine and mercurochrome for the wounds and a morphine derivative for diarrhea, which was quite prevalent among the soldiers. Many of the soldiers had problems not only with their bowels but with their urinary control. At times it was said jokingly, "It was quite clear. We are trickling across Europe." I had to evacuate some military personnel because their skin was constantly wet from urinary incontinence. The skin would begin to deteriorate, necessitating hospitalization.

I then returned to my dugout, which I shared with two or three other members of the headquarters staff of my platoon. Soon after, I head heavy shelling originating on the German side and directed at us. One of the shells seemed to land in the area of Prophet's dugout. I did not dwell on the proximity of the shelling. Prophet's dwelling appeared capable of withstanding any kind of fire short of a direct shell hit.

After the artillery barrage quieted, I decided to check on Prophet, who was located two to three hundred yards away through the forest. I could smell the artillery explosions as I approached Prophet's dugout. Two or three men, whom I had seen earlier in the dugout, were standing outside. Some smoke was emerging through the dugout's entrance.

As I walked forward, a soldier cried out, "Don't go in!" I explained that I was the medic from the 2nd Platoon and had come to see their medic. Again the soldier cautioned me about entering. He told me that I couldn't see Prophet. Surprised by the comment, I said, "Why?" He replied, "Prophet is dead!" I asked if he could share with me what had happened. The soldier responded that he would do so reluctantly.

Prophet's death was described as a terrible experience, though the actual death was quick. Prophet had been standing just inside the doorway when a shell exploded directly upon his waistline and blew him in half. The soldier was very upset by the recitation of this series of events. He had seen Prophet while the upper part of his torso was still alive. Prophet had continued to speak, oblivious to his own separated body. Within sixty seconds, Prophet was unconscious and dead. It was a terrible experience for the soldier and me. A terrible way for Prophet to die, blessed only by its speed.

As I walked away, I was assaulted by emotions. I thought this death was paradoxic: incredibly brave and concurrently awful. The memories surrounding this death exist as vividly for me today, years later, as they did immediately after the actual occurrence. Those memories haunt me. I thought I should have written a letter to his mother, but I didn't know her address or how to find it. I only know that he was from the Appalachian area of Kentucky. As a product of this environment, Prophet had led a hard but an interesting life. He was a fascinating man with an amazing name. Such are the fortunes of war.

—*The* Bulge Bugle, *February 2001*

James Graff
C Company, 134th Infantry Regiment, 35th Infantry Division

The German attack in the Ardennes was to be the last in a line of great offensives and military adventures initiated by Hitler and the German military since World War II began in September 1939. James Graff details what he and so many other unsung replacements went through to win back the ground acquired by the enemy since December 16.

AFTER LEAVING CAMP HOOD, TEXAS, with a ten-day delay en route home, we arrived at Fort Meade, Maryland. We did some training, including firing on the rifle range, then had a train ride (through New York City at night) to Camp Myles Standish at Boston, Massachusetts.

We were trucked down to the Boston docks and loaded on the British liner *Aquitania*. This ship had hauled troops to the Dardanelles Campaign in World War I. We went on board ship as advance party. I was a saltwater corporal and went to carry food to the serving line. I boarded ship December 20, 1944, and never saw so much mail: they loaded for forty-eight hours.

We had eight thousand men on board, and guess who I saw? Bill Charis, a boy from near home. I had run across him in Fort Meade, and now I saw him about every day in the chow line and the evening I got off the boat. We were packed four high without much room to move, but the monotony of it was broken by our KP work. I sure liked to watch the water, and it was pretty at night: no lights, just the sky and stars. It was a little scary throwing garbage off the fantail with no railing at night. Christmas Eve on the ship saw an uproar by the men when the order came out for all enlisted men to go to their quarters and all officers to the saloon for Christmas caroling. Christmas dinner featured pork chops.

We set sail December 22 and never saw land or another ship until we entered the Irish Sea on the seventh day out. Our destination was Greencock, Scotland, which is the port for Glasglow. The ship docked late in the afternoon, or rather dropped anchor in the harbor, and almost immediately we began to disembark. We had to walk over a narrow gangplank to a small, coal-fired British boat. We assembled on the dock and then were loaded on a train, which was to take us to Southampton. Next morning we did see much of the English countryside and took a ride through London. We detrained at Southampton and boarded trucks to a tent city. A lot of Italian prisoners were here and also colored GIs. We requisitioned a gas lantern and some fuel from the "eyeties" (slang term for Italians), and one night at Southampton we went out through the fence and went to a local pub.

The next day we were alerted for another move, onto trucks and down to the harbor and onto some small British ships for movement across the English Channel. We crossed during the night, New Year's Eve, and in daylight transferred to LSTs and were ferried to the beach and waded ashore. We were at Le Havre (France) and the whole harbor was full of sunken ships. Masts and funnels marked their graves. We marched through the town and up a hill which was pretty steep. We went into a tent city which at one time must have been a German ammo dump, drew some PX rations, and it rained.

Next day we walked down and boarded trains for a move east. Three nights and two days of French boxcars, and it was cold, and snow covered the ground after the first night. One man fell under the train and lost a leg. We messed along the tracks, with field kitchens with GI cooks and German POWs to serve. No stops to go to the toilet: just do it in your steel helmet and pass it to the door and hope somebody doesn't throw hat and all out. Kelso fixed up a hammock, but the hammock and

Kelso both fell down. Those frogs (slang term for the French people) used the throttle and the brake very hard. Lots of guys' feet began to freeze before we ever arrived at the front.

The morning of the third day on the forty and eights, we detrained and started walking. We saw our first casualty, a German corpse on a stretcher, and a sign, "Danger (MINEN) Mines." We were at Metz, an old French fortress city. We were billeted in an old cavalry barracks with a big quadrangle parade ground out in front. It was a cold, three-story stone building. Here we drew rifles and got two clips to zero them in. I talked to two guys out of 26th Infantry Division, who told of heavy fighting in the area north of here. We had known before we left the states of a German counterattack in Belgium. Now it looked like we would be part of it.

On January 8, I think, we were alerted, our names were called, and we loaded on 6x6s, open trucks, with colored drivers. It turned out to be about ninety miles in a few degrees above zero temperatures. On this trip we were to see Gen. George S. Patton, the Third Army commander; we recognized him by his pearl-handle revolvers. In Metz we were told that we were joining the 35th Division. We arrived in Martelange, Belgium, and were assigned to the 134th Infantry Regiment of the 35th Division. They divided us by alphabetical order, and I went to C Company. The chaplain of the 1st Battalion gave us some indoctrination, something of the history of the regiment and what was expected of us.

Some of us were billeted with a family by the name of Blum. This was the kitchen area of the regiment. On January 10 we loaded on quarter-ton trucks and moved out. We de-trucked in the woods and passed the battalion aid station and some 90mm antiaircraft guns being used as artillery. As yet we had not been issued any ammunition. As we moved up, we came to an 81mm mortar position, and a red-haired sergeant was standing there. Three mortars, all facing different directions, were in place. I asked, "Why are they faced in different directions?" The reply: "You damned fool, we're surrounded on three sides."

Soon we were going across an open field, and behind a wrecked barn a member of our supply group was giving us two bandoliers of ammo and six grenades. A little farther up, we met several POWs under guard of a single GI. The trail led through pine plantations, which about every quarter mile had a one-hundred-yard firebreak. In one of these firebreaks the trail wound around what I took to be some tree branches—in reality, the black-booted legs of a dead German officer almost buried in snow. Just beyond him was another corpse, lying on his back, his mouth filled with snow, with the bluest eyes you ever saw. To our left up the break were scores more of dead Germans, victims of tank machine gun fire. They had been dead for several days, but here the dead were preserved by the cold.

It was dark when we finally reached C Company's positions. They divided us up and a guy said, "I am Sergeant Storm and you belong to the 2nd squad. Walk to your right and get in a hole with a guy down there."

I walked down and someone said, "Over here." I crawled into a hole and introduced myself, and my companion identified himself as Pfc. Bruce Boyce, of South Paris, Maine. I thought here was a chance to learn what to do and what to expect. I said, "How long have you been in the line?" He replied, "Seven -----ing days," which I was to learn was a lot longer than some men lasted up here. You know, I didn't know what he looked like till morning. I stood guard that night but really didn't know what to look for.

Next morning's breakfast of pancakes, syrup, spam, and coffee was not too bad. As we were in reserve, we were able to move around some, and pretty soon I was approached by a tall, older man. He asked where I was from, and when I answered, "Illinois," he said, "Chicago?" I said, "Hell, no." He introduced himself as Bob Landrum, and I found out he had hauled corn from Mount Pulaski and Shirley, Illinois. He asked if I was familiar with traveling in the woods, and I said yes. He answered that a platoon runner was needed, and he wanted one who wouldn't get lost in the woods. Also, I would have to use a walkie-talkie radio. I answered that I would do anything to help and do the best job I could.

So I moved in with the platoon headquarters group, which consisted of Landrum, who was the platoon guide, and the platoon sergeant, Tech. Sgt. Kenneth McCrea, or Scotty, as everyone called him. I spent the rest of the day getting acquainted with my new job and my new comrades.

Next morning we were alerted to move out. While rolling our blanket rolls (four blankets and a shelter half with one roll to two men), a shot rang out along with the shout, "Medic." One man had shot himself in the wrist, accidentally or not, so our first American casualty was a self-inflicted wound.

We changed position, still in reserve; only an occasional explosion from artillery betrayed our enemy. In our new position we occupied former German holes, and these had tops. In the immediate area was a knocked-out kraut chow wagon, a dead horse, a dead driver with the lines still in his hands, and a dead German medic with glasses. Also there were two dead GIs who had been killed sometime before, as their pockets and packs had been searched, probably by the Germans.

I had to take a telephone and wire out to an outpost, and upon arriving back at the company CP, I experienced one of the oddest happenings of my overseas service. I and a company runner (Private First Class Stenis) were standing in a shallow trench about knee deep, when from the direction of the German lines came a figure. The runner called, "Halt!" This individual stopped. We gave the sign. He didn't answer. It was repeated and again no answer. I asked his name, and he answered with a German accent and German name. Stenis shouted, "A kraut!" and lifted his rifle to shoot. I knocked it down and ran and jumped on this man. We dragged him down into the CP, and by candlelight he looked like a GI, but didn't sound like one. He claimed he was out of K Company (in reserve behind us). His name was Henrick something or other. Finally, the CO called the 3rd Battalion by radio and confirmed that this man was missing. We kept him until morning and sent him back. I hope he realized how close to death he was.

Next day we moved up and dug in again. Here we found where the krauts had built stalls for their horses. They cut saplings for stalls and bedded them with straw. Grave registration crews were collecting German and American dead. They stacked them like cordwood; all were frozen solid. One officer carried a two-by-four and would break arms or legs so the bodies would lie better. I remember that Scotty, Landrum, and I all slept in one hole.

Next day we moved back to a little town and slept in an open cattle shed, and as next day was Sunday, we had church. The 1st Battalion chaplain was a good preacher and a good guy. Church attendance was a lot better here than in the States. Somebody said that "there were no atheists in a foxhole."

The next day we moved back to Marvie, the town where C Company had jumped off on January 4 when they were really ass-holed in the woods. Paratroopers of the 101st Airborne Division had held this town during the siege of Bastogne. There were wrecked gliders and C-47s (twin-engine transport planes) in the fields that were used to supply the 101st when they were surrounded. A P-47 was making strafing and bombing runs northeast of here. There was a knocked-out kraut tank up by the church, a GI Jeep and 6x6 truck knocked out by a bomb, and the barn they were next to contained several cows and chickens in their nests, killed by concussion and frozen solid.

We found a half of beef hanging in a tree. We ate it and then killed another and left it for the next outfit. Most of the civilians were gone, and what livestock was left was wandering, looking for food and water.

Today, I believe, Steinhaufel rejoined the 3rd Platoon. He had been wounded at Habkirchen. Also, a deserter by the name of Smith from Sandoval, Illinois, rejoined us. He had run off several times before, and Storm told him not to try it again or it would be too bad. When we fell out next morning, he was gone. They caught him a few days later, and he was court-martialed. These kinds of cases were not unusual, we were to find out. Many men would do anything to get out of the front line. I have already told of a self-inflicted wound; I was to witness two more such cases, one by a man, Grestbauer, who went overseas with us. Desertion was also very common, although some men came back in a day or two of their own free will.

Next morning we moved out and were to join elements of the 6th Armored Division in pushing east. As we moved into Arloncourt, we saw fifteen knocked-out tanks and a field of dead GIs. One man had a 300 radio on his back with four or five bullet holes in it. These tanks had been knocked out earlier in the campaign, but three 6th Armored tanks were burning when we came up, and wounded and burned tankers were being pulled out of a half-track. It looked to me as if the krauts had shot a lot of livestock on pulling out. We ate dinner where three dead cows lay in the street, and the blood wasn't frozen yet. It kinda pissed me off, just to kill them for the hell of it. A dead kraut was under the steps, and Nathaniel Schaeffer (from Philadelphia) got sick and couldn't eat.

We moved out into the woods and found a wounded GI on a stretcher and another limping back, hollering, "I got a million-dollar wound and I'm going to the rear." They had been hit by their own artillery. Again and again we would encounter our own artillery or tank fire and on a couple of occasions would be bombed by our own planes.

We dug in for the night next to some armored infantry. We got some hot chow up, but they only had K-rations. That is one trouble with the armored infantry. They never had a kitchen up, and maybe it was just the fault of their officers. One thing about the 134th Infantry Regiment was that we got hot chow whenever possible and also bed rolls. We were not burdened down with mess gear and blankets like some outfits. I have helped hand-carry chow and bedrolls for as much as a mile, but it sure beats cold Ks and no blankets because you had thrown them away.

That evening a kraut tank refueled just a few hundred yards from us right out in the open. We had two Sherman tanks, but they wanted us to try some 60mm mortar fire on them. Lieutenant Chappel said nothing doing. If they wouldn't fight them with tanks, he'd play hell exposing his men to tank fire just to satisfy our tankers. Although a lot of the guys won't agree with me, this was the first of many times that I saw Chappel stand up for his men, refusing to attack or commit them unless they were properly supported, a far cry from some previous company commanders that C Company has had.

Next morning we moved out to cut a highway east of us. As we moved into the woods near a big house, a German tank (maybe the one we had seen the evening before) opened up on us. There was one of our supporting tanks near us, and I guess that the kraut was really aiming for him, as he was using AP (armor piercing ammunition) rather than HE (high explosive). About three or four rounds were wild and high, the only casualty being a couple of trees. The tank crew jumped in their vehicle, as they had been standing outside, although the engine was running. They backed around and opened up with their coaxial machine gun and then "bang," their 75mm fired, and they hit the kraut, first shot. He caught fire after the third round, and we didn't see anybody get out.

Sergeant Landrum had a prayer he read to the 3rd Platoon before jumping off and one after the day had ended. This prayer service was known to a lot of attached units (such as the heavy machine gunners of D Company). We all knelt in the snow, uncovered, with bowed heads while Bob read the prayer. Private First Class Boyce was a scout one day and missed the service. He was wounded in the head later on that same day, and afterwards I heard him say the reason he got hit was because he missed the service.

Soon, we had come under German tank fire and were digging in. Our medic (Young) who had joined us a day before didn't have a shovel, and about then a shell landed in a tree among us. Kittleson (Lisbon, Illinois) was killed, and Boyce, Iacovone, Blankenship, Hammonds, Locke, Hoff, and one more were wounded. These men, with the exception of Boyce, were all men who had come overseas with me. These were our first casualties. Storm's overcoat hanging in a tree was riddled. We were under German tank fire, and if you have never faced it, is like nothing you ever saw or heard. It was zip-bang, high velocity, and no time to duck, because you didn't hear them until the shells were over you.

Again we were digging in when we heard tanks moving. A small road was near us, and a tank was coming down it, the turret turned toward us, and I thought this is it. I noticed it was an American, and it kept on going, but to this day I think it was one of ours that the krauts had captured. Evidently they didn't see us.

By evening we were on the highway. I saw a couple of krauts down the highway, but they were out of range. This, the 17th of January, was our first day of actual combat, the day of the first battle casualties. I happened to notice that the aerial on the radio was clipped short, cut by a piece of shrapnel. I didn't like that and made up my mind to get rid of this job as soon as possible. The medic and I dug in together and helped carry bedrolls and night chow (coffee and roast beef sandwiches) for almost a mile. While Storm and I were standing drinking coffee, someone walked past, and Storm remarked, "Looked like he had on kraut mess gear." In a couple of minutes someone hollered, "We got a prisoner." He had walked through two platoons of infantry and a section of heavy machine guns but didn't say anything until challenged. He could have killed a half dozen, including me, but his intention was to surrender; such was the German mind. We picked up a prisoner earlier who had hid out and followed a telephone line in, and he said, "Three years in the army and I hadn't made corporal yet, so I thought I would surrender."

We were next moved back to Michamps, a little town, and I believe we walked all the way. This town was practically destroyed. The 3rd platoon took over a house with the second story and roof shot off. It had a 105mm dud round in the kitchen, and we stayed here for several days, and it was still there when we left. Only two rooms were habitable. As I was hunting for some hay or straw to sleep on, I came across a house-barn combination which the krauts had used for an aid station. The Red Cross flag was still flying. As I opened a small shed, I noticed a blanket covering some things. I pulled it back, and there lay a dead German who was dressed in GI pants and blue knit socks. His hair was long and black, and he had died of a massive head wound. His German dog tag was still around his neck. Possibly he was a member of

295

one of the units dressed and equipped with American equipment that had spearheaded some of the German attacks in the Ardennes.

Another bizarre incident occurred while we were in Michamps. One day a Jeep pulled up in front of the company CP. Three men in it threw out a dead GI and threw an overcoat over him. We didn't know who they were, and the dead soldier was still there when we pulled out.

As the rest of the 35th Infantry Division had been moved back to Alsace-Lorraine, we of the 134th had been attached to the 6th Armored Division, and we were to replace their armored infantry, who had been pretty well used up. We even had half-tracks.

While here, we had a stove with a fire pot no bigger than your hat, so someone had to stay up all night to fire it. Schaeffer got sick, and being too lazy to go outside, shit in the corner of the room we were sleeping in.

While at Michamps, Kusch, one of the fellows that came in with us, was evacuated with frostbite and medics told him he would lose some toes. Kitchens (from Kentucky) and a Mexican boy left with frostbite soon after we joined C Company, and Lawrence left later in the month. Also there were several others that I can't remember; many had their feet frozen on our boxcar and truck rides up to the front.

We moved out in 6th Armored Division half-tracks and then dismounted and walked while they went back and let some other companies ride. The tankers were setting all hay stacks on fire with tracers because German tanks had a nasty habit of hiding in them. On this march, Staff Sergeant Sanborn was taken with one of his coughing spells. He got down on all fours and spit blood. I believed he was in a bad way.

We got into some houses. We were now in the Grand Duchy of Luxembourg. Storm threw one old lady out of her bed and slept in it. We got a bunch of replacements, and I got rid of the radio. Tom Sawyer had taken it after he had come in with us. I now was a member of the 3rd Squad of the 3rd Platoon. I was to remain here for the rest of my time in C Company except for a couple of short hitches.

I now took over the BAR (Browning automatic rifle). Its former owner, Burr, had been evacuated with frozen feet. The BAR weighed eighteen pounds without bipod, twenty with. We carried it without. I also had thirteen magazines (twenty rounds per), each weighing one pound, so I was burdened down with thirty-one pounds of equipment, to which you add one bandolier of extra ammo, forty-eight rounds, and six hand grenades, entrenching tool, trench knife, canteen, and first aid packet. You didn't have much room for personal things. I threw away my gas mask (fitted with eyeglasses) and carried two K-rations, razor, toothpaste, shaving brush, shaving cream, writing paper, and a pair of wire cutters in the gas mask carrier. These were combined with our clothes: pair of short underwear, pair of long johns, pair of fatigues, pair of wool ODs, sweater, field jacket, and overcoat, plus wool knit cap and helmet liner, combat boots, and felt-top overshoes. No wonder small arms cut down a lot of men. With all the snow, clothes, and equipment, you didn't move too fast. Armored divisions had blanket-lined overalls, which would have been a lot better. You can imagine the amount of exposure we were subject to: wet snow, wading streams, sleeping in foxholes, not being able to take off your shoes for long periods and no chance to wash your feet or change socks, and no water to drink, only coffee. We stood guard when dug in, one hour on and one off; fatigue didn't help. Through it all, hardly anyone had a cold, but I carried a jar of Vicks.

Staff Sergeant Sanborn was the squad leader, and Sergeant Loos was the assistant. As the new replacements were standing out in the street, Lieutenant Chappel, the company commander, was talking to them. He was a fairly well built man with a small mustache. He told the new men which company they were in and they should call him "Chappy" because he was a rebel himself. The lieutenant had made Sergeants Storm and Thibeault shave off their goat-whiskers (goatees) but let them wear a mustache.

Our squad got some replacements out of this group. I was to have as an assistant BAR man (Sokolowski). I asked him if he knew anything about the weapon, and he answered, "I don't even know how to load my rifle." He was a product of the army's replacement system as a so-called "retrained rifleman." He had been a truck mechanic in an antiaircraft outfit in the states. The army had many men reclassified and sent them overseas as replacements. The army brass felt that just because they were in the army, the infantry could use them. In reality, the infantryman was a highly specialized and trained individual. We had many weapons to master, plus the training to make you a combat soldier. Men like Sokolowski were next to worthless as an infantryman, and many of these retrainees were to become casualties in the next couple of days as a result of it.

Another group of men joined us this day. They were casuals (wounded who had been returned to their own units, a good practice). One was Staff Sgt. Maurice File. This man had been wounded five times and was to be hit again tomorrow morning.

That evening Sergeant Baker and I had some water heating on a stove when we observed one of the replacements using it. Baker hollered, "What the hell do you think you are doing?" and this man turned around and addressed us, "I am Lieutenant Larrieu and I am going to shave." Baker said, "I don't give a damn if you are a lieutenant, you ain't going to use our water. Put it back." To me this was quite a switch from stateside. I was to learn that officers didn't rate the same treatment overseas as stateside.

Next morning we moved out on half-tracks, and soon it became evident we were about to enter combat again. We met a Jeep with a German prisoner perched on the hood and a wounded tanker with a bandage around his eyes seated in the passenger side.

We dismounted in a small cluster of houses. Several German prisoners were standing there, and they had a German corpse on a child's wooden sled. He was one of the tallest corpses I had ever seen.

We moved out up the road with the tanks, and soon we deployed to the left of the road toward a woods. We had been informed that A Company was to flush the woods and we were to flank it. As we walked across the knee-deep, snow-swept fields, we were greeted by heavy small-arms fire. As I went to the ground, I heard the medic, Youngs, holler, "Help me, Graff; he's hit." I turned and ran back. My new assistant, Sokolowski, was lying face down in the snow. I rolled him over and we thought that he was dead, but, all of a sudden, his eyes blinked, for he had only fainted.

I then ran up a little knoll and lay down by Sergeant Baker. He was holding up a leg and trying to get a bullet through it (a million-dollar wound). I opened fire on the woods, but the BAR would only fire one round at a time, for the ejector wouldn't work. I fired the whole twenty-round magazine and dug every single cartridge out with my pocket knife. I would not be much help to our men pinned down by the fire from the woods. Finally, the fire slackened and we moved into a finger of woods. It then became apparent we had suffered considerable loss. Jones, who was Lieutenant Chappel's radio man, was killed. He had gone overseas with us. Sergeant Patrick had also been killed along with some of the new men. Some had been wounded, including Sergeant File (the most wounded man in the 35th Infantry Division).

I took the BAR and busted it on a tree, and Landrum got me a rifle off one of the casualties. A sergeant in another platoon was down in a shell hole crying, and his platoon sergeant had to kick him out to get him moving. He deserted a few weeks later, and we never did find out what happened to him. They began to reorganize, and I was sent to the weapons platoon as an ammo carrier for a machine gun.

As we were digging that afternoon, an incident occurred that was one of the tragedies of war. On January 4, C Company had been almost wiped out, with many men having been killed or captured. We had just learned the day before that six of them that were captured had been found shot to death by a small-arms bullet in the head or heart. The order had come down that if we caught anyone out of the 1st SS Adolf Hitler Panzer Division, to not take any prisoners.

As we were watching a ridge, three Germans appeared. One had on his helmet, and another had his arm in a sling. These men had been shooting at us just a couple of hours ago. Somebody hollered, "Kill the bastards!" Everyone opened fire, and two fell, but one jumped into a foxhole or hellhole. Gerstbauer, one of the fellows who went over with me, jumped up and ran up the hill and emptied his rifle in the kraut, and all the time the German was screaming, "Kamerad" (comrade, which they always hollered when surrendering) until he was killed. Bad business, but in such conditions, men's feelings and senses are sometimes dulled.

Next morning we jumped off toward the German-held town of Weiswampach, Luxembourg. As we moved out of the woods, I was with a light machine gun squad and we began to come under machine gun and tank fire. Some light tanks of the 6th

Armored Division were with us. As we struggled ahead (the snow was knee-deep and in many places deeper) the fire got heavy and accurate. The machine gun squad leader was just in front of me when all of a sudden he fell dead, cut almost in two by machine gun fire. I lay down in the snow and saw some men fall ahead of me. The 1st and 2nd Platoons were scattered out to my front, with the two machine guns right behind them. I ran back to the gunner and told him to get the gun in action, but he had frozen in the snow (not with the weather, but with the fear of combat). It affects many, and as this man was one of the new men, he just couldn't let go. Finally, I moved away from him and lay down and began to shoot into the town. Two Germans ran out of a straw stack when a tank shell hit it. Everyone shot at them, and down they went. Tank fire was hitting us and also those blasted machine guns. I could see the white tracers fly by me (our tracers were red and the Germans' white) and hear the bullets hit the snow. I saw one man throw away his rifle, pack, and overcoat and start running back near me. I pulled him down and said, "You damn fool. Do you want to get killed? Get down." It was Gerstbauer, and he said, "I've been hit in the head and I am going to the rear." He had a shrapnel wound in the side of his head. He also said that the lieutenant (Larrieu) had been blown in two by the same shell that had wounded him.

Today we were all praying. I decided to get out of here, as there was no chance of getting into the town. As I got back in the woods, I noticed another light machine gun set up and firing down into the town. I gave the gunners my ammo and moved off looking for the 3rd Platoon. I came across the weapons platoon section sergeant, and he wanted to know what I was doing, and I told him to go out there and try to get the gun in action, as I couldn't, and that I was going back to the 3rd Platoon.

I ran into Loos, and he told me that Storm and Johnson had been wounded. Storm had been hit in the butt and Johnson in the arm. Johnson had gone over with us. Loos, Sanborn, and I dug in as the tanks pulled out and left us. By now it had begun to get dark, and the executive officer, Lieutenant Neel, came around and told us to be on the alert.

After dark we began to bring in the wounded. Many had multiple wounds. One man who had gone overseas with me was hit in the leg, stomach, chest, and head. We put all of these wounded in a large, German-built dugout. The morphine the medics had was frozen. Sanborn's feet were bothering him, and he was coughing badly. He would tramp his feet, cough, and sleep sitting up all at once. I fell asleep with my face in the snow until awakened by Lieutenant Neel. I was supposed to be on guard, but sleep had overtaken me. He told us that we were cut off, and a B Company patrol had been almost wiped out trying to reach us. Soon the Germans began to shell us with the "screaming meemies". These were a multi-barreled rocket-launcher type of field piece. They sure were laying them in on us. The lieutenant came back and said we were pulling out, to head out of the woods, and when we got in the open, to guide on a village on fire, as the armor was supposed to have cleared it that afternoon. We floundered back, and of course we had to leave the wounded, who would be rescued in the morning. We left the medics with them. The rest of the night, Steinhaufel and I slept in a barn, burrowed in the sheep manure, with an old ewe and a couple of lambs.

About five o'clock our kitchen Jeep appeared with breakfast. I remember we had pancakes. The driver came back with more and said that we had been practically wiped out. Six men remained in the 1st Platoon, seven in the 2nd, and thirteen in our platoon, plus a handful of headquarters men and one machine gun.

In a couple of hours we were to jump off again to take this town, but this time the armor was supposed to support us, and we would attack from another direction. You can be assured that there were not many happy men that morning. We were certainly not looking forward to a resumption of the attack after we were all probably done.

As we moved down the road, we approached Weiswampach, and one of the tanks hit two mines. No one was hurt, but they refused to budge. Lieutenant Chappel came up, and as Loos and I were the front men, he asked us what we thought. I said, "They look like our mines, probably laid on the road early in the breakthrough." This sector had been held by the 28th Division then. He asked if we were afraid to move them, and we said, "No." So we started digging them out, and the tanks began to move. We entered the town without firing a shot. The krauts had pulled out. We could see them on a hill, and they did fire a few mortar rounds at us. A German tank was burning. I guess it had been disabled and they couldn't move it, so they destroyed it. We found a truck of German dead, for they always tried to remove their dead if possible so we couldn't assess their casualties. These Luxembourgers were pretty well shaken up. There were three girls in this house we were in, and we found a lot of German equipment and clothes upstairs. Sanborn put his frozen feet in the oven, and Loos and I cut up a lot of cemetery crosses we found in a carpenter shop. Undoubtedly the Germans were going to use them to mark graves, as they had the Prussian cross on them.

Later in the afternoon a column of tanks appeared from the west. It was a company of the 90th Infantry Division, and they were to relieve us, thank God. Guess who was riding the lead tank? Sokolowski. We hadn't missed him, and he said he had been knocked out by a screaming meemie the night before and had hidden in the woods until he saw the tanks coming. We doubted the knocked-out part, but we figured he had fallen asleep and we had missed him when we pulled out. You know, he never slept again at night in the line, but catnapped in the daytime all the rest of our days in combat. Also, he stuck to me like glue from then on to the end of the war.

We then moved out. We walked part of the way and rode on tanks part of the way back to a town called Fischbach, in the Grand Duchy of Luxembourg. We slept in a house, but a colored battalion equipped with 240mm artillery pieces fired all night. They were shaking down the houses. Here we got rid of our overshoes and combat boots and got shoe pacs.

We moved out of here and into a big house in a little town. They showed a Bob Hope movie one night in the town in a big barn. James DeVires (from Washington) and I were on guard one evening, and a German plane came over, and we could see the cross on the wings by the moonlight.

While we were in reserve here, we were treated to a bath. The men who had been in the line the longest (a group of replacements we had received were not included) were taken back in trucks several miles to an open field, where the engineers had set up a portable bath house. This unit consisted of a tent and duck boards to stand on with a series of showers powered by a generator, and we had honest-to-gosh hot water. Also included was a change of long underwear and clean socks. If you have never had to do without one, you cannot imagine our delight in having a fresh bath.

We then moved up and relieved A Company in two farm houses on the Our River. The dragon's teeth of the Siegfried Line were visible across it in Germany. Here we got a large number of replacements again, and again many were retrained riflemen. As the sole surviving BAR man in the company, I had to instruct the new BAR men in the use of the weapon. Up here was a giant Royal Tiger tank, the largest in the Nazi arsenal. Fortunately it had broken down, and the Germans had disabled the gun.

On January 31, 1945, we left the Ardennes.

INDEX

307